PRECINCT 19

PRECINCT 19

Thomas Larry Adcock

DOUBLEDAY & COMPANY, INC.
GARDEN CITY, NEW YORK
1984

For Anne and Jessica

Library of Congress Cataloging in Publication Data
Adcock, Thomas Larry, 1947–
    Precinct 19.
    1. New York (N.Y.)—Police. 2. Manhattan (New York,
N.Y.)—Police. I. Title. II. Title: Precinct nineteen.
HV8148.N5A32 1984   363—2'09747'1
ISBN: 0-385-18453-0
Library of Congress Catalog Card Number 84-6137

ACKNOWLEDGMENTS

Writers sometimes don't mind confessing that behind the scenes, as it were, there are lots of big people with lots of important help and encouragement. Without them, the authors might have just one more fish story to swap with his pals. That's why books have pages like this. Accordingly, my salutes to:

Charles Sopkin, for suggesting this book in the first place;

Liz and Jim Trupin and Kim Sykes, for supporting the project heart and soul;

"The Angel of 103rd Street," a remarkable young man whose Spanish translation and eye-opening companionship were invaluable to my travels through East Harlem.

INTRODUCTION

Like cops everywhere else in a place like New York, the men and women of the Nineteenth Precinct work under the pressure of hoping each day for the best and expecting the worst. It is a unique occupational tension, a life-and-death proposition that comes with a pension if you last long enough.

The 179 officers of Manhattan's Nineteenth Precinct are responsible for protecting the most remarkable and highly contrasting neighborhood in the world—the Upper East Side. Here live the elite from every part of the planet, in addition to the thirty-eight foreign consulates and United Nations missions. There is also the matter of Gracie Mansion along the East River, where the mayor lives.

The Upper East Side is not merely a millionaires' ghetto, however. Side by side with the likes of Fifth Avenue and Park Avenue and the gentry and meritocracy of the city are some fairly mean streets, pitiful sights and some downright vicious types. All of which makes the job of the Nineteenth Precinct cop simultaneously challenging, coveted, dreaded and confusing.

I think the cops of the Nineteenth Precinct are the best in the world. Not to an officer, mind you, but certainly as a precinct unit. There are those who drink too much, those who are full of self-pity and those who cut corners. But there are also cops like Tony Ciffo and Jack Clark and John Laffey and Charlie Leinau. Few come better than these.

I spent about a year tagging along with the cops of the Nineteenth Precinct, who were good enough to allow me to be a fly on the wall with pad and pencil. There were times when I was trusted as an outside observer and times I wasn't and that was the open-ended deal.

All of the incidents in the resultant book are real. Generally, the names of crime victims are changed to protect their privacy. A number of officers portrayed in the book are composites and have fictional names. That doesn't make their experiences fictional, however, it just makes the balance of their professional and personal lives easier.

Certain editorial changes in identities, dates and circumstances were made in the writing of *Precinct 19* in order to protect the integrity of cases pending before the courts. None of these changes alters the essential truths of the total story.

The reader will find, as did I, that the day-to-day life of being a cop in New York is a matter of slogging through violence and tragedy and dreariness and that sometimes the only human response is comedy. The cops of the Nineteenth Precinct are some of the funniest people I've ever known. God help us New Yorkers if our cops should ever lose their humanity, if they should one day stop laughing.

I've come to the point where I can pick out a cop on a crowded street, even when he's dressed like everyone else. He's as easy to spot as a bleeding man. Heavier, it appears, full of other people's sorrows whether he realizes it or not. And his eyes are always moving, sweeping the street to make note of who belongs and who bears watching.

When a cop starts talking about public perceptions of police officers, there is a certain paranoid tone to his voice. An officer named James Martin of Manhattan's Midtown North station house told the New York *Times:*

"This month we were all brutal racists, last month we were all drug addicts, the month before that we were drunks and sex fiends. A lot of times you get the feeling that the city doesn't care, the public doesn't care, that your partner and the other cops are the only ones you can count on.

"We're the most visible, the most vulnerable and the least vocal. Cops don't talk. They never know when it's going to be taken out of context, and people aren't going to understand it anyway. So you just read about it, you watch it, you put on the uniform and you go out and do your job."

I've never heard a cop's lament more succinctly expressed. Here's a hope that this book might knock a few holes into Officer Martin's outlook.

Thomas Larry Adcock

New York, N.Y.
November 1983

PART I

1

The lobby was jammed full of cops. Uniformed and plainclothed, they streamed in and out of the East Sixty-seventh Street station house, greeting one another with backslaps and fraternal insults. Their hips were laden with jangling cop hardware—guns, clubs, leather-bound citation books, handcuffs, bullets and walkie-talkies. Half the cops were waiting for the sergeant to call night-shift muster back in the squad room in the rear of the station house. The other half were from the day tour and were anxious to hit the shower rooms downstairs.

A middle-aged woman in a short double-breasted jacket of lavender suède over pleated pinstriped wool trousers, a wool jacquard knit turtleneck sweater and silk scarf and snakeskin boots stood at the tall desk. A sergeant with a belly that protruded over his belt and a sweat stain running down the back of his blue shirt listened patiently as she shrieked something about her stolen Mercedes. A small-framed policewoman made her way through the crowd to the stairway, with a fat prostitute in tow who was practically comatose on heroin.

Then the maniac wandered in and the atmosphere became unusual.

He was tall, well over six feet, about thirty-five years old. And he was quite out of his mind on drugs and alcohol and private torment. All of his clothes fit him properly, but they were torn and filthy, as if he'd worn nothing else for days and slept in the streets. To some imaginary companion, he offered repeated assurances, "I'm okay. I'm okay now."

The maniac's eyes darted from cop to cop and his whole body began shaking violently as he pushed past the uniformed men, stopping in the center of the lobby. He planted his feet firmly on the floor at a wide stance, then raised his hands and started pulling at his hair and screaming, over and over, "Fucking cops! Fucking cops fucked me up! Fucking cops . . ."

The woman in the suède jacket seemed annoyed by the distraction. She turned to look at the maniac, who returned her gaze and quickly unzipped his trousers. She swore and turned back to the sergeant to continue the tale of her waylaid Mercedes.

The maniac started shoving at the cops around him, poking them in the chest and shaking off their attempts to steer him toward the door and back out onto the street before he got himself into trouble. He lunged at a knot of young officers near the sergeant's desk and four burly men dressed in seedy jackets and greasy sweaters, not unlike the maniac's ensemble, finally managed to grab him. They looked like garbage collectors after a hot day's work. But they were cops. Street Crimes Unit—Manhattan, affectionally known by the acronym SCUM patrol.

The maniac was a regular customer.

A cop named Tony Ciffo drew the attention of the maniac, who spit his regard, a greeting that narrowly missed landing on Officer Ciffo's forehead. The tour was not off to a good start for Ciffo.

The maniac, struggling wildly under the restraint of the four SCUM patrol cops, managed to get an arm free. He swung at Ciffo, landing a jab on his chest. "What're you lookin at, eh?" the maniac screamed at Ciffo. "Wanna step outside?"

The cops ringing Ciffo offered up a small cheer of encouragement. One of them went to the front door and held it open.

"Yeah," Ciffo said to the big man with the wild eyes. "I'd like nothing better."

Tony Ciffo was about five feet nine, thickly compact and heavily muscular. His face was northern Italian, wide and swarthy but brown-hued rather than olive. His hair was a mass of light brown knots and curls, coarse enough to rip the teeth out of anything less than a steel comb.

Ciffo took off his sunglasses and carefully folded them, then handed them to another cop. Then he took a step toward the maniac, as if he were a small concrete wall that had learned to walk. The SCUM patrol cops released the maniac. Ciffo punched the big man's shoulder, causing him to spin around. Then with his right hand, Ciffo grabbed hold of his neck; with his left hand, Ciffo held the seat of his pants. As Ciffo moved the big maniac across the floor, the cop at the door opened wide the portals in preparation for an unceremonious parting.

Ciffo grunted and picked up the big man, raised him several inches off the floor and then threw him clear through the door. The maniac went stumbling and screaming down the stoop into the street, hit a blue and white Plymouth squad car at the curb and collapsed into a surprisingly small heap.

"What do you got on that nutjob?" Ciffo asked one of the SCUM patrol officers. His breathing was completely unaffected by having picked up a crazed giant and tossed him out the doorway like a bag of laundry.

"Nothing. He gets a little excited once in a while. No trouble, really, if we just turn him around and get him on his way. Thanks, Tony."

Ciffo and some of the officers looked out the door. The maniac was considerably calmer than he had been just a few minutes earlier. He'd picked himself up and walked unsteadily down the street toward Lexington Avenue, bowing at the waist to every cop he encountered along his way.

Tony Ciffo shrugged his shoulders, retrieved his sunglasses and headed upstairs one flight to the little community affairs office at the top of the landing. He shot through the door in his customary manner, like a five-foot-nine blue bullet. A thin, young rookie cop in blue blazer and gray slacks and a Gucci attaché that only a police staff lawyer downtown would dare to carry stood up from a bench and stuck out his hand. His name was Valentine and this was his first day on the transfer assignment to the Nineteenth Precinct, Community Affairs detail. A college cop from a mile off.

Ciffo stopped for a split second and pumped Valentine's hand and looked the rookie up and down, the way a cop sizes up everybody after a while, friends and collars and even fellow cops all the same. Initial distrust often paid in survival benefits. Then he said to Valentine, "Have a seat for a minute, right? I got to wash my face and take some vitamins."

He talked to Valentine over his shoulder as he barreled through the office, banging a knee against one of the four metal desks butted together. He didn't seem to notice the collision, but the desk gained yet another dent.

"Tony Ciffo's the name," he said. Then he turned on the water taps of a small basin on the wall at the far end of the office. "Not much action here usually, but we'll do our best to flush out some bad guys for you your first night, okay?"

Ciffo tossed back his head and popped a handful of aspirins, cold capsules and vitamin C tablets with rose hips, all of which he washed down with a paper cup full of cold orange water. He bent over the basin and scrubbed his face afterward, making a great deal of noise about it. When he took a toothbrush from the cabinet over the basin, Valentine took the advice about having a seat.

Besides the two men, the only other person in the room was an overweight black high school girl hunched over a typewriter adjacent to one of the desks. She was oblivious to the officers as she stared mutely at the paper in her typewriter. She wore earphones clamped to her head, attached to a radio turned up so loudly it could still be heard by Valentine, seated ten feet away from her. She listened to one of the many AM radio stations that play music highly popular with inmates prior to incarceration in mental hospitals, gangs of leather-jacketed youths with chains around their waists who like to brawl on street corners in the middle of the night and proprietors of downtown shops specializing in drug paraphernalia.

The girl seemed narcotized. She chewed gum at quite an incredible volume, too, snapping and popping lustily as she pecked an occasional key of the Royal manual standard in front of her.

Her job was to copy handwritten numbers in the columns of a weekly precinct crime index report form to an identical form in the typewriter. Clerks just like her downtown in the central filing room at Police Plaza, an office complete with radios tuned to mindless rock and synchronized gum chewing, required those reports in typed form before stowing them away someplace for yet more typing by yet more clerks onto year-end, precinct-by-precinct crime index report forms. Somewhere, someone was trying to computerize all of this on the assumption that the high school clerks could do a speedier job of it all.

The point of all the clerical make-work was to interest New York's teenagers in civilian careers with the police department. The girl who sat at the typewriter in the Nineteenth Precinct's Community Affairs office wanted to be an airlines pilot, though.

A slat in the middle of the bench where Valentine sat waiting pinched his thigh. He stood up and rubbed his leg and wondered why in the world the station house for the prestigious Upper East Side of Manhattan was so appallingly shabby.

The Community Affairs office was one of four on the second floor. It was roughly twenty by twenty-eight feet, high-ceilinged and painted in several coats of coagulated institutional green. The windows were painted over too, glass and all.

Desks in the room were eaten away around the edges by cigarette burns. Chipped filing cabinets against the walls were stuffed to capacity with the labors of semiconscious clerks; a Norelco coffee maker was wedged into a long-ago sealed-up fireplace; a G.E. battery-charge box for maintaining Point-to-Point shortwave radio broadcast power sat on a wood and steel cabinet next to the basin where Ciffo splashed.

Outside the office in the second-floor corridor, a vast echo chamber, was a cacophony of harsh noise. Cops yelled up and down the stairwell to communicate matters of intrastation business and gossip. There were also the ludicrously sterile strains of Muzak tunes, assorted ravings and cursings of manacled hookers and junkies and boosters as they were marched up and down the gritty marble stairs to and from the precinct holding cage and the constant, waspish static of hip-held PTP radios.

The place was a little short of a madhouse, Valentine thought. Yet he could see that every cop and clerk managed to zone out any sound but their own, or those sounds which applied in some way to their function or interest.

In the Community Affairs office, as in all offices on every floor of the station house, there were banks of fluorescent lights. They were the kind that allow no shadows, the kind that make everyone's skin look unhealthy. On the open wall was a display of more than two hundred mug shots, mostly of black and Hispanic criminals, a very old and peeling Police Athletic League poster having to do with a boxing marathon pitting New York cops against New York fire laddies and a coatrack next to the door. Next to the coatrack was a printed sign, black on white, containing the inspiring legend:

> Do something—
> either lead, follow,
> or get the hell
> out of the way!

The girl looked up from her typewriter and crime index forms and actually stopped chewing for a moment. "Hi," she said to the cop who took off his coat and sat at the desk next to hers.

He was tall and husky, with a round stomach and square shoulders, short red hair fringed around the sides of his head and wisped on top. "Hiya, beauty," he said. His green jacket hung behind him on the chair. He wore a polo shirt with green and yellow stripes and lit up a mentholated cigarette, a Newport. He was Detective Johnny Maguire, in charge, among other things, of easing the transition for rookie officers transferred to the Nineteenth Precinct.

"Maguire here is our Irish bumblebee," Ciffo said to Valentine as he made introductions. "And he's no relation to the former commissioner, no matter what he tries to tell you."

Valentine and Maguire shook hands. Maguire looked him up and down and offered a cigarette, which was declined. Practically none of the younger officers smoked anymore.

"You married?" Ciffo asked Valentine.

"Nope."

Ciffo lit a cigarette of his own from a pack of Marlboros in his left breast pocket. From his right breast pocket he fished out a stick of peppermint gum, which he also put in his mouth since his partner didn't approve of his smoking. Before answering a nearby telephone, he said, "It's good you're single. You won't believe the women you meet here. We got the highest divorce rate among officers in the whole damn city."

Ciffo took the call and barked hello.

"Nothing heavy here in the One-Nine," Maguire said, beginning his instruction. "But sometimes we've got fireworks. You never know. Whatever happens here is complicated, really complicated."

Maguire hadn't bothered to raise his voice to accommodate for the noise Ciffo made yelling at someone on the other end of the line and Valentine had to strain to hear, already at a disadvantage with the din from the corridor and the distraction of the tinny, muffled blasting sounds from beneath the typist's earphones. He had a long way to go before he learned the trick of filtering out superfluous sounds.

"In one day," Maguire said, "you can start with a burglary call at, say, Dustin Hoffman's pad, then you might wind up your tour making out a report on some dead bag lady who sleeps nights under the Fifty-ninth Street bridge. You just never know."

Maguire stood up. "Come on. Let me show you what I mean."

Valentine followed Maguire through the corridor and the hubbub of mingling cops and crooks and lawyers into the adjacent Detective Unit squad room, a confusion of perpetually ringing telephones and discordant desk-to-desk debates on various episodes of neighborhood violence, pilferage and chicanery. From the Muzak box high up near the ceiling molding came the theme song from a TV cop show, NBC's "Hill Street Blues."

Maguire went to a desk occupied, for the time being, by a detective wearing a suit and a haircut of remarkably good taste, given the usual standards in New York detective squad rooms. His name was Tyrone Yorio. Behind him, taped to the wall, was a photostat copy of a Manhattan detective command circular dated August 6, 1930:

N.Y.P.D. Advisory No. 3813

RE: Missing V.I.P., Joseph Force Crater, justice, New York Supreme Court.

DESC.: Male Caucasian, age 36, medium ht & wt, no distinguishing scars, no tattoos.

PARTICULARS: Subj vanished en route to Westchester County estate from chambers in city; told wife he was "going for a swim"; late inquiries indicate subj withdrew large cash sums from various bank accts in city.

REQUEST: Notify Commr Mulroony, Manhattan central D.B., ASAP.

Valentine remarked on the bulletin and Detective Yorio, looking him up and down, grinned. "We haven't caught up with him yet," he said.

"Show us the unusuals file, Ty, huh?" Maguire asked.

Yorio shoved a green cloth-bound clip book across the desk.

"Take a good look," Maguire said, opening it for Valentine.

The rookie read the first report, all about a Dutch socialite, she was said to be, who lived in a permanently leased seven-room suite at the Pierre Hotel on Fifth Avenue. Her name was Gabriella Lagerwall.

The night before, so it seemed, Mrs. Lagerwall, widow of a Swiss industrialist, was in the company of a pair of Arab businessmen—Ala Almire Alphabili and Abdul Rahan Soria by name.

The three of them had dined at Lutèce, then had had drinks at Regine's and were back at the Pierre just before midnight.

According to the report, Mrs. Lagerwall had just entered Alphabili's own two-room suite when a pair of perpetrators in ski masks and guns jumped the trio. They were promptly handcuffed and thrown on a bed where their legs were taped together and pillowcases secured around their heads.

The perpetrators then turned on the shower and a radio to cover the ruckus of ripping through everything in the suite and everything carried or worn by the estimable Mrs. Lagerwall and friends. The perpetrators insisted on calling the Arabs "prince."

Maguire stopped Valentine and asked, "Got to the bottom line yet?"

Valentine read on. When he came to the inventory of stolen goods he gasped.

Mrs. Lagerwall had lost a sixty-two-carat diamond and emerald necklace, which she said was worth "about a million" but which her friend Alphabili said was worth more like five million. Alphabili himself lost $8,000 in cash, which he had stuffed in the various pockets of his suit, a $10,000 diamond-studded wristwatch, a $4,000 diamond ring and $30,000 in cash, which was in his briefcase. Soria lost some $20,000 in cash, which he'd carried in his pockets.

Valentine whistled. "Inside job?"

"You might make detective grade real soon, boy," Maguire said.

Valentine then began the second report, this one about someone named Howard Doyle, who was executive producer of WABC-TV News. It seemed Mr. Doyle had been arrested on a weapons charge that morning at three o'clock outside his apartment building on East Seventy-seventh Street.

Doyle was colorfully garbed as he was booked. He wore a cowboy suit, complete with ten-gallon hat, fur vest, a silver and turquoise belt and fringed leather chaps. He also wore a .357 magnum six-shot revolver strapped to his waist, a gun which would have won the West and considerably more as well. The arresting officer noticed the gun when Doyle was found hollering on East Seventy-seventh and in the act, so it appeared, of pulling off the arm of Kathy Cartusciello, the young lady said to share Doyle's household.

The perpetrator took a few swipes at the officers, it was alleged, and was subsequently booked on charges of criminal possession of a dangerous weapon.

Maguire closed up the book. "Up where I live, which is Riverdale, you hardly ever hear of stuff like this."

Then Maguire and the rookie left the Detective Unit. In the corridor, a pair of cops were discussing a particularly odious rape case of a month or so earlier. The incident had occurred uptown, in a tiny Italian enclave of East Harlem, in the Twenty-third Precinct, just north of the Nineteenth's northern border, East Ninety-sixth Street.

"You know the spik bastards who raped the nun with the broomstick and carved her up?" one of the cops asked his buddy.

"Yeah."

Two small-time burglars were surprised in the act of performing their trade at St. Cecelia's Church at 112 East 106th Street. They stood on the landing of a stairway, confronted by a frail young nun, so frightened she probably would never have remembered their faces well enough for a line-up identification anyway, if only the punks were wise enough to flee right then and there. But they didn't run.

Instead, the burglars knocked down the nun, then took turns raping her. With their knives, they carved some twenty-six crosses into her flesh. Then they finished her off by jamming a broomstick into her vagina, leaving her there in the stairwell of the parish church bleeding and terrorized nearly into insanity.

When word of the atrocity spread through the Italian communities around the city—from Hunt's Point up in the Bronx downtown to the social clubs of Mulberry Street and over to Bensonhurst in Brooklyn— the newspapers were only beginning to hear about it. No one needed the papers to know that the Mafia had put up $5,000 for the privilege of meeting the two rapists.

The punks, meanwhile, had sense enough to leave town. Or to try.

One of them was caught in Chicago on a traffic violation and shipped back to New York on a no-frills flight. His accomplice was found hiding in a tenement on Roosevelt Avenue in Jackson Heights, Queens, en route to LaGuardia and a night flight anywhere.

Now they were at Riker's Island in protective, segregated lock-up after having pleaded guilty as charged. The Mafia offer still stood.

"They got their own special security at Riker's," the cop said. Other cops started listening. "And it's some goddamn Jesuit priest counselor with Corrections who won't let anybody near them because of the threats from the other spiks."

An older cop ventured his opinion. He was the old-line, old-school cop, the kind with a wide back split by sweat. He exuded squad-car odor, the smell of close quarters and Pall Mall cigarettes and coffee in styrofoam cups. Younger officers smelled of Brut.

"So nowadays," the older cop said, "we got to make appointments with a goddamn priest to get near a couple of spiks who confess to

plugging up a nun? Hell, they could clear up twenty, thirty, forty goddamn cases on the burglary load easy. And you can't even talk to them?
Jesus H. Christ, you know? It's getting so the only thing that makes
any sense at all anymore is to retire, get the hell out of this insane
asylum and take a job down in Florida with the Coconuts Police Department."

Back in the Community Affairs office, Ciffo was pounding his fist
onto the top of a desk.

"What was the call?" Maguire asked him.

"It was the Chapman broad again."

Maguire explained to the rookie, "She's our biggest complainer in
the precinct. She's always at the community meetings going on and on
about the kids in the neighborhood and how they make noise playing
ball and so on.

"Now Tony here, being our youth officer, naturally used to be asked
to the meetings. He's not allowed anymore on account of the last time
when he told Mrs. Chapman that the city had purchased four alligators
to eat all the bad children."

Ciffo felt the need to defend himself. "Well, isn't that just about
what she wants? Doesn't she want to see them all killed or something
horrible short of that? Maimed maybe. They're not so bad, you know.
Most of them are really fine kids. My God, the cranks here! They
should see the kids in my neighborhood on Bath Avenue in Brooklyn.
They'd be out there kissing the kids around here on the Upper East
Side if they could see the kids where I live.

"I don't know, I think some of these people up here are so detached
from reality it's unbelievable. I mean, I sometimes think the richer they
are the more they don't want to deal with anybody, anytime."

A couple of cops, more old-timers somewhere in their mid- to late
fifties, with plans to open bait and tackle shops on Long Island Sound
or hunting lodges up in the Adirondacks just as soon as their pension
checks started up, wandered past Maguire and Ciffo. They went to a
cabinet near the washbasin.

One of them jammed a key into the cabinet and pulled out a small
handgun and slipped it into his belt. Then he walked with his partner
out toward the hallway.

"Lemme see the extra piece," one of the cops said. "What do you
have, some throwdown?"

The cop pulled a small gun from his belt. "It ain't no throwdown. What do you think, I'm a crook? This ain't the bad old days."

In the "bad old days," some New York cops were known to carry small, concealed pistols which they would throw down on the street after they'd shot someone. Then, during the departmental inquiry which would follow, the cop could claim that the perpetrator pulled a pistol on him and he shot in self-defense.

"Jesus, what a little dink gun. What're all the rubber bands for anyway?"

"So it don't slip down into my Jockeys."

"You cheap hump. Whyn't you buy a holster? Unless it *is* a throwdown."

"It ain't a throwdown, I'm telling you. I just feel better with it."

Ciffo's partner walked in, Officer Jean Truta, her blond hair rolled up under her cap, the top of her white flak jacket peeking out above her shirt collar like a steel-lined T-shirt.

"Time to roll," Ciffo said to Maguire. "Time to go out checking on all the bad boys and girls of this great city of ours. Hold down the fort, right, Johnny?"

He caught Valentine by the shoulder and pulled him along with him. "You come on with us in the car," he said, "or we'll see what might be up for you at the desk, right?"

"You got the nice car today?" Ciffo asked Truta as they walked down the stairway into the lobby. Valentine followed behind them.

"The heater works, so don't complain," she said.

Ciffo turned around to Valentine. "Nothing but the best up here in the One-Nine."

They reached the desk and the sergeant asked Ciffo about Valentine. Then the sergeant grinned and crooked a finger at the rookie in the blazer and slacks.

"Up there in Community Affairs," the sergeant said, "you'll be doing mostly Mickey Mouse at the social clubs. Want to see what real cops see?"

Valentine nodded, uncertainly.

The sergeant waved over the very two cops who had had the conversation about the advisability of acquiring a holster for the throwdown revolver. The sergeant handed them a piece of paper.

"Need a couple of uniforms right away on a stink stiff," the sergeant said. "Take the kid here with you so he can see what that's like."

Ralph and Ed by name, the officers and Valentine left the station house, got into a blue-and-white at the curb and headed east on Sixty-fifth Street toward an apartment building at York Avenue near Rockefeller University. The sky was beginning to darken at the end of an unusually chilly day in early September.

"Ever been on a stink-stiff call, kid?" Ralph asked Valentine. He sat in the front passenger seat, twisted around to talk to the Community Affairs officer in the back.

"No," Valentine answered, "but I was at a floater once."

Ralph and Ed whistled.

"So, you know what we're after here?" Ralph asked.

"I think so."

"Sometimes this can be worse than a floater, you know," Ed warned, looking back at Valentine by way of the rearview mirror. "They tell you that? At the academy, they say you need strong feet and legs. But they should tell you that you better have besides that some pretty strong guts."

Valentine wouldn't soon forget the floater call. He had accompanied two veteran officers from a Flushing precinct house in Queens, two officers with old-fashioned big bellies not unlike Ralph and Ed. Ordinarily, the medical examiner for the County of Queens would have sent around a truck for the job, but it was a Sunday and the morgue was short-handed, so the station house obliged.

When they arrived at the scene, Valentine was struck by the large number of ghoulish neighborhood kids hanging around in the shallow waters of Flushing Bay, wading out into the murky water after a gray and greasy lump of something that used to be a living human being. The veteran cops handed the kids a grappling hook and they pulled the thing in close enough to haul onshore. Pieces of the body fell away in shreds as the boys pulled it in.

"Come on now, Valentine, leave us not be shy," one of the cops said. Then he gave Valentine a pair of huge rubber gloves with stains all over them. The gloves covered Valentine's forearms as well as his hands. He helped the cops, similarly gloved, pull to shore a carcass so bloated and discolored and misshapen that it was impossible to tell anything such as sex, race or age about something only vaguely human. And the thing smelled so powerfully that several of the teenagers who had thought the whole spectacle a matter of weekend entertainment sneaked away to vomit privately.

Valentine and the other cops rolled up the hulk in a police-issue black plastic body bag, then lifted it and set it down into the trunk of the squad car. They peeled off their gloves and tossed them into the trunk as well.

On the way to the morgue, a distance of some seven miles, Valentine received a lecture on floaters in particular and long-dead bodies in general:

"Know why it's so important to wear gloves?" one of the veteran cops asked. " 'Cause of the toxic flora. Stuff grows on a stiff and nothing's more toxic than that. We oughta get hazard pay messing around with toxic flora, that's what I say."

Valentine needed very badly to be sick.

"Happens all the time out there in the bay shallows," the other veteran cop rattled on as he weaved in and out of church traffic on a Sunday in Queens. "Guys that got neutralized last winter and tossed into the drink somewheres start popping up all over town in the spring when the water warms up."

Suddenly, the cop driving made a U-turn on Northern Boulevard and pulled into a Burger King drive-in restaurant. Valentine heard the body bag bounce in the trunk as the squad car went over a concrete traffic bump.

"Hungry?" the cop asked as he eased the squad car into a parking slot near a microphone where one could order up whoppers and milkshakes. "I get a little discount here."

Then he said, "Don't worry about the stiff in the back, kid. He won't be eating much."

Now, as he rode in the back of another squad car, this time on the Upper East Side of Manhattan, Valentine hoped to God for a little more formality to the proceedings he was about to encounter. He hoped that this time there would be someone on the way from the morgue at the very least.

The apartment building on York Avenue was squat and lime green and crisscrossed with rusting fire escapes and probably contained as many apartments as legally permissible plus several more in consideration of a hundred-dollar bill for the super and a private deal with the rental agent involved. Stewardesses and certain others would put up with just about anything in order to call the Upper East Side home.

The foyer smelled of dog shit. There the super was waiting, wide-eyed and speaking an incoherent dialect of Spanish, tinged with musca-

tel. His arms flailed as he directed Officers Ralph and Ed and the cop
in the blue blazer, Valentine, down a first-floor hallway toward the
darkened rear hold of the building, then up a spindly staircase.

A couple of cops who had heard the call on the radio were already on
hand, standing just outside the door to apartment 2-I. The unmistak-
able odor of dead flesh stung Valentine's nose. He knew the routine:
first, the uniformed officers would enter the premises and sweep the
scene for evidence of foul play; then, assuming there was none, the
officers would notify the medical examiner if that office was not already
informed; then they would make contact with the desk officer on duty;
then they would give a preliminary report of their findings to the precinct Detective Unit; then they would question a few neighbors; then
they would return to the station house and write up their reports.

Valentine saw one of the other officers with a body bag hanging
around his shoulders and his stomach began hurting.

"Better light up the cigars on this one," an officer outside the door
said.

The super used a house key to open the door. The stench was like a
mailed fist. Lighters clicked and cigars and cigarettes burned. Anything
to cover the smell. The super howled something in Spanish and retreated.

Valentine and others, hands held over their noses, stepped into the
fetid apartment. Water trickled through a radiator below the single
window, which framed a view of brown brick. Cardboard and tape had
replaced a pane of glass. There was a draft around the floorboards that
kicked up dust. Mouse droppings lay thick in the corners.

There was a cot against the wall. Next to the cot, on the floor, lay a
clarinet with a cracked reed. Above the cot, taped to the wall, were
color snapshots of a young man with red hair standing in front of a
large frame house with a veranda, along with people who must have
been a family. Ohio Gothic types. There was a snap of the young man
with another youthful, all-American bunch. Young musicians grouped
around a portable stage in a high school gymnasium somewhere far
from the glitter and sometimes the loneliness of Manhattan.

On the cot, beneath a pile of everything made of cloth that the
tenant owned, was what appeared to be an extremely thin young man
with brittle hair the color of carrots. His eyes were open, though yel-

lowed over with death. The sockets had turned black and the skin was gray. East River gray.

He had starved to death in the richest, most glamorous neighborhood in the world—Precinct 19, Manhattan.

2

Except for the big, square Dick Tracy jaw and those times he must don the official crisp powder-blue shirt, his shiny inspector's badge, the slim black four-in-hand tie and the navy twill coat and trousers tailored to accommodate a gun belt, Paul Short looks not so much like the commander of a New York police precinct house as he does the worldly proprietor of an upper Madison Avenue art gallery.

His sartorial choices tend toward hopsack blazers, silk ties of deep hues, pleated slacks and butter-soft loafers. Often, he arrives for his tour of duty at the Nineteenth with a rosebud in his lapel. His silver hair is carefully cut.

The aesthetic is important. It wouldn't matter if a commander of the South Bronx precinct popularly known as "Fort Apache" clothed himself exclusively in rayon or polyester and wore two-toned patent-leather shoes. But if a cop with visions of high command doesn't know why such fabrics do not befit an Upper East Side precinct inspector, he'll not likely get the post; and it's unlikely that anyone would think to tell him why.

But clothes alone do not make the man in the case of Paul Short.

To be a precinct commander anywhere in New York City, Short was telling Valentine one day amid repeated calls from the commissioner's office downtown on "delicate" cases and calls from neighborhood big shots and would-be big shots and brief visits from line officers handling cases in which the inspector had requested briefings, is pretty much a matter of having to switch one's personality gears, to change with the times even though you may not agree with either the times or the changes. On the whole, Inspector Short believes cops in New York, if not elsewhere in the country, are much improved.

Not that everything was wrong back when Short was a street cop, he adds. It's just that there has been a natural progression going on.

In 1954, Paul Short left his job as an airlines mechanic, where he was never once required to shoot anybody, and became a foot patrolman. "I was your regular beer-drinking, cigar-smoking cop like you don't see too much anymore these days," he said to Valentine. Officer Paul Short went to Emerald Society meetings, the principal fraternity of the main ethnic group of the New York City Police Department, and precinct dances. He got married early and stayed married. He worked hard at his job, too, and earned a reputation as an unusually tenacious cop. If a crook had Paul Short on his tail, it was like Joe Louis used to say, "He can run, but he can't hide."

There was the case of the Cuban giant, for instance:

"I was in the Bronx and that guy was the second guy I shot in my career. The other one was a taxicab stick-up artist and a junkie and isn't even worth mentioning. But the Cuban! I'll never forget it, mainly because he was enormous, close to seven feet. Also, because when I got him, it was the day before I made sergeant.

"He was a rapist, this guy . . ."

When Short says this, you understand the ferociously unspoken contempt of an Irish Catholic cop and family man for the loathsome rapist. His eyes go dead and cold and just about murderous. Valentine would see this expression many more times. And he would share the sentiment. He would also admire the control.

". . . He liked to get the nurses. Then he'd take their money by threatening to pay them another visit.

"The guy was incredible. Three times already, he'd escaped police traps."

One of those traps, the one just before Short finally brought him down, involved an apartment-house corridor. The Cuban had telephoned one of his victims and the young woman, in turn, called the police. So Paul Short rounded up the three biggest cops he could find in the Bronx and the four of them staked out the hallway on the nurse's floor. The Cuban arrived, right on schedule. When the cops moved in on him, the Cuban giant beat up the three big men and slammed past Short down the stairway to disappear into the street.

But that day before making sergeant, Short finally got his man. The Cuban, as per his habit, called up one of his victims and demanded that she meet him in a Bronx bar—with money. Otherwise, he said, she would die. Short was notified.

Posing as a neighborhood saloon patron, Short sauntered into the pub with a sack of groceries, as if he'd just been doing the day's marketing for his wife, and ordered a shot and a beer.

"The guy made me right away. Don't ask me how, but he made me. Some of these guys can smell cop. So he comes at me, this huge thing. He's a karate expert. He hits me so hard in the head I can't see anymore. I'm down on the floor and my head's split open and I can barely see. I figure this isn't right."

Officer Short peeled himself up off the barroom floor and staggered to the street. The big Cuban was in no hurry, remembering the heap of medium-build cop he'd just left back in the pub.

Short started following the Cuban, his .38 police special drawn. The big Cuban started running when he got a look at the fire in Short's eyes. There was Short, head flowing with blood, about a foot shorter than the Cuban, fully authorized to shoot to kill. The rapist, big and tough as he was, was frightened out of his mind. They ran for blocks, the dark giant panting and shouting, the loco Irish cop screaming and shooting behind him. Few things in the world are more terrifying than a stampeding, gored bull—or a cop who won't give up.

Finally, with a crack of fire that thudded into its mark, the big Cuban stumbled and fell, his legs full of lead.

"That was the easy part of it," Short recollected. "Any cop will tell you the same today. Some things haven't changed all that much. The collar's nothing sometimes compared to talking a victim into testifying against the perpetrator in court. Well, I managed to get one of the nurses to come through for us and we put away the Cuban pretty good that time."

Things were considerably different, operationally, when Paul Short cut down the Cuban as a beat cop in the Bronx. Today, Inspector Paul Short has something like seventy-two hours of paperwork on his hands when one of his men uses his gun in the line of service. There is an immediate hearing with the duty captain, or precinct inspector; there is an interview with the district attorney, then with a lawyer from the Policeman's Benevolent Association; there is a session, maybe more, with a police psychologist; there might be an interview with an officer from Internal Affairs Division; there might be a videotaping of the officer's testimony; there is a second interview with the precinct commander, who makes a decision with the officer on the question of continued psychological counseling. Back when he was Officer Short, there wasn't anything nearly like it. You just told your commander at the precinct house and then you lived with it, which was sometimes not the easiest thing in the world to do.

"I lived with that one real easy, let's just say," Short said.

In those old days of not so very long ago, the street cop in New York and other big cities around the country had profoundly more discretion than he does today. Justice, if it was justice, was swift indeed. An old-line cop worked in a system that seemed quartered by function: bust them, beat them, try them and fry them.

At times, the old ways seemed right and proper enough, even if they were a tad crude. At times, stripping away the sentiment of contemporary civil libertarianism, the old ways seemed practical. But in the long run, the percentage was not good. Cops came to work like an occupational army in a mean and beaten town. "Us against them," as Short puts it. And all that happened was that the cops were divorced from the people they served. It didn't say much for managerial methods, either.

"Way back, a cop didn't think anyone was in charge," Short said. "God forbid you should call a car for assistance. You just walked your post and took care of what came up. Guys in the cars didn't like to be bothered and let you know it by chewing up your ass.

"I don't think I even talked to a captain until I was a lieutenant. Now I'm commander of this precinct and the guys think nothing of coming in here to talk to me."

Which suits Short just fine. He likes to know what's going on and he likes the banter.

Tony Ciffo stuck his head through the door when Short recognized his knock.

"The desk's holding a delicate for you, boss," Ciffo said.

"Thanks, Tony."

Before he picked up the private line on his desk, Short said to Valentine, "We're all going to start calling him Chief-O now. Ciffo doesn't sound so good."

Short made notes on a pad with a Mont Blanc fountain pen and then hung up after some additional chitchat with the commissioner's office.

"Comes with the territory here in the Nineteenth," Short said. "We've got heavyweights. Lots of cases are delicate, referred from the commissioner or the mayor himself. They both live up here."

A series of delicates interrupted the conversation.

Short had to deal with the local exigencies of international political tensions, none of which would crop up in the course of a business day for the police chief of, say, Omaha. There were hints from anonymous callers, self-serving no doubt, that pipe bombs would be rolled into the Lebanese tourist office on Park Avenue in response to the Israeli military sorties into Palestinian Liberation Organization guerrilla camps; there would be a general picket-line protest outside the French Mission to the United Nations, the subject of which was French armaments shipments into the Middle East; it might be wise to keep an eye on the Egyptian mission due to the fighting between Coptic Christians and the majority Moslems.

The Nineteenth Precinct of Manhattan contains more than three dozen foreign missions to the United Nations or consulate offices, including the Russians, directly across the street from the Nineteenth, on East Sixty-seventh Street. Short's men are responsible for security duty, which consists of round-the-clock uniform guards in the "boxes" stationed outside the mission buildings. Most of the missions, particularly the Russians and the PLO on East Sixty-fifth Street, have their own security people working inside and quietly on the outside. The Russians are sometimes seen with submachine guns.

"So," Short said, resuming his conversation with Valentine, who was taking notes for a lecture he was preparing for a meeting of the East Side Republican Club, "in a way everything's delicate here, you might say. It's so attractive for criminals, we have to do a lot of preventative work. We haven't got time for bullshit cases. We don't cover the sheet by rounding up a few junkies or something like that. It's futile and it doesn't really help all that much.

"Well, right there is my philosophy about running the Nineteenth and it gets me into trouble with community groups all the time. If I wanted to really please the Republican Club, to name a group, I'd haul in all the *hoors* . . ."

Short says *hoors*, the way the Irish do in upper Manhattan and the Irish neighborhoods of the northern Bronx.

". . . and I'd have all the cars towed and we'd bust up all the kids' big radios. But I'd be tying up my men on bullshit that takes them to court all day and the burglars would be stealing the people blind in the meantime.

"That's the big problem here, burglary. We got career burglars. This is a very attractive place for them, like I said. Some guy goes back to Williamsburg, for instance, and he tells his pals that he scored for two grand up here and one of his buddies says, 'What the hell am I doing busting my ass for fifteen dollars on Amway Street?' So this second guy gets himself a Brooks Brothers suit like his pal and an attaché case like yours and pretty soon we've got *two* career burglars. They get on the subway in the morning and they head uptown for Fifty-ninth Street, where my command starts. It's just like they're going to work. That's a big problem and that's why we're pretty heavy on plainclothes officers here. How do you tell the bad guys from the good guys when they dress the same?

"We've got the usual sort of thing, too. Lots of *hoors* on Eighty-sixth Street. Sometimes our detectives make directs on them, which is picking them up for questioning in hopes that they can get some information helpful to some investigation. But they're pretty wise about that sort of thing. I have our uniforms run them in on occasion for soliciting, just to keep a presence, or an appearance of a presence. They're pretty wise to that, too.

"Anyway, we practically know them all by name and their career histories. There's Crystal, for instance. She got shot in the head by a john a while back, but the doctors decided removing the bullet would be a bigger risk than not. She's back there, same old corner, hooking like always."

Short shook his head.

"I don't like to get our officers too involved with the pross. You run the risk of exposing your men to corruption just once too often and it's not worth it. Just little stuff, but it's not good. Like maybe a pross will offer a feel, or maybe some hotel will pay to be left alone. You have to trust your men, but you have to be reasonable, too."

He shook his head again.

"More and more, if you want to be a good commander, you've got to think about the private lives of your men. Their private stresses. Cops are part of the society, too, you know, and they're subject to all the same troubles. Everything's seemed to change so much, you know, from the Vietnam War onward.

"Years ago, as cops, we wouldn't put up with the things we see today on the streets and now some of those things are thought to be practically normal. We've got entirely new attitudes about drugs and sexual mores and life-styles. All of that turmoil affects cops, too.

"I remember years ago that all the trouble you'd see with a cop's life is how it was going for him at home. You used to be able to tell a divorced cop just by looking at him, and there weren't too many anyway.

"Today! Hah! Today, the phone's ringing off the hook sometimes with wives and girl friends complaining about support payments being held up."

Once more, he shook his head.

"I shouldn't be talking about cops like they were only men. One of the biggest changes around here is all the women officers we've got nowadays."

At one end of the officers' locker room, men's division, in the dank basement of the Nineteenth Precinct station, Jack Clark, as usual, was complaining about unkempt colleagues. Clark works the burglary detail in plainclothes. His ensembles run toward ripped jeans, scuffed leather jackets, sweatshirts and always some sort of seedy hat. The reason for his fastidious nature is, therefore, mostly a mystery.

"Some of these guys," he says, sniffing the locker-room atmosphere, "don't hit the rain room too often, if you catch my drift."

He had a special contempt for the man who lockered next to him, a sweat-soaked officer whose locker door hung open, its contents ripe with the same fragrance that affected its owner. He had just placed the uniform he'd managed to pick off his body into the locker.

"What's that uniform?" Clark asked. "You shoot it out of a gun into the locker?"

"Hey, Clark, you keep your damn locker the way you want to and I'll keep mine the way I want."

"Okay," Clark said, "just so long as nothing jumps out of yours and bites me."

"Take a look at one of New York's finest," another cop said, swinging open the doors to an immaculate locker, one that Clark would approve.

The inside of the door was plastered with five pages of the September '82 number of something called *Beaver*, the "wildlife" magazine. The photo spread in question consisted of five color poses and one black-and-white of a dark-eyed and obviously authentic brunet model to whom the magazine had given the *nom de plume* Nina.

Nina was almost wearing a red teddy with white lace trim. The straps were loosened down around the shoulders of the fetching femme, the bodice dipped below high, tiny breasts with prominent dark red nipples. The bottom edge of the garment grazed her navel. She wore dark hose with black elasticized tops and spikey black leather pumps. A puff of red feather accented her bouffant hairdo.

She had a taupe beauty mark below one eye and dazzling white teeth, perfectly straight and even except for a bit of space between the two bottom front incisors. The lower portions of the photographs were explicit enough to be of some use to Nina's gynecologist.

There was a block of text accompanying the layout, which explained Nina's favorite fantasy, the one about taking on more than one stud at a time.

"Doesn't look like any cop I've ever seen," one of the cops in the locker room said.

"Sure about that?" the cop with the open locker asked. "Little bitty thing around here, not even five feet? Not a bad cop, either. She was decorated not long ago for bringing down three strong-arms."

"She's not at the One-Nine anymore," another cop said. "Haven't you heard? She's been transferred downtown to Public Morals."

The cop laughed and added, "When word about this gets around, boy, there's going to be some heavy dung going to hit the old propeller. You heard it here first."

The delicate was very old and very rich and she hadn't shown up at the appointed time for dinner in Southampton.

The Nineteenth was full of them. Rich old women who lived out lonely marriages for the big payoff: wealthy widowhood. Trouble with them was that they went a little loopy from all the wasted years and now here they were with plenty of cash, but very little sense. They were perfect marks for all manner of smooth scam, the more exotic the better. Mostly, the old family retainer from some Park Avenue law office would settle accounts when they got their teats caught in the wringer, so to speak. But sometimes the police were unavoidable. That's when the commissioner's office would call up Paul Short.

There was a day when a delicate case meant something far more important to Paul Short's job than what the term meant for him today. There were the days back in Harlem, in the sixties, when his exploits were the stuff of cop movie legend. In fact, his partner then was Sonny Grosso, creator of TV's "Kojak." The "Kojak" pilot written by Grosso, *The Marcus Nelson Murders,* was, in fact, the story of Grosso and Short and their incredible adventures as two of the most productive narcotics cops in New York City and, therefore, the world.

There was the Frankie Paradise case, for instance:

As a narc, Short worked out of the city-wide Major Violators Squad. He'd been after Frankie Paradise for months, knowing that somewhere in the city Paradise had the biggest stash of heroin anyone had known about all in one place since the French Connection bust.

Paradise was a slippery character. He had a half-dozen Cadillacs, but he never used them. He went everywhere by subway, which was how Short knew the stash had to be somewhere within the city limits. The problem was to find Paradise's safe house, which is what it had to be, since Paradise liked to sleep with his stash to know it was safe and sound.

For months, Short and his partners worked an "A,B,C,D tail" on Paradise, meaning four different cops would be used to follow him, the four in communication with PTP radios and alternating to throw off any suspicion of a tail, any sign of the same man in close proximity. And for months, Short and the others were frustrated by Paradise's uncanny ability to make them. Before Short and the other tails gave up, Paradise had taken them on a tour of all 239 route miles of the New York City subway system, through all three separate lines several times, through all 458 stations and back again to point zero.

Frankie Paradise didn't seem to have a weak spot. Could that be?

Short thought about this for a while. It didn't add up. He'd been a cop long enough to know that everybody has a weak spot. If he could touch that spot just right, even a smooth operator like Frankie Paradise would sing himself right up the river. Finally, it occurred to Short that Frankie Paradise had the oldest and the biggest weak spot in the annals of crime history: a dumb blonde for a girl friend.

Instead of shadowing Paradise, Short went for a tap on Blondie's telephone.

Among other calls that Frankie might not be so happy to know about, Short discovered that Blondie's assistance in Paradise's informal pharmaceutical enterprise was to provide certain inquirers with five numerals. Over and over again, Blondie would issue the same five digits.

These days, maybe the telephone company has high-speed computers and possibly someone who knows how to operate them in order to isolate a set of five digits attached to a small collection of exchange codes. Back in the days when Short was chasing after Paradise, though, he had to rely on the inevitable slip-up on the part of the dumb blonde girl friend. His patience was rewarded.

One fine day, Blondie said, "RAvenswood . . . whoops, I'm not supposed to say that . . ."

It was all Short needed to know that the safe house was in the Ravenswood district of Queens. He checked through telephone company records and located an address.

Then, armed with the necessary court papers, Short paid a visit to the house one night while his partners resumed playing subway games with Frankie Paradise. He secreted himself in the closet of one of the several bedrooms in the large Queens home. And there he stayed for ten days, waiting for the mouse to enter the trap.

Paradise was nabbed in the act of retrieving a kilo of heroin from a false bottom to one of the bedroom dressers. Short made the collar with no resistance, though plenty of grudging respect for his prowess and patience. Paradise had in his pockets at the time about $50,000 in cash, a pittance in comparison to the value of the heroin in the dressers.

Now, with nearly thirty years on the job, and assignment to a gentler sort of precinct, Short was confronted with the case of the vanished dowager.

Her name was Eleanor Moore Montgomery, aged eighty-eight. Ten days earlier, she was to have arrived at a Southampton dinner party. On the day she vanished, the doorman at her apartment building, 875 Fifth Avenue, flagged her a taxicab. Presumably, she was taken to her garage, at First Avenue and Seventy-second Street, where she would take out her Mercedes and motor on out to Long Island alone.

A former fashion editor at *Vogue* magazine, Mrs. Montgomery had been lately fascinated with Eastern mysticism in the person of one Panna Kamla, who had his own room in Mrs. Montgomery's spacious apartment.

The two of them, in fact, Mrs. Montgomery and Kamla, were co-authors of a coffee-table book few had ever heard of, *The Meaning of My Mantra*, all about the Kamla worldview. The book was a sort of bible for the foundation Mrs. Montgomery had established, along with her guru, Kamla.

Kamla was unavailable for questioning.

"Sometimes it's first thing in the morning when the cop has to go to the morgue," the desk sergeant was telling Valentine. "So what's good for him is good for a Community Affairs guy, right?"

Valentine nodded and was off once again with the fun-loving Ralph and Ed.

The New York Medical Examiner's Office is situated in a big, battleship-gray hulk of a building at Thirtieth Street and First Avenue in the Kip's Bay district of Manhattan, near the Bellevue Hospital complex. The saloons and restaurants serving the neighborhood of resident physicians, medical technicians and interns reverberate with tales of visits by the likes of Valentine the rookie cop.

Valentine walked into the building and found it full of white-smocked medical personnel and cops getting signatures for deposits of corpses that had found their way to the morgue. The smell of the place was a blend of formaldehyde and dead wino.

There was a main bank of steel beds and vaults in a cavernous room with slippery, immaculate tiles. An orderly helped an intern and a cop locate a vault containing the body of the young man who had died in the little apartment on York Avenue, the musician from Ohio.

The body, with its toe tag connecting it to the Nineteenth Precinct, was shifted onto a steel surgical table with sheets cascading over the sides to the floor. Then the body was wheeled into a small operating room off the main bank. Whenever there is an unwitnessed death, anywhere in New York City, there is at the very least a preliminary autopsy performed, even though the cause of death might be clear as day. On such rules of *pro forma* are thousands of careers built in New York.

Valentine watched as interns scrubbed up. Then for the next quarter of an hour or so, he watched with increasing wooziness the routine incisions made on the body of the young man with the gray skin as his body was probed for any signs of evidence that would indicate foul play.

Blood was drained through the arms by a pair of tubes implanted in the dead wrists. Tissue was extracted from the roof of the mouth and the frontal portion of the brain for later chemical analysis.

As they worked, the chief resident made oral observations about the young man they examined. Another intern operated a tape recorder to preserve these notations. Valentine could hear it all, distanced as he was from the mass of toxic flora that lay dead on the operating table, for the interns spoke into a microphone suspended above the corpse.

"In this case," the chief intern intoned, "there isn't a great deal more fluid to be extracted from the body. But it's been my experience that there always is something in there, always something a little wet left inside a body that's been dead for days, even months."

For the benefit of the novice observer, the intern continued:

"Now, we're going to have to do something a little unorthodox here, something we didn't do customarily in medical school. What we have to do is drain the pelvic fluids by way of the penis."

Valentine was confused.

"We take a suture . . ."

Valentine's eyes were perversely glued to the grisly procedure. A flaring pain shot through his own pelvis in some involuntary physical sympathy.

". . . and wind it around the base of the penis. Then we wrap it up tight."

The intern wound the suture around the corpse's penis a half-dozen times, then wound the other end around his fingers.

"Right," he said into the microphone. "Now, I'll hold it taut while my associate works on some pressure points at the neck. I'll wait for the signal."

The other intern fingered the corpse's neck. Then, suddenly, he yelled, "Pull!"

The intern with the suture wrapped around his fingers gave a fierce tug. At that precise moment, as the dead man's penis was yanked hard, there came from below the operating table, hidden under the draped sheets, a bloodcurdling scream of pain. For several horrifying seconds suspended in time, it seemed to Valentine, the scream floated from the dead man's own lips like some nightmare come true.

An orderly crawled out from beneath the wheeled operating table laughing gleefully.

Valentine, the butt of the joke, very nearly fainted.

Ralph and Ed were laughing so hard they almost fainted, too.

3

"You're not married, if I hear right."

"No," Valentine said.

"Course not. You wouldn't be sitting here in this dump with me now, would you? Not if you had a good woman to go home to."

"That would depend a lot on the woman, I'd say."

Keenan laughed, but the joke was a sad one for him. He ordered another schnapps and lager, his fourth setup. He drank the liquor down quickly and his lips stretched back as it burned nicely in his throat. He sipped the lager. Keenan was a thirty-eight-year-old cop with sixteen years on the force, a wife and two kids at home up in Riverdale. His wife, Mairead, was expecting their third.

They sat in a dingy saloon in upper Manhattan, far from the Nineteenth Precinct and its chic streets. Keenan stopped at the place most days after work, the Hibernian by name.

"Wouldn't you?" Keenan asked.

"Wouldn't I *what?*"

"Ah listen, I can read your mind, college boy. You went to college now, didn't you? Sure you did." Keenan waved his hand, unsteadily. "What I meant was, if you were me, wouldn't you work up an awful big thirst every day and come into a place like this?"

Keenan was currently assigned to the "bow-and-arrow squad," which meant that he would not be allowed to carry a gun until such time as his attitude improved. Usually, bow-and-arrow duty lasted for a specified time and for a specific reason or reasons. That was bad enough.

You take away a cop's gun and you take away the pride and trust he's won in being allowed to carry it in the first place. In Keenan's case, bow-and-arrow was indefinite. A depressed cop endangers the public.

"Yeah, maybe. Maybe I would come into this place, just like you," Valentine said. "Yeah. Sometimes drinking is the answer."

Keenan slapped him on the back. "You don't look any worse for the wear yet, but you sound like you've been run over a few times yourself, eh, college boy? Hey, supposing I told you I had some college myself? Surprise you?"

Valentine shook his head.

"Ah, 'tis true. This business takes the finer edges off anyone, real quick. That's what's happened to me. Besides which, the company I keep at home and the company you can start keeping as a cop ain't too fuckin' mentally stimulating sometimes.

"Anyway, I like you, college boy. You're going to be good for my intellectual development."

They ordered another round. Valentine was astonished by Keenan's capacity.

Keenan looked at the mirror that backed the bar, looked at the images of all the bottles, all different colors and shapes and infinitely more where they came from, all of them reflected in the glass. He swirled his beer. Then he turned to Valentine on the stool next to his.

"I wanted to be a writer when I came over from the other side, that's the truth," Keenan said. "So you want to know how it was then, or do you want to know how it was I got to be a fucked-up cop?"

"Whatever you want to tell me, I'll listen."

"Then I'll tell you both tales, my friend." Keenan ordered another round of drinks.

"When I came over, I was just old enough to have the memory of it burn into my brain for good. We sailed over, just like in all the movies. I was ten. You can't imagine how it was for a wee boy. I come from a small village outside Dublin and all my life I was hearing about this place, New York and America. I was warned about America, I met the Irish-Americans when they came back to strut around, I saw all the cinema I could, I decided America was the only place in the whole world to be and, please God, I hoped my father could see his way to getting us all over there.

"Well, by God, he did get us over."

Keenan stopped talking for a few seconds and his eyes misted. Valentine looked the other way because he was embarrassed by Keenan's intimacy. Well, he'd agreed to go along with Keenan for a few lifters, hadn't he?

"One day, I was on the boat with the family, actually going over the seas to America. And we sailed into the harbor at New York and I saw the Statue of Liberty with the sun settling down behind her.

"I'd seen the pictures of this a thousand times in books and on the television in Ireland, but the pictures didn't do justice to the experience. That's how I decided I wanted to be a writer. For justice."

Keenan laughed and Valentine asked him, "What did you do about it?"

"I read a lot, everything I could get. And I did well in school. Then I went to college. Tuition was free at City."

He wiped his upper lip and drank with the satisfaction of a powerful need met. Keenan was telling someone exactly what he wanted. Valentine was the new guy at the station house and Keenan had caught his ear before anyone could warn him off.

"Also, I had to get a job because Mairead was pregnant. And of course, that meant marriage. So I married a little girl from the very next village over from mine. Something had to give, and it was college because I had to be practical, see. I was studying to become a journalist."

"So instead you became a cop."

"A telephone installer first, my friend. You know how it is. You get something good for yourself and then you take the police exam and wait to be called. It takes a while, right?"

"Why did you want to be a cop?"

"A fine question! And coming from a cop himself. Well, it's deserving then of a fine answer, but I'm sorry I haven't got one. Maybe I wanted to be a cop for justice, too. Maybe I wanted to be a cop because every little boy in the world wants to put on the blue uniform and wear a badge on his chest and a gun on his hip. Maybe I wanted to impress Mairead back in our courting days. Maybe I wanted to help people. I forget just which it was."

"Sounds to me like you're about ready to quit the force."

"Oh no. You'd have me wrong. I can't quit being a cop any more than I could quit my wife or my kids. That's the way I'm constructed."

Keenan tossed back a final schnapps. Time to get home.

"But I wouldn't mind changing a thing or two," he said. "I'm like

most cops in this city. I spend years making good, clean collars and
nobody gets hurt. I spend years making things good for my wife and my
babies. For that, I get no recognition. Now I wonder why it isn't just
the other way around?

"So I come here after work. I come here because I'm in a position
where I can either drink or cry. Drinking is so much more subtle, isn't
it?"

By nine o'clock in the morning, it was eighty degrees and the humidity level was nearly the same. By midafternoon, just before the night
tour, it was so bad in Manhattan you could lift the heat with your
hands.

Keenan woke up at half-past two in the afternoon, his head heavy
with alcohol and nine hours of breathing air artificially cooled and dried
by a machine wedged in the bedroom window of his apartment. He
thought the same thing he thought every day when he woke, what he'd
watched on television in the living room, where he'd fallen asleep.
Sometimes it occurred to him in the haze of arousal that Mairead must
have moved him into the marital bed sometime after the second episode of Mary Tyler Moore; sometimes it occurred to him that he
hadn't made love to his wife in a very long time.

Mairead had long ago left the apartment with the children. They
would be in the nice, safe park down below, the children playing with
the other boys and girls in the sandbox. Mairead would spend the
afternoon in artificially cheerful conversation with the other housewives.

He looked out the tightly sealed bedroom window, down to the
wide, rippled Hudson River and out over the New Jersey Palisades.
Keenan had been to Jersey several times, on trips down to the shore on
steaming days like this, and he'd been upstate and over the border once
into Ontario. Otherwise, his travels had yet to include anything of
America much farther west than his bedroom window.

Keenan showered quickly, dressed and had time enough to fix himself eggs and bacon. He took an elevator down to the underground
garage and fired up his air-conditioned Ford for the drive over the
Henry Hudson Bridge down Manhattan's West Side Highway, over the
potholes to the exit at 125th Street, where he drove crosstown to the
East Side. He liked driving through the blight of 125th Street. He liked

the sense of threat he felt in Harlem in the dog days of summer. At least it was something real, something palpable; it was life.

Tony Ciffo sat on a beach at Jacob Riis Park in Queens, where it was cool and the air was salty dry. His hair curled tighter in the sun and his skin grew browner by the second. He looked at his wristwatch and swore. Next to him was a pleasant, attractive, intelligent woman. She was a blond psychology student who happened also to be his partner, Officer Jean Truta.

They packed up their things and left the beach. Towels and swimsuits in canvas bags changed places in the back end of Ciffo's brand-new Renault Fuego with four forward speeds on a stick shift with NYPD duffel bags containing starched blue summer-issue short-sleeve shirts, summer-weight navy-blue wool twill pants, shiny black oxfords and bulletproof vests.

Then Ciffo and Truta headed into the city. They would have a ride-along that night on their tour, Valentine.

Philip Leland Hehmeyer hadn't felt like going to work at the World Trade Center that day, but he did. So many people depended on his being there. And anyway, it wouldn't look good if he took a day off for no good reason after having been elected just two months ago chairman of the New York Cotton Exchange.

No good reason.

In an hour, the New York Stock Exchange would close with the official gaveler's thudding finale of a remarkable week's trading. Despite the recession of August 1982, the Dow Jones industrial average had soared a whopping eighty-one points. President Reagan and his staff were jubilant and press conferences were hastily arranged in order to trumpet the success of the Administration's economic policies, evidenced by the record-setting confidence of Wall Street, no less.

Not everyone was a celebrant of the remarkable week's trading. Hehmeyer's experience was not the stuff of White House hurrahs. On Monday, he personally lost nearly $64,000 in cotton trading, though he managed to cover it; the losses of his clients would be greater and he would have to face their wrath soon; he made some money on Thursday in gold; but today, Friday, by his penciled calculations, his personal losses in futures trading would be $58,803.75.

He totted up these losses in a sleek and sweeping office high over the most important city in the world.

On "Black Friday" of 1929, financiers and brokers like Philip L. Hehmeyer crept out onto ledges outside their windows and leapt to the street to die. Back in '29, the windows of office buildings in New York's Financial District were so constructed as to provide easy access to suicide. In the World Trade Center of today, it is impossible to actually open a window without special tools.

Besides, it was 1982, not '29. And Hehmeyer knew that no matter what, he always had his luxurious apartment on Sixty-second Street just a few doors east of Fifth Avenue and Central Park, his antique Jaguar motorcar, his collection of paintings now on loan to museums throughout the United States and his venture capital investments in dozens of new and thriving small businesses.

And he had his business ability. How else had he managed to keep the firm going back when his two former partners were indicted on charges of plotting millions in phony tax losses by manipulating the market for crude oil futures? Philip Leland Hehmeyer had kept his head. He alone ran things until his partners were cleared. Then, in 1979, he split from them and became independent.

Phil Hehmeyer was by every measure a winner.

He lived on the Upper East Side, in a fabulous stone town house in a neighborhood where some of the wealthiest people in the world lived.

He was quick and smart; he had a million stories from his days as a Memphis newspaper reporter and the year he captained a sailboat from New York to St. Thomas, remaining in the Virgin Islands to manage a saloon; he was an outstanding amateur golfer and a pal of Jack Nicklaus, the pro, whom he personally watched win his fifth Masters championship in 1975 in Augusta, Georgia; he frequently went tarpon fishing off the Florida coast; he loved the primitive pleasure, the manly camaraderie of sitting in a swamp blind at dawn with a shotgun at the ready for the first sign of geese breaking across the sky; he belonged to a country club out on Long Island and a chic health spa in Manhattan.

He worried about his business losses in the philosophical way traders must worry about such things, so his friends said. What worried him more today was the big picture, the real news beyond such titillations as a presidential press conference. The collapse of the Mexican economy, for instance, which just that week was evidenced by a fall of the peso's value every bit as precipitous as the boom of numbers on Wall Street's big board. He was so worried, he was reading, for the third time, Adam Smith's book *Paper Money*.

He worried, too, that he smoked too many Winston cigarettes and that no matter how hard he tried, he just couldn't seem to shake the habit.

There was Dom Perignon champagne in his office, for occasions when the market was good. Otherwise, there were the makings for bullshots—vodka and beef broth. Hehmeyer didn't know which to drink today.

The night before, he had put his fiancée since Christmas, Susan McCadden Carr, the twenty-five-year-old daughter of a prominent cotton magnate from Mississippi, into a taxicab. She was headed to La-Guardia airport for a quick trip South to make arrangements for a family funeral. She would be back soon. Their wedding day was two weeks off.

He hadn't felt much like going to work, for he knew it would be a bad week for him. Nobody likes to show up for his own beating. But so many people depended on him.

Sometimes the burden of other people's expectations were an awful lot for him to shoulder. He was thirty-seven years old.

"Achtung!"

It was the sergeant's little way of calling order to the night-tour muster. Officers Ciffo, Truta and the rest stiffened for a few seconds, then resumed slouches. Blue-shirted backs were beginning to perspire. The sergeant, who strongly resembled Art Carney as Ed Norton, studied a clipboard full of special notices from Inspector Short's office, one of the few in the station house chilled to meat-locker temperature.

The sergeant called roll. Everyone seemed either "here" or "present."

"Okay, let's see about any special instructions today," the sergeant said, noisily riffling through the papers. "Oh yeah, up there at the Greek Embassy, watch out for people backin' into the place."

Laughter as he searched the day's hot sheet for bona fide memoranda.

There was still the matter of a fellow by the street name of "Kano," very much wanted for murdering a family of four by setting their apartment on fire; known to be heavily armed. . . . There was a lunatic hanging around lately outside Jacqueline Kennedy Onassis' apartment house on Fifth Avenue at East Eighty-sixth Street, "posing as some kind of cockamamie author, so you're welcome to scoop up the little scribbler and set him on the Toonerville Trolley to Ding Dong School." . . . And, as usual during the start of the afternoon rush hour, "try to scare the living hell out of the squeegee boys at the Queensboro Bridge."

That seemed to be all of an official nature.

"Remember now," the sergeant said, "you got to get them there shoes shined up. Now, we don't got no wax here, so's you're going to have to spring for it yourself. But you notice we do have this electronic buffer right here in the muster room that I'd like you all to get to know real well.

"Okay, that's all. Have a good tour."

There is an important rule of thumb strictly observed by police officers all over the city of New York, even on the Upper East Side: when you're in the vicinity of a clean, safe toilet, use it, no matter what. You never know when you may see one again on your tour. Ciffo went upstairs to the second-floor men's room while Truta went out to Lexington Avenue in search of an available squad car to begin the rounds.

There was a new bit of poetry inked upon a fresh coat of paint over an often-painted section of wall above the officers' latrine:

> They paint this place to hide
> the pen, but the
> Shithouse poet has struck again!

Down on the street, Ciffo joined Truta in a dented squad car. The air conditioner blasted hot air instead of cold, just as it had the other night. "Typical New York cop car," Ciffo said. "Nothing but the best for New York's finest." He worked the dial on a portable radio to a top-forty soft-rock station, then started to light up a Marlboro. Truta glared at him and put away the pack with a roll of his eyes.

"Okay, let's go," he said. "Look out, desperadoes, here we come!"

"Queensboro?" Truta asked.

"Absolutely. I feel like striking fear into the hearts of our little squeegee pals."

Truta navigated the squad car through streets clogged with shoppers, businessmen, clerks and rich Upper East Side matrons with Caucasian facial features and skin darkened incredibly by a combination of chemicals and unnaturally long periods in the sun, precisely timed. They had trails of unusual brown spots on their necks and collarbones, leopard-like, and they carried multitudes of brightly colored paper bags chock full of a day's purchases.

The rich women with the bags loading down their tanned arms passed by Bloomingdale's on Lexington Avenue at Fifty-ninth and paid little heed to an obese blind woman with torn hosiery and many similarly bright paper bags. The blind woman's bags, however, were creased and somewhat dog-eared from many trips about town with the things she needed to perform each day for her living.

"She's called 'Baby,' " Ciffo said of the blind lady. "She doesn't like to be called a bag lady."

Baby was singing an especially rousing rendition of "Tomorrow" from the hit Broadway show *Annie*. There was a cup nearby so that people could make contributions. Few did. None of the rich women with bags did, as if somehow repelled.

Baby had chosen the name for herself back when social workers somewhere in the Midwest—she doesn't remember exactly—had her sterilized and took away her out-of-wedlock infant. Baby chose her name because, she said, "I'm a lady who likes babies, so I'll be called 'Baby.' "

Once, Baby ventured inside Bloomingdale's after a day's performance on the street outside. She went to the doll department at Christmastime. She held a doll in her arms and ran her fingers over the doll's plastic face, felt eyes and a nose and lips and a chin and throat, hair and belly and legs. Store detectives, acting on the complaints of customers lucky enough to have eyes that worked but who were sickened by the sight of a blind woman feeling a doll's face, escorted Baby back out to the street.

Baby never complained about it. The cops in the Nineteenth Precinct look out for her, figuring that she probably will need protection sooner or later in a neighborhood full of people who can't stomach her appearance.

At the bridge, Truta and Ciffo used the car to chase youngsters and others not so young who swooped in on commuters with squeegees and pails of soapy water and scrubbed automobile windshields whether or not the driver agreed to such a service. The wipers would scatter fast and the game was afoot.

Occasionally, Truta would close in on a gang of squeegee-wielding miscreants, trapping them in an apartment-house driveway. Ciffo leapt out of the passenger seat, his nightstick raised. He snarled and the youngsters ran some more.

Then it would happen all over again until about half-past five, when the traffic moved too briskly for the youngsters to dare approach the cars.

A call came over the radio.

"Undesirable needs a sweep. Vicinity Madison and Sixty-first."

Truta reached for the radio microphone when Ciffo failed to make any move. Ciffo groaned.

"SU-8 can take the undesirable," Truta radioed back to the dispatcher. "Tell me what you can."

"God, I hate this," Ciffo said, talking over the dispatch.

". . . just hanging around, not doing any harm or anything, a white female in her thirties, well-dressed, writing things on a pad and sitting in stairwells."

"What'd I tell you?" Ciffo said.

Truta responded to the dispatcher, "Got it. You need a hear-back?"

"Discretionary."

Truta drove to an art gallery in the Sixties, between Madison and Park avenues. Ciffo grumbled all the way. In the stairwell of the gallery, closed for the day, was the woman described by the dispatcher. She wore a long, quality denim skirt and a clean white blouse. Her hair was brown with streaks of silver, drawn back neatly in a bun. Her skin and eyes were clear. She held a small pad of paper and a pencil and made notes of things she saw as she looked around her. She jotted down names and numbers of things, occasionally a scribbled line of something to describe a stoop or a window or a plant.

She had several large paper bags with her, which were set out on the steps of the stairwell as she sat, crouched just below the surface of the street to make her notes. Officers Truta and Ciffo approached her, carefully.

"Hi," Ciffo said, "how are you this afternoon? Hot, isn't it?"

The woman didn't answer his question, but was put at ease by Ciffo's manner. Then she smiled at Ciffo and said, "I suppose someone has complained about me again?" Her voice was a cultivated one. There was no trace of a hard life in it, no rasp of cigarettes or liquor.

"You know, I got to tell you that you have to leave the stairwell here and move along now," Ciffo said. "I hope you don't mind too much."

The woman rose gracefully, gathered up her bags, her pad and pencil and said, "Of course not." She smiled with great dignity.

Ciffo and Truta returned to the car. They circled the block a few times. The woman walked, stopping occasionally to make notes. She never looked directly at the squad car that followed her, but she was aware of it.

"Poor thing," Ciffo said. "She wouldn't have hurt anyone. It's always the same old thing, even when they're just starting out. The owner of the gallery doesn't want her around and he sure as hell doesn't want her pissing in his stairwell and disturbing the customers the next day, so he calls the cops."

Ciffo reached for a cigarette, but left the pack in his pocket. "I wonder what in hell her story is. She looks okay now, but she's off her nut and she's got herself her first set of bags. Now she's a rookie bag lady. God, what's going to happen to her after her first winter on the streets? You want to find out, but you just don't have the time to find out about everything you see.

"Sometimes you make it a point to find out anyway. You make the time. And then they don't want your help. Maybe they know there isn't anything we can do, really. They don't want anything to do with us. We try to be nice to them and I guess that's about what we should be doing under the circumstances."

Jean Truta, the psychology student, is getting her academic training in a very practical way by being a cop. Most particularly by coming into contact with bag ladies and other strange fauna of the Upper East Side.

"This is an ironic city in a very ironic world," she said. "The bag ladies. They either belong in mental institutions, or they were in them before and they weren't properly treated; which makes me wonder if they ever should have been put into existing mental institutions in the first place. You could go round and round—"

The police dispatcher's voice crackled again over the radio.

"Shots in the lobby of apartment building . . ."

Ciffo grabbed the mike and listened. He jotted down the house address, East Seventy-ninth Street at Third Avenue.

"Two squads confirm respond. Backup required . . ."

"SU-8 will back up," Ciffo said.

"Roger. Backup SU-8."

Truta yanked the wheel of the squad car hard and turned east, driving straight and fast down a tree-lined street. Ciffo flipped the sound and light switches below the dash.

Sirens blooped and screamed and the muscles tensed in Truta's neck as she drove, all her training concentrated on the immediate job of making good time safely, responding to the unknown moment, a moment that must be presumed to be extremely dangerous. Ciffo did what the nondriving partner is supposed to do under the circumstances of the call. His eyes swept the sidewalks and cross streets for signs of anyone who might not be able to hear the squad car's warning system or see its lights. If he saw something, he would alert the driver, but the two would not speak until they arrived at the scene. Each needed absolute concentration in these critical minutes of response time.

All around the speeding blue-and-white, its top lights blazing in an early gray twilight, the people of blasé Manhattan stood transfixed. Heads popped out of apartment windows. Diners stopped eating and watched the street scene from the bistros. Children and adults alike on the sidewalks, their eyes huge, watched the squad car sailing swiftly through the street, the officers inside a blur, the siren and the lights piercing the calm bustle. In New York there is no other shared experience so exciting, so riveting, so seductively thrilling as the sight of a squad car rocketing through the streets; everyone is most alive when his mortality, or a cop's mortality, is in the balance.

The silence inside a speeding blue-and-white is a terrifying and exhilarating thing. There is the sensation of a red heat that spreads through the body, a sensation that does not change, no matter how many times a cop finds himself hurtling through and over Manhattan's avenues and streets in response to violence somewhere in the night. Taxicabs and limousines and trucks and ordinary automobiles screech to curbsides, some of them, anyway, braking and yielding to cops rushing to danger, perhaps to their deaths. It has happened so often.

There is a frozen moment of unspoken tribute offered to cops by every New Yorker whose flesh goes bumpy at the sight of the frantic blue-and-white racing by: "I hope they catch him! Glad it's not my job!" And God help the New York cops, they love it.

A half-dozen squad cars were already converged on the scene by the time Ciffo and Truta arrived, blazing red and white lights flashing atop the vehicles drawn in a semicircle at the curb, beneath a long green awning at the front of a luxurious apartment building, at the foot of a long red carpet where tenants alit from Cadillacs and Lincolns and sometimes Rolls-Royces. Glass panels on either side of a double-door entrance were shattered, shards of destruction blown everywhere inside the lobby. Something with a wide-range blast had powered the explosion, possibly an automatic weapon of some sort, probably a shotgun.

Plainclothes cops, their badges flying at the ends of brass chains tucked inside their shirts as they walked the streets unobtrusively watching for people with larceny on their minds, combed a parking garage at one side of the large building. A pair of uniforms checked a rear garden. Another team questioned a very frightened, elderly doorman, who had seen nothing from the chair he occupied just inside the lobby.

No one, apparently, had been hurt.

"Probably a passing car," a cop said. Others agreed.

Though it was unlikely the gunman was inside the building, as he clearly had shot from the outside and the doorman had seen no one enter through the lobby, uniformed officers with guns drawn did a floor-by-floor search of the building—just in case anyone had heard anything; in case anyone had a suspicion that might turn up a lead.

Nothing.

Random violence that might always be a mystery is not yet the norm for the Nineteenth Precinct, but it is certainly routine. If cops thought about it too long, they would be no good. It's too spooky.

Philip Leland Hehmeyer had bolted the door of his fourth-floor apartment when he returned home at the end of a long and very dismal day, the sort of day when a commodities broker finds the two principles of his professional performance most taxing. To do the job, one has to put on a show for one's clients; one also has to put on a show for oneself.

Hehmeyer had been good at performing for a very long time.

He had lived well by it.

Near a wall of framed newspaper clippings of Jack Nicklaus' championship rounds in Augusta was a blackboard. There was also a gun cabinet containing the weapons he used in swamp blinds.

Hehmeyer wrote two sentences on the blank slate:

> Someone had to do it.
> Self-awareness is silly.

4

Ciffo took the wheel for the drive back to the "house" at East Sixty-seventh for the dinner break. Truta sat on the passenger side humming along with the radio.

At Third Avenue and Sixty-fifth, a car with California plates pulled alongside Ciffo and Truta after having made an illegal right turn on a red light. The driver, a middle-aged woman wearing a blond wig and sunglasses with red plastic bows, threw her hands up to her cheeks when she saw the police officers in the squad car next to her. She pushed a power button on the arm console and the driver's-side window whooshed down. A blast of iced air escaped her car.

"Oh my goodness," she said to Officer Truta, "I'm sorry, I forgot. In California, you can make a right on red."

Then the California woman noticed Officer Truta's gender.

"My goodness, you're a lady!" she said.

Officer Truta blushed.

Then the Californian said, "Say, you're cute!"

Ciffo told her to take it easy on the right turns while in New York.

"Okay, well, ta-ta, officers!" Her electronic window whirred up and she was off.

Dinnertime at the house is spent by most officers in the third-floor lounge, which is air conditioned and which has a nonprofit communal coffee urn, color cable television atop an abandoned green steel cabinet too rickety to hold drawers full of files anymore, two folding steel cafeteria tables of the type seen in public high schools everywhere and an eclectic collection of overstuffed chairs, wood frame couches and permanently scorched aluminum ashtrays. Officers on break sit mostly alone, or with their partners, munching sandwiches brought from home or slapped together by the counterman at a delicatessen on Third Avenue.

Down in the basement, some officers use the police gym to work out during breaks. Periodically, most of the newer officers work out at the first sign of occupational hazard—a puffy stomach from all the riding and waiting in squad cars, from the sandwiches, from the free doughnuts here and there throughout the precinct. Ciffo went downstairs to lift weights while Truta, in the third-floor lounge, opened up a brown bag containing mostly fruits and low-calorie items.

One of the officers in the lounge had been good enough to stop by a Burger King that day before work to buy a half dozen or so pairs of special red and blue cellophane eyeglasses secured in stiff white paper with drawings of hamburgers on the sides. The glasses were necessary for optimum appreciation of *Gorilla at Large,* the three-dimensional movie scheduled that night on WOR-TV. A few other officers had brought special 3-D glasses as well and there were about ten pairs circulating around the lounge as the film began.

The movie—starring Lee J. Cobb, Cameron Mitchell, Raymond Burr and Lee Marvin—concerned the escape of a gigantic circus gorilla who enjoyed biting and pummeling human beings and a love triangle involving the beautiful female trapeze artist, a shady ringmaster and an earnest young swain who was the only man in the world who truly understood that the beast was a gentle fellow deep down inside. The story and the special effects held about two dozen New York cops in an amused thrall during a break in the day's crime wave.

Down on the first floor, meanwhile, Keenan worked the complaint desk.

This is a small room containing a tiny, beat-up wooden desk with drawers full of a variety of printed forms. On top of the desk is a green and gray Smith-Corona manual typewriter, its keys coated with dust and grime. Keenan's job was to enter the appropriate data in the forms when incensed citizens made their way through the lobby and past a confusing and somewhat threatening sign pointing to his desk. The sign has large block lettering and an arrow beneath pointing the way. But instead of reading COMPLAINT ROOM, HAVE A SEAT, the vandalized sign reads DEATH SQUAD, HAVE A SEAT. Beyond the sign is a wall plastered over with wanted posters for various killers, armed robbers, extortionists, psychopathic revolutionaries and rapists. In almost every case where the poster photograph shows the alleged perpetrator to be black, there is a crudely scrawled addendum, "Send back to Africa."

An upset citizen would have to go to the complaint desk to register objection to such things as motorists who attempt to run down pedestrians. Usually, the citizen can barely contain his rage and operates under the belief that he is the only pedestrian who has ever had an encounter with a murderous motorist. And usually the officer who must work the complaint desk is, like Keenan, on bow-and-arrow duty. The citizen is upset. And certainly Keenan was upset at the ignominy of having to type up complaints, which were, practically speaking, little more than receipts for use when and if the incensed citizen cared to spend a grueling day of noise and red tape and delays at the civil complaint court on lower Broadway, business hours only. Mostly, the complaint forms were eventually discarded when the citizen calmed down over the next forty-eight hours and figured the percentage of justice to be gained against the irritation factor in dealing with minor court bureaucracy.

After taking a complaint from a particularly incensed citizen who wished to give a complete physical description of a motorist he claimed had leapt out of a car after having a door kicked and dented by the complainant, who the driver had allegedly attempted to run down in cold blood, Keenan had had enough. He needed air, he needed freedom from tension and chickenshit. He wanted badly to punch the last complainant in the face, but he did what he was supposed to do by giving the citizen an official piece of paper that seemed to satisfy the situation, at least that night. Keenan said the perpetrator might be prosecuted for criminal threatening. He advised the complainant, now solemn with the thought of facing the mad driver again in a courtroom, to go through the legal system by showing up in civil court first thing on Monday.

Keenan waited for the complainant to make his way slowly out of the precinct house, then he left himself and went for an ice cream. He returned with a cup of Sedutto double chocolate fudge and sat on the precinct-house stoop, alone, spooning thick confection into his mouth.

Tony Ciffo, his capillaries aglow from the exercise down in the gym, wandered out onto the stoop. He felt so good he thought he might talk to Keenan.

"How you doing?" he asked.

"Not good, Tony. I don't know what the fuck life means anymore. Do you?"

"The marriage, huh?"

Keenan didn't say anything. He didn't have to.

"Well, good luck, pal," Ciffo said. "It's kind of like a prison, isn't it? I'm just glad I did my time already, that's for sure."

"Yeah."

An extremely attractive young woman passed by on the street, the sort of sleek woman who predominates on the Upper East Side. College-educated, a professional woman, a cultured woman, a woman who talked about something other than the grocer and the children, a woman who might show a man like Keenan that the world is a very big place with many things to do.

But the chances of Keenan hooking up with such a woman for anything more than a short-term sexual fling, if even that, were remote. Keenan knew it and watched her pass. Perhaps the woman knew it, too.

Keenan called to her, "What do you think it means?"

She turned. Ordinarily, a woman like her would ignore a conversation struck up on the street, but the man sat on the steps of a police station. The man was a cop. "What?" she asked.

"What does life mean?" Keenan asked.

She turned on her heel and continued down East Sixty-seventh toward Lexington, then right, perhaps to the subway station at Sixty-eighth Street or perhaps to Hunter College and some affair far beyond Keenan's world.

Ciffo walked down the stairs to the street, then turned and looked at Keenan, who was staring blankly at his ice cream.

"Listen, pal," he said to Keenan, "life is more than a cup of ice cream."

Keenan said, "It's half a cup."

Philip Hehmeyer, the young, hardworking, highly respected tycoon soon to be wed, sat in his expensive, tasteful apartment, alone. He wasn't receiving. He wasn't answering his telephone. He drank into the night.

When he'd had enough—quite enough—he took his favored shotgun from the cabinet near the mementos of Jack Nicklaus' smashing victory at the Masters, the one he used to hunt geese.

Then he walked into his kitchen. He put both barrels of the shotgun into his mouth and pulled the triggers. His body collapsed to the floor in a heap. Brains and blood spattered the room.

Hehmeyer lay there until the following Monday. Someone noticed right away that he hadn't shown up for work. His telephone was of no use. An associate went uptown to his apartment and checked, knowing that Hehmeyer, smart and professional though he was, might be a very troubled man.

A "family spokesman" informed the Nineteenth Precinct detective squad that Eleanor Moore Montgomery had apparently become confused while driving through Long Island. All was well now and she was home on Fifth Avenue, safe and sound. Nothing was mentioned of Panna Kamla.

Officer Cibella Borges of the Public Morals Division, lately of the Nineteenth Precinct, had been telling cops for days now that she hadn't posed for any magazine called *Beaver*. Whoever "Nina" was, she said, there was nothing in the magazine about her being a cop.

Maybe this "Nina" chick was Cibella Borges' *Doppelgänger*, her exact double. That had to be it!

Now the press was calling. The *Daily News* and the *Post*, the city's tabloids, were already speculating in big, black, lurid headlines that played over and over again in Cibella Borges' dreams about her being a "cheesecake cop" and the true identity of "Naughty Nina." Now they wanted her to make a "clean breast of it," as the *Post* put it with a smirk.

Deputy Police Chief John Guido told reporters about his receiving "anonymous calls" alerting him to the magazine layout. The press didn't bother challenging the legitimacy of anonymity in this case. Guido, unchallenged, said that if Officer Borges didn't happen to have an exact double who happened to have posed in the buff for the likes of *Beaver*, then she was in very serious trouble. She might be found by departmental trial, he said, to be guilty of "conduct unbecoming to the department" and subject to punishment ranging from a reprimand to outright dismissal.

Why, supposing Officer Borges *was* the model in the pornographic photo spread, reporters were told! The first time she had to testify in a case where she'd arrested someone on a morals charge—a hooker, say, or maybe even a pornographer—the defense lawyer would simply have to trot out the September '82 number of *Beaver* and ask the good officer about *her* moral standards.

Meanwhile, though never much of a mover in the newsstands around the city, *Beaver* magazine was having something of a bull market at the Nineteenth.

A newsstand operator on Fifth Avenue by the name of Frank Senior sold out within an hour of the *Beaver* delivery. "I guess the cops bought them," he said.

Meanwhile, for those cops who could manage to remain clothed while associating with publishers of magazines featuring photos of naked women in variously compromised poses, there were several more games on the season schedule for the Nineteenth Precinct men's softball club, whose membership included many readers of the September '82 issue of *Beaver*. The sponsor of their club was *Penthouse* magazine, a circumstance not considered compromising or even titillating by Deputy Chief Guido or the city's tabloid headline writers.

Dory Smith had been raped.

For three years this single fact of her thirty-two-year-old life dominated her thoughts and her identity. Friends would bring it up when they talked to her, trying to help; and if her friends didn't bring up the subject, Dory would herself, sometimes with total strangers.

Friends invited her to lots of parties right after it happened. Always, the parties included a lot of nice men. Dory's friends tried to help in this way. Dory was certain the nice men had been told of her tragedy because they always seemed so uneasy around her. Usually, she would say to them, "You don't know this about me, but I was raped once." Then would ensue several hours of conversation, during which these nice men would shrink from even the mildest, the most normal party flirtations when it came to A Rape Victim.

Gradually, her friends drifted away and Dory was saddened by it, though at the same time oddly relieved. There seemed to be no more common ground in the relationships. She wondered, was it because her friends hadn't also been raped?

Sometimes, she dreamed of her rapist's face. And the dream was sometimes quite the opposite of nightmare. She would wake, sexually aroused and ashamed of herself. She would then take a very long shower, but it didn't help her return to sleep. Horrible nightmares would have been far more restful, she thought.

For the past year practically the only people she saw were her co-workers and the members of her therapy group. Her colleagues were all women and, like her, seamstresses hired at very low pay by a theatrical costume shop. The owner was a homosexual man whom she would see a few minutes each week when he came by with the pay envelopes. Her therapy group was composed entirely of women, including the psychologist. Dory didn't much like these women because she felt oddly insulted to be among them. They were all either ugly or obese or loud-mouthed or in some other manner repulsive or at least off-putting. Dory Smith was an attractive woman, quiet and intelligent. She wanted to be an actress. She didn't belong with these ugly women.

And yet, she hadn't been to an audition since the rape, though she still told her married sister back in Missouri that she simply had to remain in New York, where the "chances for my break" were. Her sister argued that Dory lived a "grasshopper's life," what with her low pay, most of which went for rent, and her hermit's existence.

Dory agreed with her sister, although she offered an explanation for her pathetic situation. She wrote to her sister to inform her that no matter what she might read of the glamour of New York, especially the glamour of the Upper East Side, where she lived in an apartment the size of a Missouri kitchen, it was entirely possible for an attractive young woman to go weeks without having a substantial conversation with anyone. Once, Dory wrote, she had gone without speaking a word to anyone at all for four straight days. She could have talked to someone, Dory told her sister, if she was willing to run the risk of being raped while taking an evening stroll on Fifth Avenue or the risk of idiotic chatter by hanging around in Upper East Side singles bars.

Dory's sister never asked in letters about her "sex life," as she used to put it before The Rape. Dory's sister wrote to her as if there was no such thing as a male of the species.

No matter how many times Dory would write in her letters of how lonely she was, how much she would like to meet a good, gentle man, there was no response from her sister. Soon, Dory's sister would go the way of her friends.

One spring morning Dory read a newspaper story about the New York City police auxiliary. There was a photograph accompanying the story, a picture of men and women who worked in precinct houses throughout the city for no pay, assisting the police in things such as traffic control and certain station office duties and crowd duty. She remembered how really sensitive the two police officers had been who came to her apartment the night she was raped. Dory wanted to meet good men, men with whom she could feel safe and men who might understand that crimes happen to good people like her, who ought not to be further victimized by their friends' pity.

She thought about joining the Nineteenth Precinct auxiliary unit for several days. Then she went ahead and did it and didn't tell her sister.

5

Generally speaking, the New York City mugger is young and male and remarkably able-bodied. He is either unnaturally afraid of working for wages or salary, or he is wildly unsuited for straight jobs, or there don't happen to be such things in the scope of his friends, family and associates; in any event, he requires a steady cash flow to support a fondness for drugs.

Like the rodent, the mugger customarily shuns daylight and he is not apt to stray too far from home on his nocturnal prowlings. Mostly, he travels in packs of like-minded fellows, all of whom are savvy to measuring the prospects of everyone on a given street in terms of exactly who might give exactly what sort of trouble if requested to surrender money or jewels.

Like the practical businessman, the mugger likes to ply his trade for maximum return on minimum risk.

Unless he's psychotic. Or frightened.

Otherwise, a good cop, even a mediocre cop, can easily spot a "mope" out "scoping for a score" in most quarters of New York. Cops who work Community Affairs details and speak before neighborhood clubs and civic organizations are constantly offering up the same picture of the New York mugger. Elderly women are warned that they happen to be the muggers' number one choice, followed in descending order by elderly men, children with lunch money, women of any age so long as they don't look too athletic and men smaller than them.

New York City, with its huge numbers of pedestrians day and night, is a muggers' paradise. Everybody knows it, victim and mugger alike. Everybody watches everyone else and some are pretty good at prevailing over the odds of being hit in the head or knocked off their feet and robbed.

In the Nineteenth Precinct, though, muggings tend not to be so mundane as in the rest of the city. For one thing, the potential stakes are much more rewarding for the mugger. For another, the Nineteenth Precinct mugger is the elite craftsman of his guild. Just as the Upper East Side in general attracts the best and brightest and richest of the city-at-large, so, too, does it attract the wiliest of criminals, muggers included.

Mrs. Quent sat in a canary-yellow silk damask chair near a bank of windows on the twenty-first floor of her apartment building on East Eighty-fifth Street just off Park Avenue. She wore an elaborate sort of oriental robe and a boa. Her hair was stiff with too much spray and, in the frenzy of preparing herself to receive Officers Basil Reece and Dennis MacDonald, not to mention the circumstances of violence, her lipstick strayed rather wide of the mark and there was a small blotch of eyeliner on the very thin bridge of her very aristocratic nose.

Behind her, through the window, was a stunning view of Central Park and its reservoir. Robert Redford, when he was in town and staying at the apartment he owned on Fifth Avenue at the corner of Ninety-fourth Street, ran around the reservoir daily. Once, Mrs. Quent had seen him, though she herself was hardly a runner. She said her heart did "a little race of its own" as she watched the movie star's blond hair bouncing along and a few other parts of him that bounced as well.

She confessed this to Mr. Peters, her "companion," as she introduced him to the officers. Mr. Peters was with her the day they saw Redford, though he was hardly a runner either. He had a "condition" that prohibited his moving about too quickly.

Mr. Peters sat on a matching canary-yellow chair at the opposite end of the windows, a cane held between his legs. His right foot was bound in gauze and an Ace bandage and it rested on an antique mahogany footstool shaped like an Indian elephant. He wore a maroon smoking jacket, silk with black lapels and maroon piping, and pajama bottoms that were black with a dark red paisley design shot through.

Mrs. Quent was English, upper-crust, elderly and extremely well-preserved. Mr. Peters was about sixty, with artfully cut silver hair and soft, pink flesh that spoke of *haute cuisine* exclusively and many decades of martinis. He drank one now. It was half-past three of a steaming hot afternoon.

A Puerto Rican maid of about fifty, wearing a long black dress, a starched white apron and sturdy shoes, admitted Officers Reece and MacDonald. Reece sat on the edge of an antique chair and opened a note pad full of forms. He picked out the robbery report form and waited, ballpoint pen clicked into position. MacDonald asked the questions.

"First of all, are you all right, Mrs. Quent?"

"We're waiting for the doctor now," she said, waving a paper fan in front of her face.

"That's right," Mr. Peters added. "I telephoned the doctor first, then the police second. You gentlemen were the first to arrive."

"You look all right and I hope you are," MacDonald said.

"Well, we'll see."

"Okay. Now, what's missing?"

"Besides my purse, you mean?"

"Well, yes. Your purse and what was inside."

"Oh, that purse was a lovely thing," she said.

"The one we purchased in London last time?" Mr. Peters asked her.

"The very one." She turned from Peters to the officers. "It was a French purse with a lovely clasp to it. I bought it for fifty pounds, I think, which seemed dear. But it was of very high quality and quite a bargain, actually. . . . But, oh well, you really don't have time to hear about that, do you?"

"No, ma'am."

"Well now. What was in the purse?" She fanned herself.

Mr. Peters took up the task of detailing the inventory of the purse.

"There were the credit cards, mainly," he said. He waited for Reece to find the line on the report form that had to do with the listing of missing property. "There was the Ferragamo card, then one for Bonwit Teller . . . Lord and Taylor . . . Bloomingdale's, of course . . . Altman's. . . . Let's see now . . ."

"How do you spell Ferragamo?" Reece asked.

Mr. Peters, accustomed to spending a great deal of time coping with small matters, was patient with Reece and spelled out the name of each account slowly.

"I got to learn this paperwork," Reece said.

"Yes, I quite understand," Mr. Peters said.

MacDonald asked, "How old are you, Mrs. Quent?"

"Oh, I won't tell you my age. Just put down, oh, sixty-five or maybe seventy. Oh! Well, I'm 'over sixty-five.' Can't you just put that in your little form?"

MacDonald shook his head yes and Reece wrote, his pen hand sweeping over the form until he found the space for the victim's age.

"Now tell us what happened," MacDonald said.

"Oh, I really should wait until the morning to report this all. I'm not actually up to it now, you know, but Mr. Peters says one should get to these things immediately."

"Just what happened, Mrs. Quent?"

"Oh yes. Well, they knocked me."

"Ma'am?"

"They knocked me about the shoulders and arms and then down I went, right on my bum."

"And they stole your purse."

"Yes, that's it."

"And where did it happen?"

"I was walking down Lexington Avenue, near Eighty-fourth Street, and they approached me from the opposite direction. And they knocked me."

"There was more than one perpetrator?"

"Perpetrator?"

"More than one mugger?"

"Oh my yes. There were two of them."

"Could you describe them?"

"Well, I should say I could. But then I would be describing half the good boys in the neighborhood."

"Could you just describe them?"

"They were such wicked boys! I just want their mothers and fathers to know!"

She pumped her fan very rapidly.

"These wicked boys," she continued, "smiled at me in the nicest way. And I thought they were so well-bred the way they smiled. You know, Officer, in my day, they would have worn caps and I suppose boys like that would have taken them off before a lady. You don't have time to hear that, do you?"

"Well, no, ma'am."

"They were blond boys, no more than fourteen years of age, I should say. And they had blue eyes. They were darling boys, so it seemed. But they were wicked, so wicked and diabolical!

"They were by no means ruffians. I should think their mothers and fathers are quite well off. They didn't seem to be wanting for anything —except to knock me down and pinch my bag, that is.

"Both of them wore rugby shirts, one was red and navy and the other was blue and yellow. And those khaki mountain climber shorts, the sort I saw one day in the men's shop at Saks." To Mr. Peters, she added, "I almost bought a pair for you, deary."

She asked MacDonald, "Do you know about skateboards?"

MacDonald did.

"They each carried a skateboard. Then when they knocked me, they got up on those contraptions and flashed clean away."

MacDonald and Reece said their good-byes. Mr. Peters even rose to see them to the door. Mrs. Quent remained in her canary-yellow chair with her fan, waiting for the doctor.

Down on the street and once again in the ovenlike squad car, Mac-Donald told Reece, a rookie assigned him for the day, "I've heard something about these kids, I think. It happens in waves like this. We'll see if it fits a pattern. And maybe we can spot them while we're out today."

Miguel arose at two-fifteen in the afternoon, alone and swimming in his own sweat in a filthy twin-size mattress on the floor of a tenement cellar. His head was throbbing from all the beer and the noise of the previous night, which, in Miguel's case, had extended through dawn of this new day.

His pal Herman slumbered on, about eight feet away through the blackness of the cellar, on his own filthy mattress. Neither one of them had dared return home, for fear their mothers would scream at them, then slap them, and then, worst of all, begin their nonstop prayers to the blessed Virgin Mary for deliverance from the afflictions of the world and from those born of accursed wombs.

That's what Miguel's mother had said. "Accursed wombs." She

spoke both of her own and that of Herman's mother, even though she didn't know the woman. She knew Herman, though, and Herman was as bad as her own son.

Once, Miguel had argued the case with his mother. How would the Blessed Virgin know anything about an accursed womb, Miguel asked? After all, hadn't *her* womb delivered the world its Savior? Miguel's mother had slapped his face and then gone into the kitchen to pray all night and the next day, too. Miguel didn't buy any of that Catholic stuff, though he still got the shivers when he saw a particularly gruesome crucifix hanging over someone's bed, but he did have a moral sense that included a commandment against slapping his mother to make her shut up.

Miguel's father wouldn't say anything. He was no longer able to challenge his nineteen-year-old son physically anyway, nor did he any longer have the heart. What was the use?

Herman's father had long ago given up on New York and returned to Puerto Rico for good, abandoning the family he had brought to New York in the first place. Herman wasn't so bad, really, as everyone would later say. It wasn't that. It was just that he was mentally slow and prone to admire a pal for the things he didn't have in himself—quickness, strength, respect, *machismo*. He would follow Miguel to the ends of the earth. Miguel was several years older than Herman and already a legend in East Harlem, a man of destiny. A wise and good man, by Herman's lights.

Miguel had promised to get Herman laid last night for the first time in his life. And true to his word, as Miguel almost always was, Herman got laid. It was a fairly sweaty affair and it had its moments of embarrassment, but on the whole it was well worth it, as Herman received the congratulations of all Miguel's hot-eyed pals, now his pals, too. Herman was moving up in the world, as long as he stuck by his hero, Miguel.

The girl wasn't one of the neighborhood punchboards, either. She had come from Washington Heights and she was very pretty.

Her name was Rosalina and she was one of Miguel's many female admirers. She met Miguel one day down in Washington Square Park in the Village after watching him for about an hour as he tossed a Frisbee back and forth with a friend. Miguel was nearly naked, wearing only a tiny pair of cut-off shorts and tennis shoes. His graceful, muscular body

was very exciting for Rosalina, so exciting she was ashamed of herself
and told the priest all about it the next day at confession.

But anyway, she was in love. In a matter of forty-eight hours, Miguel
had managed to compromise her iron-bound rule against sexual inter-
course with any man short of her husband, whoever that might be. If
only it could be Miguel! Miguel had succeeded where so many other
hot-blooded swains had failed. Miguel told Rosalina he loved her crazy.
It had to be true!

And so they had become, in Rosalina's term, "lovers." And so they
were, to Rosalina's mind, engaged. Never mind about a ring.

She had come across town to meet Miguel on the night that she
would, unbeknown to her, make Herman a man and herself something
less than a lady. Rosalina splurged on a taxicab all the way from the
Heights because she didn't wish to run the risk of soiling her dress on
the subway and bus combination she would ordinarily take. She had
bought the dress and the new open-toed pumps and the white gloves
on the occasion of Miguel's asking her to a nightclub on East 103rd
Street.

Rosalina was soon embarrassed to be so overdressed. The other girls
wore the standard-issue female adolescent evening ensemble in East
Harlem: sharply creased designer jeans, stiletto heels and tight-waisted
white or yellow or beige blouses loose on top to show off round young
breasts encased in black lace push-up bras. The "nightclub" turned out
to be the back room of a candy store that did most of its business in
pornographic comic books printed in Spanish, loose Kools three-for-a-
quarter, nickel bags of marijuana and the occasional .22-caliber pistol at
the bargain rate of $30.

The back room vibrated with rock music blasting from an enormous
set of speakers attached to a stereo system Miguel had stolen, piece by
piece, from shops down in the Nineteenth Precinct just below Ninety-
sixth Street, the "DMZ" of the East Side, as the rich folks in singles
bars joked. Miguel had heard the joke a million times. He was offended
at first, but gradually his offense slipped away, each time he mugged
someone with that attitude after sizing them up in the singles bars,
after maybe charming a woman or two. He had to be careful about
that, though. He knew he looked good, but he knew, too, that he didn't
sound good enough yet, not by a long shot.

There were drugs of every description being passed around and
plenty of beer, which is all that Miguel ever took for himself. When

Rosalina walked in, resplendent and out of place in her dress, she nearly cried. The girls laughed aloud and Miguel's pals whistled and made obscene mouth noises. But when Miguel walked to her, the commotion ceased. He told her she was the most beautiful woman he had ever seen, took her lightly by the hand and introduced her to everyone in the room as if she were visiting royalty.

Rosalina never felt completely comfortable and she knew this night might begin the end of her engagement—how could she marry a man who would consider this den of thieves a place to take his fiancée? She was nonetheless charmed, as usual, by Miguel. He danced with her and everyone in the room stood back against the walls to watch them, the royal couple. She did not approve of the place, but Rosalina would enjoy of it what she could before returning home. She knew nothing of Miguel's promise to Herman.

She drank a lot of beer that night, at Miguel's suggestion, and she smoked a bit of grass. It helped. She would confess her sins, but Lord, it helped.

Rosalina had few defenses to guard against what Miguel promised was a "surprise" in honor of her presence, in an alleyway at the rear of the shop. She went with him, of course. Out in the alleyway, in a gypsy cab owned by a friend of Miguel's, Herman waited, naked and highly aroused. Miguel had told him that Rosalina was finally ready to make him a man.

Miguel had also told his charge that he must understand the contradictory nature of women: you had to fight them always. No matter what, you had to wrestle with women, especially when it came to sex. They would scream, they would strike you, they would do anything to keep their legs together, but all of it was a lie. They wanted it. Herman shook his head in understanding of this deep mystery of life. He was ready.

Miguel opened the back door of the cab and slipped his hand over Rosalina's mouth before she screamed, as he knew she would. "Just enjoy it," he hissed into her perfumed ear, "or you'll die." Then he shoved her into the cab and Herman began wrestling her. She tried screaming again, but Miguel was quick with a leather sap and she was thus persuaded to suffer this hell.

Herman raised her dress and tore through heavy pantyhose, then through elasticized panties. Sweat poured from his brow. He squeezed Rosalina's breasts and hurt her, though he didn't mean to. When he caught sight of her black pubis, he started grunting incoherently. Then he heard laughter and looked up to see that everyone had stolen out of the candy shop to watch the show in the back of the cab. Rosalina wanted to faint, but fought against it, believing that if she lost consciousness Miguel or one of the savages watching her disgrace would murder her.

"Do it to her!" Herman heard Miguel shout.

So he did it. He was clumsy; he wasn't so sure Rosalina wanted it as much as he did, but Herman did it. When he was through, everyone cheered and Herman grinned proudly.

When they were alone, Miguel kissed Rosalina on the cheek. He could not force any words from her, though. She would never speak to him again, of course. He put her into a taxicab and paid the driver enough to get her home. All the way across town, Rosalina prayed to God to strike Miguel dead.

That had all happened last night.

Miguel sat up on his mattress. He lit a cigarette and briefly his subterranean world could be viewed. Cans, mops, rat droppings, an enormous furnace, a rotting wooden stairway to the lobby of a decrepit tenement run by a super Miguel supplied with drugs for assorted favors in return, such as the use of the cellar and the super's keeping his mouth shut about it.

Miguel didn't like what he saw. It wasn't nearly enough for him. He was wasting his time fooling around in East Harlem. There was nothing there of any value. Down in the Nineteenth was where a man of Miguel's abilities should be. Down below Ninety-sixth, where the money and the glamour were.

He smoked.

When Herman woke, Miguel took him to breakfast and began telling him what they would be doing that night down in the Nineteenth.

"Me, I ran an elevator at a private men's club, worked around the place at whatever there was and I learned to be a gentleman," Mac-Donald was telling Reece as they drove around the streets of the Upper East Side, on the look-out for blond, well-fed teenagers on skateboards looking to rip off old ladies' handbags. "It was pretty good work, then I took the police test and waited and got my assignment.

"I love the police work. I especially like working the Nineteenth. I've worked other precincts where most of the time you're arguing with people on jobs. Here, you get a chance to do your work like a gentleman. How do you like the job so far?"

Reece shifted in the front passenger seat. He was a huge man, quiet and deliberate when he talked.

"Something like your work in the club," Reece said. "I'm learning from the others here. I'm only twenty-three. I'm maturing real, real fast on this job."

MacDonald stopped the squad car for a few minutes outside the Lebanese Mission to the United Nations on East Seventy-sixth Street. "I'm going to say hello to my regular partner. He's working the box here today."

MacDonald introduced Reece to Officer Seamus Weir, who stepped out of the police booth in front of the mission, pushed his hat to the back of his head and said, "What a drag tonight. Looks like a nice summer rain, so there's no broads out. They're afraid of getting their feet wet, I suppose."

Weir stood between his box and the squad car at the curb. An exceptionally attractive young woman walked behind him, toward the avenue, wiping the tip of her nose with her finger.

"Oh, yeah. Go ahead and pick your nose in front of me," Weir hissed. "Man, oh man, does it seem to you that there's some sort of weird increase in the number of nice-looking chicks doing really disgusting things?"

MacDonald turned to Reece and said, "Listen to this guy. Working in the box all day makes even a guy like that frustrated. You'll get your turn, all right. Just wait. My advice is to watch yourself when you get assigned to the Russian box around the side of the mission. It's filled with lice."

To Weir, he said, "Easy night, or what?"

"I hope, man. Today, they bombed some synagogue in Paris, so I suppose I might see some pipe bomb rolling down the street at me. At least I'll know why. They've got a big do tonight here at the Lebanese. It's 'Feast of Fitur' you know—"

MacDonald turned his attention to an R.I.P. call on the squad-car radio. Weir quieted.

"R.I.P. is for 'Robbery in Progress,' " MacDonald told Reece. "Or 'Rest in Peace.' Take your pick."

Then he radioed a response:

"Unit eleven is right around the corner from that R.I.P."

"All yours, eleven. Need one back-up unit . . ."

Reece jotted the address in his note pad. MacDonald stepped on the accelerator and the squad car roared down the street to the avenue, then downtown to East Sixty-fourth Street. No lights, no siren. And high hopes of making a red-handed collar.

According to the dispatcher, neighbors reported two men going through an empty town-house window. The block in question, between Madison and Park avenues, was filled with town houses worth millions of dollars, the contents hard to get at—though not impossible for the elite of professional burglars. Making a collar under such circumstances would guarantee several letters of gratitude from the neighborhood and, if the arrests managed to clear up a number of unsolved high-ticket burglary cases, maybe an officer's career could get a nice boost.

MacDonald eased the car to a halt a few doors west of the empty house. Occupants probably out to Southampton until sometime after Labor Day . . . second-floor windows standing open, unusual . . . iron grille work leading to open windows, perfect for illegal entry . . .

"Here we go," MacDonald said, tapping at his bulletproof vest. "Quiet and steady as she goes, all right?"

Reece, even though a rookie, was obviously a good pick as an officer. He hadn't been through anything like this, but he was able to keep the presence of mind a cop has to have when the threat of physical peril is thrown in his face. He was nervous, but it made him alert and careful. His eyes would miss nothing.

Reece held a corner of the iron grille for MacDonald, who hoisted himself quickly through a window. Then Reece mounted the grille, now held by a neighbor. He, too, popped through the window, catlike.

A small group of neighbors, hushed, gathered discreetly in the street to wait for the officers to emerge, possibly with a burglar caught in the act.

The door of the town house opened and MacDonald marched two boys, about twelve years each, out the door in front of him. He carried his nightstick at his side. Reece followed.

Then MacDonald lectured the boys, "Next time your ball bangs through a window like that, you just lost a ball. Get it?"

The boys were cool and insolent. One of them wore expensive running shoes, easily $100 the pair. This one said to MacDonald, "Just call Bill Walters. You know him?"

"Don't hand me any names. Names don't mean anything to me, kid. Except yours. What is it?" MacDonald opened a pad of juvenile report forms. "And your partner's name, too."

"Will there be a record?" the boy with the overpriced shoes asked.

"No, not this time. Your parents will be notified. You're in the system, though. Next time, we go the whole route."

"You don't have to call our parents. Just call Bill Walters."

"We'll call your parents."

"We know our rights."

"Good for you. You know your names?"

MacDonald got the names, then he and Reece got back in the squad car and resumed patrol.

"God, these kids are wise up here," MacDonald said. "They pretty much know nothing's going to happen to them. And what they do is scare hell out of people when they pull something like that.

"Sometimes I like to say that every call up here is E.S.P., 'East Side Paranoia.' A house like that is worth so damn much! There's so much to lose! Well, a lot of times a call turns out just like this, nothing. But you always have to be prepared. That's how you're going to live to retire from being a cop. You prepare for the worst every time. And when you get a light one, well, you loosen your bulletproof vest maybe and you wipe your brow and you're thankful it was a light one."

Officers Jimmy Sullivan and Mike Ward took one final job before rolling back to the house for a cool shower before heading home. The day was routine and hot. The temperature still hovered in the nineties, even though the sun had set. The humidity level was in the seventies.

The call would be easy. A report from another mugging victim.

It would not, however, be comfortable. The old lady involved, Mrs. Helen Braunstein, had the heat on in her apartment on Park Avenue at the corner of East Eightieth Street. Sullivan and Ward exchanged pained glances, then sat down to a huge dining-room table at Mrs. Braunstein's direction. They sweltered. She talked.

"Well, I was just preparing something for Henry and me. Life must go on, after all," she said.

"Can you tell us just what happened?" Ward asked.

"I put out my arm to stop one of them from running right into me on his skateboard. The other one grabbed my clutch bag and they were gone. It was instantaneous. Never in a million years would I have suspected them. They were nice-looking boys. Blond, very fair, about twelve, I think."

"Now, what are you missing?"

Henry Braunstein wandered in, a cloud of cigar smoke preceding him. He moved slowly in his house slippers.

"Well, my clutch bag, of course. And eighty-five dollars. And my faraway glasses. That's what I call them, the glasses I use for seeing far away, you know."

"Yes, ma'am."

Her husband said, "You had eighty-five dollars on you? Why were you carrying so much?"

"Because I had to market for two days," she said.

"So, you couldn't have written a check?" Braunstein turned to the officers. "Tell her. She could have written a check. Am I right?"

Ward smiled.

"I thought you'd complain," Mrs. Braunstein said to her husband. To the officers, "He always complains like this."

"What bag did they steal from you?" Braunstein asked her.

"My small one."

He turned to Ward and Sullivan and said, "She made that one herself."

"The bag was worthless," Mrs. Braunstein said.

"What do you mean?" Braunstein sputtered. He caught his cigar before it fell from his mouth. "She made it herself, officers. It was white with little pearls on it. I loved that bag."

"The important thing here," Ward said, making some final notations on the robbery form, "is that you didn't get hurt, Mrs. Braunstein. You've got to be aware, all the time you're out, especially when you get up there in years. I'm just glad you didn't get knocked down."

Hurriedly, Ward and Sullivan made their way out of the Braunstein apartment. There is a realistic fear of suffering heat prostration under such circumstances.

Soaking wet with perspiration, Ward and Sullivan needed desperately to get to the station-house locker room. But first, there was a special call.

Sullivan drove the squad car to the nearest telephone booth. Ward got out. "I'll drop the dime this time out," he said. He dialed the station-house desk sergeant, then returned to the car and told Sullivan,

"We go to Tricia Nixon's apartment building, where some guy needs to get into his sister-in-law's apartment because she might be dead. Nice and delicate."

The apartment house was a high rise on East Eightieth Street near Second Avenue, a nondescript gray brick affair with nondescript men in suits and sunglasses sitting around the lobby earning their livings by watching the comings and goings of folks who lived near an ex-President's daughter. Ward and Sullivan were taken to an upper floor of the building by the superintendent, accompanied by a nervous middle-aged man.

"She just returned from Minneapolis," the nervous man said, "where she was in a hospital for alcoholics. She seemed all right, but now she's not been heard from. My wife is out of her mind with worry. We call, we come by, but there's no answer."

"Take it easy, sir. We'll be able to get in now. You've done the right thing. The super can always call the police in cases like this and we'll be able to take a look," Ward said.

The super opened the door with a pass key.

Inside, there were only the most expensive of furnishings. The walls were covered with excellent and valuable art. And everywhere, strewn across the floors and all the furniture, were empty liquor bottles.

"Jesus!" the man said. "This is worse than I imagined."

"Well, we'll see if it's the worst," Ward said.

He and Sullivan proceeded to make their way through the rubble of bottles and glasses. They searched through a well-stocked library, through closets brimming over with furs and gowns and expensive suits, through the well-appointed kitchen, through all the rooms that they would never have for themselves and their families.

"She was last in Minneapolis?" Ward asked the nervous man.

"Well, we heard she came back to New York."

"Nothing much we can do," Ward said.

"I guess not," the brother-in-law said. "God, I need a drink."

Ward and Sullivan, the ashen-faced brother-in-law and the superintendent returned to the lobby in silence.

Outside, the brother-in-law reached into his pocket and pulled out a huge roll of currency. He said to Ward, "May I make a contribution to your pension fund?"

Ward looked at the money for several seconds and then at the man offering it. The brother-in-law wiped his upper lip.

"You keep it," Ward said.

Miguel and Herman sat on a bench in Carl Schurz Park and looked out over the river. Herman smoked a joint and the sweet smell of marijuana made a haze that shimmered off into the heat of the early evening.

"You sure, Miguel?" Herman asked, puffing furiously on the joint.

"Of course, my friend. I am sure. I have been watching that place for months now."

"I don't know."

"You don't know what, dummy?" Miguel said. "You don't know that we've been living like two-bit spiks up there? We got to change our ways, man."

"Yeah, I guess so."

"I know so."

"Whatever you say, Miguel."

6

Officer Jack Clark made his way down the dark, dusty stairway from the "Penthouse," more officially known as the plainclothes burglary detail squad room up on the fifth floor. He stopped at the second-floor corridor to gossip and noticed the platoon of auxiliary cops pouring out from the big room used for suspect line-ups.

Keenan was wandering around. "What's up with the hobby cops tonight?" Clark asked Keenan.

"Movie premiere at the Gemini on Third Avenue. They're going to do the crowd control," Keenan said.

Clark shook his head. "I just don't see it. What possible beneficial use is served by these hobby cops? Jesus! Can you imagine if . . . oh, construction workers, say, had an auxiliary? Can't you just hear the auxiliary construction worker walking up to a site and saying to the real guys, 'Say, there, big boys, we're going to lay a little beam for you, free.' "

Clark's boss, Sergeant John Laffey, walked out of the men's room and said to Keenan, "You know, I don't know if this is a cause-and-effect thing, but the more Clark here talks, the more I want to go take another dump."

"I mean it," Clark said, "what the hell are they going to do tonight? Keep the folks from getting near the celebrities? Let's suppose there's some nutjob comes along, like they do whenever there's celebrities all together in one place. Remember John Lennon?

"So the nutjob gets shoved maybe by one of our hobby cops here.

You think the nutjob is going to stop and say to himself, 'Hey, wait a minute. This is an auxiliary officer. A fine, upstanding, public-spirited citizen who doesn't carry a gun, just somebody interested in safeguarding democracy.'

"So who's the nutjob in that case? The psycho or the guy who puts on a fake policeman suit with a little bar of small print that says auxiliary and goes out in the street like a target and doesn't even have sense enough to get paid for it?"

Laffey said to Keenan, "There isn't another sergeant in the whole damn city who wants Clark. I get him. I'm able to tell you who's the nutjob, all right."

Keenan wasn't listening to either one of them. His attention was distracted by the sight of one of the auxiliary cops, the posterior of the auxiliary cop to be exact. A woman. Keenan could have sworn he'd seen her somewhere before. The short, thick blue-black hair, green eyes and the slender figure, especially the switching posterior. The auxiliary uniform didn't do much to flatter that figure. But Keenan remembered now when he'd last seen her, dressed in a summer blouse and shorts, crying.

"See you guys," he said to Clark and Laffey.

Then Keenan followed the group of auxiliary cops down the final flight of stairs into the lobby, floating along after them as if drawn by some mysterious magnetic power. It was a very odd feeling for Keenan. It had been such a long time since he'd been so excited by the mere sight of a woman. His wife, his drinking, his job, the kids, Riverdale and its monotony, his unfulfilled dreams. They had all taken a toll, had dulled his most joyous of human senses.

She stood off by herself, away from the group. The talkative hobby cops milled in a tight circle in the middle of the lobby, waiting for transportation to the Gemini, which seemed appropriate to Keenan. They were mostly youngish men, the sort of narrow-shouldered, slack-jawed, no-chin guys you could arm with good long flashlights and be certain of having a crack squad of movie-house ushers. There were a handful of women as well, but she seemed different, a woman who seemed comfortable in her femininity as opposed to the muscular women auxiliary cops who bound their breasts and tucked their hair carefully and tightly up under their hats.

She was alone, her hat in her hand. She seemed amused by her own presence in the police lobby. Amused at herself, at her being dressed in blue twills with a whistle on a stout string secured to the epaulet on her left shoulder.

"Excuse me."

She turned.

"Excuse me," Keenan repeated, his face shot red and his hands and armpits sweating, "but what's your duty tonight?"

She looked as if she didn't understand.

"Oh," Keenan said. His right hand touched his hip where his service revolver ordinarily was kept. "I'm a cop."

Keenan reached into his back pocket and brought out a black leather wallet. He flipped it open to show her his shield.

"I'm with the auxiliary," she said. "Dory Smith."

Keenan took her hand and shook it.

"Tommy Keenan," he said.

Then neither one of them said anything. Four of the auxiliary cops nearest the door left to climb into a squad car. Keenan had to speak now or maybe he'd never see her again.

"Pardon me for askin' but you've been here before, haven't you? I recall. You were cryin'. What was it?"

"Three years ago," she said. "I was assaulted. And sure, I came here all right."

"What happened?"

Dory took a deep breath. "I was raped."

"Oh, I'm sorry," Keenan said. "How are you now, dear?"

She smiled. Usually, a man would go mingle with someone else once this was learned. This cop seemed genuinely interested in her well-being.

"It's not been easy, but I'm getting better. At least I think I am. My friends aren't doing so well, though, those that are left anyway."

"I'm sorry about that, too. You shouldn't be bitter. It's a waste of time."

"I'm sure you're right, Officer. But it seems unavoidable sometimes."

Keenan smiled. "Sure, I know what you mean."

Most of the group of auxiliary cops started moving toward the door. Dory Smith moved along with the group, with Keenan striding alongside.

"Look," Keenan said, red-faced again, "when will you be finished up? There wasn't much talk between us, but it was better than most of the talk around here. Maybe we could talk some more, tonight some-where? Wherever you like."

She stopped and smiled at him. "I was raped, you know," she said.

Keenan thought for a moment. "One way or another, we've all been raped, now haven't we?"

"Eleven-thirty."

Then she was gone.

With the auxiliary cops cleared out of the big two-room suite on the second floor, Detective Marty Gill started arranging things for a line-up that night. He set chairs in a row in the back room, one for the suspect and about eight others for white males of average build with mous-taches, which was the shorthand description of the perpetrator cooling his heels in the precinct lockup.

Gill and two detectives from the city-wide robbery squad had a live one this time, a guy that might clear as many as two dozen cases from their load.

"You can go to the well only so many times," Gill said to Valentine, who had picked that night to hang out with the detectives. "This guy's gone too often. He's knocked over shopkeepers and clerks here in the Nineteenth, and down in the Seventeenth and Midtown North pre-cincts, too.

"We're having the line-up for him here because it's pretty easy for us to get his type from the armory over on Park Avenue."

The Seventh Regiment Armory on any given night has a hundred or so likely line-up prospects, young men playing squash or the like who get five or ten dollars apiece and a good story for their wives or girl friends for sitting around in a room while people look at them through a two-way mirror.

Day-shift line-ups are generally held in the Seventeenth Precinct, in the East Thirties, Forties and Fifties, where there are plenty of messen-gers who like the idea of earning lunch money for a quick sit at the station house on East Fifty-fourth Street. Times Square was the place for line-ups if freakish types were necessary to flesh out the general description. And up in the East Harlem precinct on 102nd Street, Puerto Ricans wandered in every night volunteering for line-up duty.

"One thing we don't use in the line-ups anywhere is cops," Gill said. "That's because a lot of judges in the city believe that anybody can

pick a cop from a crowd. Something about the way they carry themselves. I agree. I think I could pick out a cop on a beach in his briefs,
you know?"

Thirty-eight potential courtroom witnesses were on Gill's list, which
he compared with the list held by the two special Central Robbery
Division detectives. "The big job is going to be to get them all down
here on a hot night to sit around looking at some guy they've been
having nightmares about anyway, you know?

"I mean, I been doing this long enough to know what's going
through their minds when they come in here. You'll see. They're
scared, like somehow the guy's going to see them through that glass
that's just a mirror on his side. They know in their heads that it's a
mirror to him, but the last time they saw this character, he was holding
a gun on them that looked to them like a goddamn cannon.

"People really do have nightmares about this sort of thing. And they
don't want to relive them. I don't know if I can blame them."

Gill went to the holding cell to check on the suspect. Valentine went
along.

"Look at him," Gill said. The suspect sat on a chair in the cage, a
man maybe five-foot-ten with a droopy brown moustache. His clothing
looked like it might have been of good quality once. "His family won't
have anything to do with him anymore. He's a misfit."

The suspect stared at Gill and Valentine, but it was doubtful that he
could focus. His eyes were watery and senseless.

"The guy's been doing drugs for a long, long time," Gill said. "His
family's had him in and out of hospitals all over the country, but it's a
lost cause. Good family, too. I've known this guy for a while now and
I've been after him. So finally I've nailed him and I've got a line-up
going and we're going to put this one away. And what do I think about
him? I can't help feeling sorry for him, that's what."

Gill shook his head. He exhaled a weary breath.

"When this guy first started," Gill said, "he had a good car and good
clothes, good everything. A Rolex watch this guy had, for crying out
loud. Think a guy like me's ever going to have a Rolex? What the hell
does it mean with this guy?

"I don't know. It's all gone for him now, all of it and all the money
he borrowed from his family, too. He sold it all because he's a junkie.

"Here you're looking at a guy who wasted his time. That's what cops deal with mostly, when you come down to it, guys who waste their time. What a goddamn pity."

In all, thirty-eight of the fifty-one people who swore they would do their duty as citizens and come by the precinct house for Detective Gill's line-up actually followed through. A good ratio, especially for a night of good television and a sky that threatened rain.

One by one, the shopkeepers of the Upper East Side entered the squad room and peered through the glass at the men sitting in a sort of semicircle, the perpetrators and the decoys instructed to stare at themselves in the mirror that was their side of the glass.

Thirty-three shopkeepers were dead certain that the sorrowful man with the droopy brown moustache was the man who had stood across the counter from them one day, gun in hand, threatening to kill them unless they turned over all the money in the till. Most of them took several quick looks through the glass, as if they were afraid of arousing anger in the sad-looking man who once, incredible as it seemed at this moment, had made their blood race with fear for their lives and treasures.

He didn't look much like a desperate gunman now; nor then, actually, though no right-minded New Yorker sees much percentage in challenging the sincerity of an armed man, especially one whose finger trembles at the trigger. He looked more like someone's terribly troubled younger brother. He looked helpless and doomed and ultimately pathetic, as if he knew exactly what people thought of him as they inspected him through the trick glass, as if he were an insect or a reptile.

His name was Tim. And he had come to perhaps the end of an odyssey that can only be understood as an irony of innocence, a special sort of lousy break that afflicts some of the most respectable families.

For the past several years, Tim had subsisted on the Upper East Side. He lived in a series of apartments east of Third Avenue in the Yorkville district, where rents can sometimes be cheap and where the more obviously disreputable sorts have long encroached on the better sensibilities of others. (The German-American Bund once held rallies to praise *der Führer* where now stands a branch of the Israeli Bank Leumi.) Mostly, his parents paid the rent for him, as an insurance policy against Tim's coming back to darken their door in the tonier environs of Lenox Hill. They'd had quite enough of their only son—their only ripple in two placid and abundant lives.

The estrangement began almost the moment Tim graduated from high school, where he'd been an excellent though unimaginative student, and began classes at Columbia University, which might as well have been a different planet.

It was the early 1960s. Tim attended his classes at Columbia, read dull textbooks and listened to dull lectures. None of it was anywhere near as compelling as the street politics of the day, the great struggles for civil rights at home and an end to the war abroad. Scholastically, Tim got along for a while, barely.

Like lots of other privileged students across the country in those times, Tim was swept up in the excitement of momentous causes and the chaos of assassination, forbidden heroics of anticolonial guerrillas in a country he'd never heard of before, racial conflicts and urban rioting, violent music and violent protest against cops and anyone else in authority—and drugs, which sometimes offered a context for it all. The world was exploding with change and it would never again be the same; yet everywhere, colleges offered up the same old gray lessons, government leaders continued to blame all troubles on communist bogeymen and parents were frightened to pieces by the sudden passion that seemed to seize their children, passion they often considered to be personal threats.

All the security and sophistication and opportunity and material comfort available to families like Tim's were no guarantee against the pain of passage through the 1960s. Nothing in Tim's life could prepare him for the maelstrom of divergent thought on the Columbia campus or the exotic street life of nearby Harlem. And nothing could have prepared Tim's parents for their son's attraction to a culture that ran so wildly counter to their own.

The Columbia campus was a bazaar of radical politics and hundreds of social activist movements; neighboring Harlem was a vast drug emporium. Forbidden thought, fueled by drugs, was a thrilling intoxication. And disastrous for a rich kid from the Upper East Side who couldn't possibly avoid minefields in such unfamiliar terrain. Already, Tim was a man and this was only his first cross-cultural experience. Was the world of his parents real—or were Columbia and Harlem real? Or was there no reality? Growing up in Lenox Hill is as insulating in its splendid way as growing up in some quiet Middle Western suburb.

Tim grew up in a community where Sunday brunch in chic neighborhood restaurants was a family routine. His mother played bridge on weekday afternoons with other idle women, or else she took tennis lessons. The corner delicatessen stocked Iranian Beluga caviar. The coffee table in the living room was strewn with copies of *The New Yorker, Town & Country* and *Saturday Review*. His father had a job that left him with clean fingernails at the end of the day. Tim's wardrobe was acquired mostly at Barney's and Paul Stuart with his father's Diners Club card. Never did it occur to Tim that certain allegiances were implied by all this. And few could predict a decade following the Eisenhower years when everyone would have to choose sides on almost everything.

Ten weeks after starting at Columbia, Tim's friends included a voodoo queen from 125th Street, a Marxist revolutionary who belonged to something called the "Mad Dogs" and a drug baron who convinced him that blowing grass and dropping acid and shooting silver into his veins now and then made profoundly more sense than bombing Asian jungles in the name of a holy war against communism.

Tim's parents were like a lot of others of the Upper East Side's moneyed and educated households. They held the notion that they were basically liberal-minded on social issues, but always they voted on the basis of what they might stand to lose if the subjects of their egalitarian sympathies gained on them too quickly. In the superheated 1960s, much of Tim's generation looked on such time-worn hypocrisy as a newly discovered frontier of intolerable evil.

Angry words between fathers and sons in the 1960s were like stabs to the heart. The first time Tim came home to denounce his father's "bourgeois mentality," a hard line was drawn. Tim's mother and father retreated into the rigid ideological sureties of Americanism, so-called, and seemed to know what it meant. Tim soon came to believe most truly in whatever fierce and friendly brand of convictions were close at hand.

Strong ideas filled an intellectual vacuum in lots of households, Tim's included. With few guideposts for handling inflammatory rhetoric and scary ideas, family loyalties and tolerances became the first casualties of the nation's first living-room war between the generations, a war compounded by televised carnage from Vietnam. So it was at even Tim's house.

While Tim and his passions were unacceptable to his parents, he was welcomed warmly in every place his parents and their ilk were considered the enemy. His father and mother began drinking heavily; Tim began using drugs rather heavily. And so the world foundered.

With each of his drug episodes, Tim consolidated his rejection of home. And with each new drug episode, he was dazzled by what he took to be life on the cutting edge of a vast social changeover—or so it seemed to the media.

In a few years, at the very height of the war in Vietnam, Tim's college career sputtered to a finish, along with several million of his brain cells.

Then of narcotic and economic necessity, Tim became a fairly successful subdealer of marijuana, Quaaludes, LSD, heroin and, toward the end, cocaine. He was the perfect distributor for a while, the product of a rich white family just when others like him were fascinated with the concept of drugs as recreation. His drug baron friend, black and inarticulate, needed front men like Tim for the emerging new mainstream American market.

Tim serviced the Columbia campus, easily identifiable to his clientele as the nonstudent hanger-on with the Jaguar and all the pocket money. But his market expanded from the campus back to the familiar environs of the Upper East Side, where Tim took a succession of apartments, each one a step down from the last as his own personal drug expenses rose and as more and more respectable types such as himself entered the business and cut into his territory.

As Tim filled more and more of his idle hours—and days and weeks —with drugs, he grew increasingly detached from friends and associates and increasingly irrational and irresponsible about business. Selling illicit goods, such as drugs, has always been a business that requires trust and dependability. Those successful in the business are, by and large, those whose use of the product is the least—or nonexistent. The successful drug dealers in New York deal in cash and lots of it. Dealers on the skids begin using product as currency and they begin selling off their possessions for their cash. Tim was slipping very fast. His customers abandoned him far more swiftly than had his parents in earlier years; his friends had better things to do than hang around with Tim, and holding down a job was an idea that never occurred, not any more than getting straight.

Tim became a burglar and a stickup artist.

He knew enough to stay around the Upper East Side, where he

could still look like he fit the neighborhood. And he stuck to nonviolent methods of raising cash for his drugs and other of life's necessities. He stole old lady's purses and he pried open apartment doors in buildings that catered to young single professionals who were mostly absent during the business hours.

When he came across a pistol in one apartment job, he began carrying it with him wherever he went. No particular reason. One day—he can't remember just when—he walked into a shop on Lexington Avenue and pulled the pistol on the owner and walked out with nearly $900 in cash. The experience was considerably less wearing on what was left of his nerves than the anxiety he knew each time he popped open an apartment door.

So he held up dozens and dozens of shops after that and his income soared. Fencing jewelry and small appliances stolen from young urban professionals—"yuppies"—was very profitable.

With a larger income, Tim spent proportionately more on drugs. And then something snapped. He stopped caring about his appearance and was evicted from his apartment for panicking the other tenants by running through the corridors screaming and howling in one of his more terrifying hallucinations.

When he was busted in the Seventeenth Precinct by a pair of plainclothes officers from Central Robbery Division, Tim first heard himself called what he had indeed become—a "dirtbag."

And now, tonight at this lineup, thirty-three solid citizens, his parents' sort, were ready to go to court to testify that Tim was also an armed robber.

He'd been allowed to call his parents that night. They declined to speak to him.

When the lineup was over, Detective Gill took Tim back to the small holding cell in the precinct house. Later that night, he would be returned to Riker's Island, first stop on what would be a long and lonely journey to Sing Sing Prison.

Tim sat on a stool in holding, a steel wire mesh box four feet by six feet by seven feet high on the second floor of the station house. As a boy, he'd seen the holding cell when he and his sixth grade classmates took a school field trip through the Nineteenth Precinct house. A grinning, pot-bellied policeman, a friendly Irish cop, showed the kids how the door opened and shut and warned them to "keep your noses clean now so's you stay out of the slammer." Tim laughed bitterly now.

The case against him was ironclad. He would be up the river for years, held forcibly in a place where hours and days and weeks become indistinguishable, where time is wasted, where drugs and cigarettes and liquor are coins of the realm.

Five and one half blocks from the Nineteenth Precinct, Tim's parents drank cocktails on the terrace and didn't speak of their son. To such people, the present and future become wasted if there is no reconciliation with the past.

"You ever try to tell parents how to raise their kids, though?" Detective Gill asked. "I can't do that, you can't do that. Nobody can do that. So like I said, we're dealing with people who have wasted their time."

"I know the feeling," Joe Simon said.

Detective Simon spoke to Detective Bill Lent, whose thickset body had collapsed, with a dull thud, into a wooden chair behind a gray steel desk in the PDU quarters. Lent rubbed his eyes and pinched the bridge of his nose, an attempt to make the pressure of a day on the witness stand down in Manhattan Criminal Court go away.

"Jesus, I'd sooner run all over town on the streets on the hottest day in August than be on the stand," Simon said. "You go to court and take all the raps from the lawyers for every damn word misspelled in your paperwork. It's agony, man."

"Oh yeah," Lent agreed, "that's the way it is. There's just two ways a perp can maybe beat the rap. He can get his mouthpiece to either attack the merits of the collar, or the cop personally.

"Well, I suppose if I was the perp I'd do the same. What could I lose, you know? Maybe I could shave a couple years off the sentence by attacking the cop personally in court. Hell, it's not going to add years, that's for sure.

"I tell you, Joe, I call that kind of system 'taking a bite out of the Apple,' you know?"

Simon nodded his head, wearily. "Amen."

Lent leaned his head back, resting on the chipped aqua wall behind him. Above his head were wanted posters for one William Morales, the Puerto Rican urban guerrilla fighting for the island's independence from the U.S. by planting bombs in New York saloons, and a murder suspect called "Frenchie" Hernandez who wore a muscle shirt in his photograph and was said to be a frequent patron of Midtown gay bars.

The PDU was quiet now. Lieutenant Stein had gone to dinner, the sergeant's office was empty, three other detectives were busy with a welter of paperwork. Detective Herman was busy taking a complaint from an attractive blond woman who claimed that her ex-husband was harassing her and her young son.

"What's the case, anyway?" Simon asked.

"The slasher from the pleasant little uptown family. Nice folks. This guy and his two sons and his wife sucking up booze all day long for years and years and he's the one who's usually on the receiving end of it.

"Once, they castrated him. No shit. They actually carved his balls right out of the old sack. Another time, they took an ax to his head and cut him up so bad that little pieces of his skull came out.

"That's not all. Man, over the years, they've knifed him in the gut and taken out his intestines and ripped him so bad the doctors had to take out most of his stomach.

"So one day, this guy finally says he's going to cut his old lady's throat, which he does. They're all drunk, as usual, and the guy takes a big old butcher knife and stabs her five times in the back of the neck and then slashes her pretty good around the front.

"His sons take off after him and the guy slips them by jumping through the kitchen window. The super of the building sees him going down the fire escape with blood all over his hands, right?"

Lent took a long sip of coffee.

"So now I've got the job of finding this rum-dum who's scared shitless, right? So what I did was find out who his buddies were, who he used to run with when he wasn't drinking with his family. Well, I came up with the name and location of his best pal, a rum-dum just like the perp. The two of them are like twins, both run over by life, you know?

"So I told the perp's buddy, 'Look, do your pal a big favor, man. There's an order out in this city that if any cop finds him, they're supposed to blow his damn head off. He's a dead man. I can't do anything about the order to kill him, but I might be able to protect him if you bring him here to me and only me. Man, don't let him get tangled up with any other cops. Another cop will kill him. I sort of understand what the guy's been going through. Just make sure he gets to me, all right?'

"Well, it worked. I scared the guy right into my lap, right? So what happens in court today when I tell this story?

"The judge asks me, 'Is it true, Officer, that you said to this man's friend that there was a police order out to kill him? Where do you get off telling that to anyone?'

"So I tell the judge, 'Look, Your Honor, no one ever told me I had to tell the whole truth and nothing but the truth except here in court, where I always tell the truth. But out there? On the street? So what if I tricked a guy into walking into the station house so I could make a collar where nobody gets hurt?' "

Simon almost fell off his chair laughing. "What happened?"

"The jury loved it."

"We don't hurt nobody, Miguel?"

"We don't have to, my friend. We don't have to."

Nonetheless, Herman worried about the suspicious lump under Miguel's shirt. Hadn't Miguel always managed to control the situation, though? Hadn't Miguel always managed to have things go exactly the way he wanted? And hadn't Herman always benefitted by friendship with the dashing Miguel?

Now, though, there was that bulge under his shirt. And Miguel was watching everyone as they walked through the park, sizing them up. Herman didn't want trouble. He didn't feel safe outside his own neighborhood uptown. Here, everyone spoke English, all the time. How could anyone feel comfortable?

"Listen to me, Herman. Nobody gives a fight here. They're rich and they're insured and they know better. They just hand it over."

Miguel's words calmed Herman. Sure, Miguel knew what he was doing. As usual, he had only to trust Miguel.

"Okay," Miguel said. "That one."

He pointed to an attractive young woman, maybe thirty years old, an Anglo, professional, the sort of Upper East Side woman who writes long letters to relatives in the Middle West hoping to dissuade them of exaggerated notions of crime in the Big Apple. She walked purposefully, sure to be leaving the park for home at this hour, going on half-past eleven.

"Come on, Herman."

The two rose, Herman a little dizzy from hours of smoking marijuana. Miguel was tense and alive, his strong, slim body moving through the shadows of the park like a long-legged cat of the wilds.

They followed the woman out of the park, staying a full block behind. She didn't see them. They kept close to the walls of the big stone apartment houses on East End Avenue. And she didn't hear them. Their sneakers muffled every step.

She turned into a doorway at East Seventy-ninth Street.

"Come!" Miguel whispered. "I know that place. No doorman."

Miguel took a knife from his belt. Herman's face, if it could have been seen, went white. He followed Miguel, though. Miguel knew what he was doing. Herman looked around the street as he followed Miguel, hurrying now to keep up with him. No one. A taxi two blocks down. Parked cars. A couple of winos down the way. No trouble, just like Miguel said.

Miguel went through the door, followed by Herman.

She went through a second door into a courtyard just as they made their way through the door that hadn't quite swung shut yet. Miguel rushed to this second door, caught it. Now they were behind her. Now she noticed them.

Her hand was in her purse. The purse dropped to the ground. In her hand was a set of keys.

Herman breathed a sigh of relief. He thought she might have a gun in her hand. Now Miguel would just have to take the purse. Like he said, she'd just hand it over. No trouble.

"Hey, this I like," Miguel said, closing the distance between the woman and himself. He put the knife against her breasts. Then he put his left arm around her shoulders and drew her face to his. He kissed her, thrusting his tongue into her mouth. "Yeah, this I like very, very much."

He dropped his left hand from her shoulders and it trailed down the young woman's back. She started to scream, but Miguel pressed the tip of his knife between her breasts and instead she sucked in air, terrified.

"Pick up the purse."

Herman obeyed Miguel. Miguel ripped a gold chain off the woman's neck. Then to the victim, Miguel said, "You're going to get it now, baby." He grasped the top of her shirt and started ripping it.

Someone screamed.

It wasn't the victim.

It was someone from a window overhead.

"Leave her alone! Leave her alone! You scum!"

An old woman's croaky voice.

Herman grabbed at Miguel's arm, was afraid when he couldn't find it in the darkness, even more afraid when finally he did manage to catch it. He felt Miguel's fear.

"Leave her alone. You scum! I just called the cops!"

Miguel and Herman looked up. One by one, the window ledges filled with the young woman's neighbors. Lights were popping on, each one seeming like some gigantic, accusing search beam that trapped them over and over again in white glare. Then one by one, the windows filled with shouting, cursing neighbors.

Now it was Miguel who followed as Herman fled the courtyard and the blaze of all that dangerous light. The young woman, so meek and frightened only seconds before, stood in the light and the might of her neighbors' avenging shouts, her shirt torn, her fists upraised. She shrieked threats of her own at the retreating figures of those who would have raped and robbed her.

They clattered through the small lobby, then out the second door into East End Avenue. Instinctively, they ran uptown. Uptown, where it was safe.

Only the winos they saw earlier were in their way. The shouting neighbors could no longer be heard. Maybe they would get away. Herman made a vow to himself as he ran, his lungs bursting and his feet pounding heavily over the pavement, that he would never again leave where he belonged, East Harlem.

Then someone shouted. A command.

This time, it was no old lady in a windowsill; nor was it a chorus of hollering neighbors safe from on high. This shout came from the street.

"Freeze!"

Herman's head spun around. He looked straight past one of the winos, his tall form partially illuminated by a streetlamp. Then he looked back at the wino, heard him shout, "Freeze!"

It took several suspended seconds for Miguel and Herman to realize that the wino was a cop, that he had the drop on them. Then they saw another wino, another cop. The back-up man, maybe ten feet away near a skinny plane tree in a planter box. There was the dull sound of a squad-car siren from somewhere nearby.

Herman heard a growl from Miguel. He turned to see Miguel turn up the edge of his shirt, saw him thrust his hand into his belt, saw the big gun slip out.

Miguel growled again.

He and Herman took off up the avenue, Herman with his hand clutched over Miguel's arm. Then Miguel broke free of the grip and twisted around. Herman turned his head.

"Freeze! Police!" one of the cops shouted.

Miguel raised his gun in the direction of the shouting cop.

Herman saw the plainclothes cop, legs spread, knees bent, arms out-stretched, a glistening .38 police special held in both hands.

"Freeze! Police!"

Miguel's hand jerked the big gun.

There was a shot. Not from Miguel's gun.

Another shot and Miguel fell to the sidewalk.

Blood flowed from Miguel's neck, poured out onto the sidewalk.

Herman dropped the woman's purse. He had forgotten he held it.

The cop with the drawn gun approached slowly, aimed his gun alternately at Herman and at Miguel's sprawled body. There was the smell of gunpowder streaming from the .38.

Herman's hands were high in the air.

A pair of uniformed cops jumped out of the squad car that roared up the curb and one of them snapped the steel bracelets on Herman's wrists. The other plainclothes cop, his voice amazingly steady despite his heaving chest, stood close to Herman's ear and said, "You're busted, creep."

The other plainclothes cop stood over Miguel, his .38 still held in both his hands. His eyes were wild with fright, nearly brimming over. At his feet, Miguel was dead. Officer Dominick Salvato had killed him.

A uniformed officer used a handkerchief to pick up Miguel's weapon. It was a pellet gun.

7

Mairead Keenan tried to imagine exactly what her husband was doing right this very minute as she sat on a flower-patterned Early American couch, hands folded in her pregnant lap, eyes fixed on the brass clock that was the centerpiece of her freshly spray-waxed coffee table.

It was nearly half-past eleven, which she knew to be Tommy's quitting time this week.

The house was, as usual, antiseptically clean. Each night after trundling the girls off to bed, Mairead performed a manic cleaning routine. It didn't matter whether Tommy was home or not. What mattered at that time of day was the cleaning. Her mother in Ireland, back home "on the other side" beyond the Atlantic, used to instruct her daughters, "The body responds to regularity in all things."

Thus, every stick of furniture in the large Riverdale apartment was wiped and polished nightly, every square inch of floor was swept or vacuumed or scrubbed. Then the kitchen was washed down, followed by the sterilization of both bathrooms—each equipped with toilets ever on guard against incursions of bacteria with their supplies of inky blue, chemically treated tank water.

After this, Mairead would shower for perhaps the third time of the day, then dust her body with talcum and, if Tommy were home, perhaps daub some Paris Moon behind her ears. Whether or not he was there for all this, she would slip into a peignoir and take her place, rather regally, in what she insisted on calling the "parlor." Each night she had visions of engaging her husband in the sort of sophisticated, witty and tender conversations she was forever reading in her substantial collection of romance novels. But mostly, Tommy was gone, and even when he was there, she mostly read her novels anyway.

If Tommy were home, in his usual place in front of the twenty-five-inch Early American console color television set with remote control unit, she would attempt one of her idealized conversations, usually opening with something like, "I know this is silly of me, darling, but a little chat could be amusing." Her husband would look at her for several seconds, then roll his eyes heavenward and say something like, "Nobody who lives on planet Earth talks like that." And then he would return to the business of the television schedule.

And so one by one, Mairead added little tasks to her evenings, until she developed her elaborate household routine, which served both to justify the purpose of her life and to blot out the dreary facts of her life —the constant din of television, the job of marketing for food and preparing meals that never varied from the fourteen-day menu recommended by Betty Crocker for maximum nutritional balance, the afternoon gossip with the other mothers down in the park, her husband's customary absence and his sexual frigidity.

Among her lesser routines was the reverent way she ran her fingers over two of the picture frames on a section of parlor wall devoted to important Keenan family mementos. One was a very large framed montage of snapshots taken of a towheaded boy named Sean. He would have been a high school senior now. He was the Keenans' first baby, dead fourteen years tomorrow. Only once since the funeral at Good Shepherd had Tommy Keenan made any reference to that morning they found little Sean in his crib bed, his skin blue and cold, inexplicably dead. If Mairead broached the subject, her husband would silently leave the house.

The other picture frame contained a photograph of Tommy Keenan at the age of twenty-two, his hair so thick and his face ruddy and unworn by the work that lay ahead of him. It was his police academy photograph and the retoucher had made his teeth impossibly white, his eyes blazingly clear and brave and his cheeks miraculously free of the acne that used to plague her husband back then. Below the photograph was a copper plate containing his name, the date he was officially sworn in as a police officer of New York City and a poem:

A Policeman's Prayer

Dear Lord, be with me on my beat this day,
    and every day.
Grant that each weary block I walk may ease
    a brother's way.
Let me be kindly to the old,
    and to the young be strong;
But let me triumph over those whose acts
    are cruel or wrong.
And when my own last summons comes and I stand
    in Your Court,
Lord, may my rest with You be long,
    my punishment be short.

Mairead closed her eyes to stem a flow of tears. She wanted with all her heart to believe Tommy was punching out, or whatever it was that the men did when they quit their tours. She wanted him to be walking to his car, getting in and driving straight home to Riverdale.

But she knew better.

She wiped an eye and returned her hands to her lap. She looked at the clock—a wedding gift from her mother, with the inscription "For all time"—and tried to imagine what the Nineteenth Precinct station house looked like inside. She'd seen the old limestone building only once, and then from a car window. That was five years ago when Tommy had last taken her anywhere besides package tours to Ireland, where he spent all day and all night in the pubs and she visited her mother and girlhood friends, family gatherings—his—or Emerald Society dinner dances, which Tommy believed were politically important for whatever chance he might have one day at significant promotion within the department.

Tommy had driven past the precinct house on East Sixty-seventh Street that night so that Mairead could see the place where he was determined his career would finally take off. "The mayor lives in the precinct," he told her excitedly, his arm slipped over her shoulder as she peered through the car window, "and the commissioner, too. A cop can get himself a little notice here, his work can mean something when the right people see it and all the right people are here to see, right?"

They were late for the theater because Mairead had been rushed through her cleaning routine. Otherwise, Tommy might have shown his wife the precinct house, his new surroundings, his new lease on life.

He wasn't cross with her for making them late, though. Nothing could spoil his fine mood, it seemed. He was so full of himself that night. And Mairead thought it might well be the first night in a very long while when they would make love properly, when she wouldn't have to coax a half-dozing man from the parlor sofa and drag him to bed and then do what she had to do to satisfy her own cravings. Yes, it might be the night she would be fulfilled and yet unashamed. She might not have to confess that week to the priest, who agreed with her each time that making her husband's penis hard when he was woozy with sleep and liquor and then pushing it between her legs was an awful lot like rape.

The day before, Tommy had come home with a pair of tickets to the Broadway musical *A Chorus Line.* Mairead nearly fainted with surprise and joy. She knew all about the play, of course, from talking with the women in the park. But never did she think her husband would take her to see such a thing.

"And we'll have dinner afterward, too," he told her. "It's a celebration."

Then he took his wife into his arms and they danced across the parlor to an imaginary song. The dance was over when Tommy banged his knee on the Hoover upright.

The dinner was at a place called Mama Leone's, a cavernous Italian restaurant in Times Square popular with tourists and infrequent the-ater-goers from the suburbs. To Mairead, it was elegant and magical, as if she'd actually stepped into one of her paperback romances. She was swept away by the excitement of the play she'd just seen and by the sight of the strolling violinists in their tuxedoes and starched white shirts.

The occasion was Tommy Keenan's reassignment. For far too many years, he'd worked the city-wide Sex Crimes Squad. Now he had won a spot in the Nineteenth, a prestige precinct.

Whenever he talked of his work, Mairead wanted to cover her ears with her hands and scream. It was horrifying, sickening. All the perversity in the world! But that night, at the magical restaurant, Mairead had no trouble listening to her husband's proud talk of the future, of the things he wanted to accomplish as a police officer.

Her mind drifted as he spoke. She felt girlish listening to him, ador-ing him, and it seemed as if she were returned in time to one summer night in Gaelic Park in the Bronx. She had let Tommy Keenan, the boy she'd only just met that night in the park, make love to her. He was good to her. He was strong and he knew it and held her as if he thought he might break her in two. She did not confess this sin to the priest.

A month later, she told Tommy Keenan that she was pregnant. "Are you sure?" he asked her. She assured him that the doctor was as certain of it as she. "I'm so happy," he said. And he proposed to her.

They were married at Good Shepherd Church in the Inwood section of upper Manhattan, where one of the younger priests who knew of their whirlwind romance and guessed what might be at the root of it took Mairead aside and whispered in her ear, "The second child takes nine months, the first one can come anytime. So don't you worry now. You just make your husband a good home."

Sean was born and then he died. And time, like a vandal, passed.

That night on the town five years ago, Mairead knew even while it was happening, could never be the same as the night when Mairead and Tommy were so innocent and so passionate, that night in Gaelic Park.

She was an uneducated girl from a very tiny village back on the other side. But one night in New York, she had loved Tommy Keenan and considered the pleasure of it a solemn compact. She would make a life for them, a home, and she would try to be a useful and understanding wife to a policeman.

Over the years, Mairead understood her husband far better than he realized. She knew about his work, about what he saw assigned to the Sex Crimes Squad. And she understood that what he saw was wrecking his life and probably hers. She knew it every time she saw the agonized confusion in Tommy Keenan's eyes as he looked, with an odd contempt, at her naked body.

But that night at Mama Leone's, she believed, was truly a night that would change the years of trouble, a night when Tommy Keenan might put his pains and memories behind him. That night he looked like his rookie photograph when he smiled, when he talked.

When they returned home, Tommy wasn't interested in making love to his wife. And for the first time, Mairead complained—and bitterly.

And Tommy Keenan said, just before he left her to go out drinking alone, "Sex with you only means a dead baby in the morning."

Now she sat, waiting.

The baby kicked and Mairead allowed herself to enjoy the sensation. It had happened sinfully, as with the girls. Mairead had dragged him from couch to bed, his breath thick and stinking of beer, and she'd stroked his penis until he was hard enough to fill her.

Another baby, this time maybe a boy. This time, maybe Tommy might get better.

She watched as the clock struck its soft eleven-thirty chimes. Then she leaned forward for the tenth time and straightened the magazines on the coffee table—*People*, the *Reader's Digest*, *Good Housekeeping* and the *Catholic Messenger*.

This time, just maybe Tommy Keenan would get into his car and come straight home.

"*¿Habla inglés?*"

Herman stared into the cop's face. Reflected lights from the flashing red of the squad cars that filled the avenue played in the big cop's eyes. The cop held Herman's upper right arm in a very tight grip. Herman's wrists were bound even tighter, with steel cuffs. More cops arrived, cars full of them. Herman was surrounded by an army of blue uniforms now, police badges, drawn nightsticks, drawn revolvers, the smell of leather and gunfire, the vengeful sounds of a swarm of neighborhood onlookers who formed a semicircle around the scene of the crime.

He tried to answer. Herman's mouth opened, but he couldn't form words, not with Miguel's dead eyes looking up at him from the bloodspattered sidewalk. His thoughts were in Spanish, but he spoke English to the cop squeezing his arm.

"So fast," he said, his voice soft and reedy. He looked down to Miguel. "It all ended, so fast."

"The creep speaks English," a cop said. "Go ahead and read him."

Again, the cop with his hand clamped over Herman's arm asked, "*¿Habla inglés?*"

Herman looked up and nodded dumbly. The cop squeezed his arm hard.

"Yes," Herman said.

"All right," the cop said. "Listen up, then."

He cleared his throat and sounded almost brotherly as he recited the Miranda warning to Herman, who trembled at the words and was suddenly thankful for the support of the cop's fingers dug into his upper arm:

"You have the right to remain silent. . . . Any statements you make may be used against you in a court of law. . . . You have the right to an attorney before answering any questions, or to have an attorney present at any time. . . . If you cannot afford an attorney, one will be furnished you free of charge. . . . Now that I have told you this, do you understand your rights?"

Herman understood. He'd heard the words dozens of times in his young life, mostly spoken by tough-talking actors in TV cop shows. Now it was real, depressingly real. Herman and the cop were players on a very real stage. And the semicircle of curious onlookers was their audience.

The crowd cheered when the cop finished reading Herman his rights.

Older officers appreciated the irony of this. A cop named Collins said, "Listen to the rubbernecks, will you? I'm old enough to remember when the Supreme Court handed down the Miranda warning law and everybody thought it was a big hot victory for the radical-liberals. Nowadays it's the voice of authority."

A testament to the power of video imagery. After a few hundred thousand cop dramas where a staccato-voiced heavy snaps off the Miranda and then packs the thug off to the slammer, the reading of constitutional rights against self-incrimination and statutory rights to legal counsel ceases to be a libertarian pronouncement and sounds, instead, like something ruthlessly fascist. In New York, neighborhood crowds turned out on the occasion of a fresh neighborhood crime often cheer what they believe to be at least the *sound* of swift justice and the only sound they might hear is the reading of rights to a suspect spread against a wall.

Herman was shoved into the back of a squad car and taken off to the precinct house for booking, during which time it would be discovered, to no one's particular surprise, that he didn't have any people at home who were able to hire him a lawyer. Toward morning, he would be taken to Riker's Island until court arraignment and subsequent trial, during which time he would meet a lot of the guys from his neighborhood. In the meantime, his name would go into the overnight hopper at the public defender's office and someone who never heard of him would draw the assignment. And Herman would talk to a lot of officers and detectives at the Nineteenth, "so I can get some very heavy shit off my chest."

On East End Avenue, a couple of detectives did the forensic evidence tasks, but just the basics since there were four eyewitnesses to the shooting. They bagged up Miguel's pellet gun in glassine, photographed his body from all angles, chalked the outline of the body and photographed that while the medical examiner's crew was wrapping up the remains to haul off in the meat wagon.

Gradually, the crowd began dispersing.

The woman whose bag was stolen was interviewed and comforted and told to expect a call in the morning from a detective.

Officer Dominick Salvato wanted to be sick.

"It's your collar all the way, Dom," his partner told him.

"Thanks," Salvato said. He reholstered his .38 and discovered that his entire body shook just like his right hand.

"Let's go to the house."

"Yeah," Salvato agreed.

He felt a lot of hands on him, his fellow officers helping him into a squad car. Everyone knew the private little hell in store for Dominick Salvato.

He was a cop who'd just killed someone he didn't know, a boy whose life, no matter how wasted, would no longer have the chance for redemption. In television shows, the cop who shoots down the menacing punk is supposed to be a big hero. And we can all see it coming from a long way off anyway. In real life, it doesn't play anything like that. Real life is far too much for television to handle, and far too fast.

Dominick Salvato sat in the back of the squad car, which was hemmed in on all sides by other squad cars and by crowds of cops and civilians moving through the avenue. He felt hundreds of eyes burn into him. Fellow cops, strangely speechless as they looked at him; neighborhood residents, their faces a mix of admiration and gratitude and fear; the men in the medical examiner coats as they walked by with a dead boy in a body bag, the thin, flat lump on the stretcher. They all took a look at the guy who just killed someone, as if he'd done it wantonly, as if he was proud of himself, as if he knew much more than what he saw in that few life-and-death seconds on a darkened street.

What he saw was a frightened figure, two of them. One aimed a gun. Dominick Salvato was frightened, too, and did what he had to do to protect himself and maybe others, other cops, people who lived in the neighborhood. He didn't know.

The boy he'd shot, Miguel, had raised a pellet gun. It wouldn't have done much harm, given the distance between them. But how could he have known?

Salvato would be told later, by the department lawyer from headquarters and by Inspector Short and by his partner, that he was clearly in the right. He would learn that Miguel was an animal.

But Salvato knew, too, what it was like to watch a boy's eyes close in death by his hand.

"It was all . . ." he said in the squad car on a steaming summer's night. "It was all, so fast. It ended so fast."

Herman had said the same thing. Salvato could think of nothing else but the same, the speed of a deathly moment.

Dominick Salvato didn't feel anything at all like a hero as he rode, in silence, to the precinct house. Heroes don't feel like vomiting.

They sat in a booth at the back of an all-night luncheonette near her place, which was a railroad flat on Ninety-fifth Street near First Avenue. Keenan's hands were sweating. He tried to decide what he wanted to have happen with the rest of the night, if anything.

"How long have you been a cop?" she asked.

They were the first words between them for some time, since they had spoken briefly back at the house and she'd given him the location of the restaurant and he'd suggested that she go along and he would meet her later. Dory Smith's hands were sweating, too, and her heart pounded. She was attracted to Keenan, excited by her first night as an auxiliary cop, even though she'd done nothing more than stand on a curb near some klieg lights in her uniform and occasionally ask someone to stay behind the wooden police barricade. It was a polite crowd of gawkers who happened by the theater premiere.

Keenan smiled. "Long enough so that no one thinks to ask what I might have been before I was a cop. Nobody's ever surprised that I'm a cop, either. It shows, I guess."

Dory smiled. "You're a thoughtful one, aren't you?"

"What do you mean? Thoughtful for a cop?"

"And paranoid."

"Yeah, maybe paranoid, too. You know what they say. If you're not paranoid these days, you're not thinking straight."

She considered this and then answered, "In this city, maybe you're right."

"How long have you been in New York then?"

She resented the question, even though she knew such resentment was unfair. Keenan asked her innocently enough, but even relative newcomers to New York bristle at being revealed as immigrants.

"About five years," she answered.

"And you want to be an actress, I suppose? A good-looking girl from the heartland and all?"

"It's not so unusual."

"No. Sorry." Keenan knew his talk was clumsy. "No more so than wanting to be a cop, I expect."

A heavyset waitress shuffled to their booth and took a pencil stub from behind her ear, held it over a smudged pink and white pad. "What'll it be, dearies?"

Keenan ordered coffee and a tuna sandwich, which he didn't want. He wanted beer. Dory Smith ordered eggs and tea.

"What's it like?" she asked.

"What, tuna?"

The waitress laughed and tapped him appreciatively on the shoulder as she waddled off to the kitchen.

"Oh, I know what you mean," Keenan said. "What's it like being a cop, eh?"

"No, what's tuna like?"

"Yeah, I thought I'd like you," Keenan said. He folded his arms in front of him on the table. "The way I figure, everything that goes on between men and women comes down to how funny it is they ever get together in the first place. It's the laughs that are the important things."

"Are you married?"

She said it calmly, which surprised her. She supposed he was and she supposed there might be a point at which it was every bit as important as laughs, even though she told herself now that it didn't matter. Why should it matter? Were they doing something wrong?

Keenan answered quickly and struggled to keep his face from becoming any hotter than it was.

"Yes, I'm married. Yes, I'm unhappy. No, I'm not thinking about

divorce. Yes, it's because of the kids and I know all about how that's
not a legitimate reason these days. Anything else you need to know
about it?"

"What's her name?"

Keenan wiped his forehead. "Mairead."

"And your children?"

Keenan told her. He told her their ages, too.

"What's in store for us?" he asked when she stared at him blankly.

"I don't know. What's it like being a cop?"

"You change the subject awfully damned fast, don't you?"

"I'm thinking about one thing and I want to hear you talk about
something else, that's all."

"Jesus help me. Women!"

The waitress set down their food, almost breaking the plates. She
winked at Dory and walked away.

They'd taken a few bites when Dory asked, "You'd rather be someplace else, right? Maybe at my place having a drink?"

"Maybe."

"So maybe we'll go there."

One of the enduring mysteries of life's annoying moments in New
York is the insistence of Manhattan car owners on equipping their
vehicles with burglary alarm systems that scream unendingly into the
night, touched off by the slightest jostling of the car. Never in the
entire history of auto burglar alarm sirens has the contraption led to the
arrest of a burglar.

A hefty percentage of the time the siren is set off accidentally by the
owner, who becomes furious with the hardware for making all the
commotion but who is still incapable of understanding how the thing
could possibly annoy anyone else.

If anything, the auto alarm siren is the burglar's best friend. If a car
starts shrieking, there is an automatic warning to all within hearing
range, which is considerable in a city where conversations on the sidewalk echo up and down buildings, to steer clear of a place where a
criminal—and maybe a criminal with a gun—is plying his trade. A
telephone call to the police, if ever made, will usually be placed long
after a burglar's one or two minutes' need for completion of the job,

and it will be handled as a low-priority complaint about excessive noise by the officer on the switchboard.

It is surprising that burglars themselves don't set off alarms when they find a car with something inside worth stealing. It is not so surprising that New Yorkers awakened by a siren that has shrieked on in the middle of the night become sometimes so frustrated that they themselves jump into their jeans and sneakers and take a baseball bat down to the street to bash out the windows of the offending car, whose owner is probably off somewhere sleeping peacefully.

Keenan pointed all this out to Dory Smith as they left the luncheonette and walked up First Avenue from Eighty-eighth Street toward Dory's apartment on Ninety-fifth. The shrill blare from a white Jaguar cut through his head like a nail. Dory covered her ears as they walked.

A young woman, yelling something up the avenue in the vicinity of the Jaguar, raised what appeared to be a crowbar over her head, as if to bring it smashing down hard on the hood of the sports car. Her threat of vandalism met with the shrill blare of the Jaguar's driver, a very drunk, middle-aged blond woman with a white fur wrap around her shoulders.

The driver and the rudely awakened young woman with the crowbar stood hollering at one another across the hood of the car, which made nearly as much noise as the women.

Keenan began trotting toward the scene, toward what might turn out to be an altercation. He stopped when he saw a squad car pull out from a side street, lights flashing.

Officers Tony Ciffo and Jean Truta stepped out of the squad car. Truta held her hands up, flat-palmed, to the young woman with the crowbar.

"We'll take care of it," she said. "Don't make it worse for yourself, okay?"

The crowbar was lowered.

Ciffo looked at his wristwatch. "How long has it been going off?" he asked the young woman, a tenant of the apartment building near the shrieking car.

"About a goddamn half hour! What are you going to do about it?"

"I'm going to write up a summons, ma'am," Ciffo said.

He stepped around the front of the car and held a hand out. The blond woman with the fur wrap caught it just in time to keep from falling.

"This your car?" Ciffo asked her.

"Yeah, of course."

"Can you turn it off?"

"That's what I've been trying to do, Officer." She waved a small key in her hand and then climbed back into the car and ducked her head under the dash. "The little devil is somewhere around here, I don't know."

Ciffo counted to twenty. He didn't like drunks, especially drunk women.

"We've got a complainant here who says your burglar alarm has been going beyond the ten-minute limit prescribed by the law," Ciffo said.

The blonde popped her head out the door of the car. One of her breasts bobbled out the top of her gown. She worked it back inside.

"I'm doing my best, Officer."

"Have you got some identification?" Ciffo asked.

"Identification?" she said, filling the air between them with liquor fumes. "Officer, I'm not so sure I even exist!"

Ciffo counted to twenty again. It was useless talking with her. He leaned against the Jaguar while she fiddled with her key under the dashboard.

The complainant walked sternly away from Officer Truta and said to Ciffo, "Officer, I want you to shoot the car."

"I can't shoot a car, lady. Sorry, but it's slightly against the rules, you know?"

"But I want that siren killed! Who do you think pays your salary anyway?"

Ciffo counted to twenty. Officer Truta suppressed laughter and wrote up the summons, attaching it to the Jaguar's windshield.

Then, suddenly, the siren died.

The drunken blonde stepped out, victorious.

Ciffo stopped a cruising taxicab and made sure the blond Jaguar owner had sufficient carfare, then sent her along home. The Jaguar would be towed and the fine would have to be paid—in full and in cash —if she ever wanted it back. Maybe she'd learn a lesson if it cost her a few hundred dollars.

Keenan passed by with Dory Smith and they each looked as guilty as if they'd just boosted something from a shop only to run right into a cop on the street, namely Tony Ciffo.

Seeing Ciffo there looking at him suspiciously, Keenan felt the need for some sort of comment.

"Don't worry," he said to Ciffo. "It's not like I know what I'm doing."

Then he and Dory hurried along to her apartment.

8

There is a man called Joe—just that and nothing more—who summers above ground on the Upper East Side and winters below ground, about twenty-six blocks south and a few blocks crosstown in a steam tunnel that runs under a hotel famous the world over.

As far as the cops are concerned, "Joe" is good enough, so long as he minds his own business and doesn't hurt anyone. Joe knows the rules and he observes them. Besides, it's against his nature to hurt anyone. And besides, he forgot his last name.

He sleeps, like the troll of the nursery story, beneath the Queensboro Bridge on First Avenue at East Fifty-ninth Street. Joe knows the long-established customs of the "house," as it were. He cozies up against the east pylon with the rest of the men, leaving the west side for the women who have no homes.

Joe stays dry on rainy nights and relatively unnoticed in these bridge shadows. He is also pretty much ignored by passersby, young couples with plenty of money in their pockets to spend at all the bars and nightclubs nearby.

Within a few blocks of where Joe and the others slumber in dark huddles, there is a cluster of comedy showcase clubs—Dangerfield's, Catch a Rising Star, the Comic Strip and Who's on First. Here would-be comedians try out their repertoires and rarely stray from six-joke categories—drugs, bodily elimination, Jews, genitalia, the agony of dating and the funny things that homeless people like Joe do and say every day on the streets of New York.

Joe doesn't care what they say about him, as long as they don't hurt him. He had a friend once who was stabbed while he slept on a bench down near Madison Square Park.

His winter digs consist of bundled newspapers tucked into a niche of a steam tunnel that runs past an elevator specially built to carry Franklin D. Roosevelt in his wheelchair up to the presidential suite of the Waldorf-Astoria Hotel from a specially built railroad siding. Joe remembers voting for Roosevelt once, which he says is about the time he forgot his last name and maybe his first, too, though "Joe" sounds right.

Near where he sleeps in the winter, in the tunnel, Joe heats food on a particularly hot section of steam pipe, which is part of a vast system that snakes out in all directions from Grand Central Station to supply heat to most of Midtown Manhattan. He even has a sort of washing machine rigged up in his niche, in the form of a rubber hose attached to a pipe valve that leads into a bucket where the steam bubbles through a load of water and clothes. There is a steam main farther down that serves as a drying rack.

"Don't like it in them steam tunnels," Joe says, sucking audibly before the words whoosh out. He has a tracheotomy hole at the bottom of his neck and speaks by drawing air into his stomach, then belching it out in short phrases. "Too goddamn hot."

He takes more breath.

"But thank God the pipes is there . . . I'd freeze here under the bridge. . . . But I'd rather be under the bridge . . . if I could, all year. I like the Upper East Side."

Joe likes the Upper East Side because he can make the most money panhandling for the least effort. He doesn't look threatening and he doesn't drink, which is especially unusual under the circumstances.

"Don't like the taste. . . . Puts you off your toes anyway. . . . They can get you when you're not careful."

Joe gets a little over $300 monthly as a disabled veteran. The checks are mailed to a sister in Brooklyn, who needs most of it for medicine. Joe won't stay with her because "I can't stand the old bitch." Not regularly anyway. But on winter days when he can't get through the unmarked brass door on the Forty-ninth Street side of the Waldorf to descend into his niche, or when even the doorless opening to the tunnel system at the lower level of Grand Central has been sealed off by security men, Joe relents and travels to Brooklyn.

"Don't like it, though. . . . The goddamn subways are dangerous, I'm tellin' you!"

If he's at his sister's home, Joe spends most of the time in a warm bath.

"You never know when you get the chance next. . . . You got to stay clean as you can. . . . Like everything else uptown, you got to be the best. . . . So I like to be the cleanest bum in New York.

"I keep clean and I keep myself uptown . . . often as possible. I stay safe there. Down in the tunnels one winter . . . some guy comes up to me . . . no cop uniform or nothin', but he says he's a cop. . . . Says he's plainclothes, like this one cop I know uptown . . . and he says I got to pay him or move along, that's the law. . . . So he takes seven bucks off me.

"Things are gettin' pretty bad . . . when a bum gets ripped off in a tunnel under the Waldorf, for God's sake."

The plainclothes cop Joe knows is named Ed Smith, with the Nineteenth Precinct Street Crimes Unit—the SCUM patrol. Smith was instructed in the finer points of blending into the street scene by none other than Joe the bum.

"He's one of my contacts, you might say," Smith said. "Joe hears a lot and he sees a lot and no matter what he looks like, he's not stupid or out of his mind. He's just ignored. It's like he's air or something, like he's blind and deaf.

"So anyway, I talk to him once in a while. He teaches me things about being invisible. And once he came across some really good skinny, which gave me a really great collar.

"From Joe I learned that you do three basic things so no one pays attention to you. One, you lie down and act like you're dead. In this city, almost everyone will walk right by. In the Nineteenth, they might think to call the precinct house or something and report the nasty old dead person. Second, you lie down and act like you're stoned and nobody wants to touch you because you're a dirtbag with no money. And third, you look at people's faces. Everybody, and I mean everybody, is intimidated when a bum looks at them. Maybe it's guilt. Yeah, I think it's guilt.

"Also, it's important to remember your place. When you're a bum, you're always deferring. That's if you want to stay on the street. If you don't defer to people, if you start making trouble, that's when they come after you with the nets and bag you off to Bellevue. You know?

The Toonerville Trolley to Ding Dong School. So you defer. You don't go walking down the middle of the street whistling a tune. It doesn't look right. You hug the curb, or the buildings, on the shady side of the street. Out of the way of everybody. You sort of crouch, too. People expect bums to crouch. And shuffle."

All this instruction has been important to Ed Smith's career as a SCUM patrol cop. When he first started out, back in the Times Square precinct before his transfer to the Nineteenth, Smith didn't have the finer points of being a bum firmly in mind. The test came one day as he lay in a gutter at the corner of Seventh Avenue and West Forty-sixth Street.

"I was on a post watching for the punks who snatch chains," Smith said. "It was a Wednesday, when the ladies from Jersey in the pant suits come over on the buses for the matinees. So I'm lying in the gutter, sort of, waiting for trouble.

"From the corner of my eye, I see this guy moping along, you know? He's scoping out the crowd and he's waiting for his moment. He's not noticing me at all and everybody's stepping all over me, so I figure I'm doing all right. I see this mope ready to rip off this lady and I'm ready to jump up and nail the guy.

"Just then, the lady passes by me and stops. She leans over and talks to me.

" 'Can I help you?' she says. 'Are you all right, sir?'

"I said to her, 'Get away, lady, I'm a cop.'

"But now it's too late. I see the mope has me made when he spots us talking, even though he can't hear what I said about being a cop.

"See? I wasn't invisible. You have to get to the point where people just don't care about you, so they look right through you and don't even feel sorry about you. You have to force them to ignore you before you become invisible."

Joe taught him well and it paid off one morning shortly after dawn, on East Seventy-ninth Street. Smith saw them, but the eight of them must have thought he was invisible.

". . . Conduct prejudicial to the good order and efficiency of the department."

He read it through half-frame spectacles, waited for Officer Cibella

Borges or her attorney, both of them seated across from him, to say something in response.

First Deputy Police Commissioner William Devine asked Officer Borges if she understood. She said nothing. Her attorney said he understood the "allegation here."

Officer Borges, even though she'd been around lawyers long enough to know how they could make even the most incriminating set of facts seem utterly insignificant, could not now understand the percentage in prolonging this process. Her attorney had advised going the whole route—departmental trial, the works. And she had agreed. But now, in the cold light of the confession she'd just made to Commissioner Devine, it seemed such an empty exercise.

"Allegation," her lawyer said. Her confession was, in lawyerese, a mere "allegation."

". . . I'm certain," he'd added, "that when the extenuating circumstances are known and weighed against Officer Borges' exemplary record, she will be cleared of the charges. And there is the matter of timing, as we have said. Cibella Borges posed for these pictures before she was sworn as an officer . . ."

But it was all words. A lawyer's words against the evidence of the pictures in that magazine.

Cibella Borges wanted more than anything in the world at that moment to crawl into a hole and die. That morning, she'd joked with the photographer who took her pictures, a scrawny young man she'd met one day walking on the Upper West Side, along the Columbus Avenue "quiche belt." Then after she'd talked with him, she cried and said, "I don't think I'll ever be working as a cop again."

Commissioner Devine and her lawyer were talking. Her lawyer penciled the charges on a notepad as Devine read it again from a typed report. It had all been decided, even before she came in to own up to it all!

"Conduct prejudicial to the good order and efficiency of the department."

She asked what would happen next, interrupting her own lawyer.

The press would be notified, Devine said . . .

If it were a male officer, the department brass would be hiding it from the press!

. . . and then there would be a hearing set before Departmental Trials Commissioner Jaime A. Rios.

It would all cost so much money!

"My hospitalization?" she asked. "Meanwhile, what about my medical care? I told you, it's very important to me just now."

Devine said he would look into that matter, nodding to her lawyer. He didn't know that the department could withhold fringe benefits as well as salary.

Up until now, he had been courteously patient. Now Devine looked at his wristwatch and made sure that Cibella Borges and her attorney noticed his concern for time. It was three forty-five on a very gray, wet afternoon.

Officer Borges rose from her chair and wobbled slightly. Her lawyer held her elbow. She seemed even smaller than her four feet, eleven inches. So tiny and fragile. She thought about all the money she would need for her defense. She thought about blowing her brains out.

She could pass the hat up at the Nineteenth Precinct house, among the female officers anyway. And who knows, maybe a few of the guys might kick in.

Maybe she could win the support of somebody like Gloria Steinem! After all, there was the Linda Lovelace case. All Cibella Borges had done was pose for a magazine.

And what about the guys who just so happened to have seen her in the magazine? What were they doing reading *Beaver* anyway? Or what were they doing *while* they were reading *Beaver?* She knew damn well the magazine was all over the city, in every precinct house in all five boroughs, probably. The hypocrisy made her as sick to her stomach as her own damn foolishness.

A year and a half on the force, down the toilet. The meritorious citation for helping to apprehend three gun-wielding stick-up artists. Her green belt in karate. That didn't matter. What mattered was the fact that a bunch of cops saw her naked in a magazine that most people never heard of and complained about it.

Well, maybe it would all wash away. Maybe she could make them see, make them understand.

First of all, she wasn't even a cop when she posed for *Beaver.* She taught typing and self-defense at the Police Academy, that's all. When she posed, her job at the academy was just a job. She might as well have worked at the YMCA.

On top of it all, she had applied for a police officer slot, only to be rejected for medical reasons.

Her lawyer had said the department would have a very, very rough time dismissing her for something she did *before* becoming a cop, even if it might possibly reflect badly on her subsequent position. Her lawyer had already let this fact leak to the press and, in response to reporters' questions, the brass agreed with her lawyer that firing her outright would be very tough indeed.

Officer Borges allowed herself to smile.

Between the sympathy she might arouse among women officers and feminists generally and the legal technicality of her status with the department when she posed for *Beaver* . . . perhaps, just perhaps, she might beat it. Maybe she could hold on to the job that made her mother so proud of her, the job that made her the neighborhood hero-ine, the job with the big future.

As she walked to the door leading out of Devine's office, Cibella Borges' mind was filled with the confidence that truth would out, that justice would be done, that a good officer like her wouldn't be let go because of a particularly delicate indiscretion. She would be able to tell her story. Any woman would understand.

But why?

She shook her head, but this basic question wouldn't go away. She couldn't convince herself of any reason she tried. And her confidence evaporated as quickly as it had swelled.

She thought for a moment of the men she knew who had tattoos on their arms, or chests or the backs of their hands. Stupid, juvenile de-signs like hearts or snakes, skulls and crossbones, sailing ships, anchors, mermaids and knives. Most stupid of all, some girl's name from their adolescence, usually accompanied by flowers and lies like "forever." How embarrassed the men were for these indiscretions. But no one punished them for being young fools, no one took their jobs away as long as they kept their sleeves rolled down.

The tattoos would last as long as the skin they covered. But how long would a magazine last?

Cibella Borges could walk on a beach and no one would know she once posed for lewd photos in a filthy magazine. A man with a tattoo had a permanent, blazing neon sign of stupidity—for which he'd had to pay! At least Cibella Borges could say they'd paid *her*.

A scribble of fear played through her head.

. . . What if they found out the other thing?

Detectives Matty Monahan and Charlie Leinau drove down the FDR Drive along the East River, Leinau at the wheel. Their destination was Police Plaza in Lower Manhattan. Their guest, in the back seat guarded by an extremely red-faced young officer sweating in his blue uniform, was one Monique Mansfield, a platinum blonde whose fetching *décolletage* was the cause of the young officer's color and perspiration. Miss Mansfield smirked and crossed her legs.

It was a baloney bust, if Monahan and Leinau had ever seen one.

Monique had taken a call to some freak's apartment, hadn't enjoyed the scene too well and then had left with a little hazard pay—the customer's Ming dynasty vase in the vestibule gallery. The creep noticed it was gone right off and managed to slip out of his rubber underwear long enough to call the Nineteenth and report a burglary. A couple of uniforms bagged her two blocks from the freak's town house just off Madison Avenue in the Seventies, which is a neighborhood where you don't see too many bouffant blondes in spike heels, black mesh stockings, leather double-slit skirts and off-the-shoulder chain-link blouses walking around in the middle of the afternoon with priceless Chinese vases under their arms.

There was no place to hold Miss Mansfield at the house, as the last available spot for a female prisoner had been taken by a junkie with dry heaves and fairly violent hallucinations. Lieutenant Stein didn't think too much of having her hang around the PDU squad room, so Monahan and Leinau were elected to take her downtown and while they were there they could attend to some paperwork anyway.

"I'm thinking seriously of taking that terminal leave plan, you know," Leinau said. He shook his head up and down.

"Oh Jesus, here we go again on the second anniversary of Leinau threatening to quit."

"No, no. This time I mean it. Jesus Christ, who needs all this shit?" Leinau looked into the rearview mirror. Monique had taken the remark personally and looked hurt. "Sorry, old girl."

"Hmphh!"

"So twenty years and I'm out on my pension," Leinau continued with Monahan. "Sounds good. You got to do something for money and to keep busy, though."

"What would you do, you hump? The only thing you're fit for is being a cop and living vampire hours. Christ, what do you sleep, two hours a night or what? No wonder you think like this."

Leinau waved his hand.

"Everybody's got to settle down, pal. Vampires, too. Listen, you know where the old New Rochelle Creek bait and tackle shop was?"

"Yeah."

"Well, nobody's been there for years, right? The place burned to the ground. I figure I get the place and start up the business again."

"This I got to see. Leinau selling fucking worms up in New Rochelle."

"On the whole Sound, close in, there was only that place and City Island where you could buy worms. Don't sell worms short, Monahan. I could make a fortune."

"Yeah, you and Ralph Kramden. You'll die of boredom first, you hump."

"Maybe. And maybe I'd die bored and rich."

"Leinau, you're just going to die on the job, period. And it's going to be old age because you're too fucking weird to be killed."

Leinau waved his hand again.

"Okay," he said to Monahan. "You think you pay a lot for steak these days? What about a pound of worms? You pay maybe six bucks for a pound of top sirloin at the old Sloan's, right? Figure out what a pound of worms costs, buddy—at the rate of three bucks for a dozen of those suckers."

"What'd you say happened to the bait and tackle shop?"

"Burned to the ground."

"You better first see about why it burned, that's my advice. Maybe someone fucking torched it because it belonged to some dick like you with enemies five or six miles long, you know?"

Leinau pulled off the FDR and took the exit ramp that ran into Park Row. In a few minutes, the squad car rolled into the underground garage at Police Plaza.

"Up off your keister, sweetheart," Monahan said, looking back at Monique Mansfield. "It's upstairs we go, kiddo."

On the way up the elevator to Central Booking, Monique licked her lips and sidled up against Monahan. Monahan laughed at her. Leinau studied her face.

Upstairs, Leinau took her to the fingerprint desk and began rolling her palms and tips through black ink, all the while studying her vaguely familiar face. Monique was clearly rattled by this, unaccustomed as she was to having men stare at her face rather than her bust. She was nervous and quiet as Leinau pressed her fingertips into the neat squares on the white three-by-five FBI standard print identification forms, left and right.

"Say," Leinau finally asked her, a bell ringing somewhere inside his head, "you female?"

A very indignant Monique Mansfield tossed her blond tresses over her back and said, "Yeah, what you think, copper? What do you want, proof or something?"

"Wait here," Leinau said. He gave her a wet towel so she could wipe up the mess of ink on her hands. "Just wait right here."

"So where would I go, already?"

"Yeah. So wait."

Leinau walked over to Monahan, who was busy with a couple of large black books, property of the Major Crimes Squad. The mug shots weren't helping, nor were the psyche sheets of known torches in New York City.

For months, Monahan had been after someone he knew only as "Kano." He'd put a lot of money out on the street to various informers in the Nineteenth, as well as the Seventeenth and Twenty-third precincts. He'd come up with a street name, Kano. And he kept hearing that Kano was extremely dangerous. A "human bomb," according to one of his stoolies, who never went anywhere without a couple of revolvers tucked inside his shirt, a hand grenade clipped to his belt and a carload of dynamite, gasoline cans, waterproof fuse wire, blasting caps, asbestos gloves, an M-1 carbine with telescopic sights and a Uzi collapsible submachine gun.

But Monahan was chasing a phantom, he began to think. Every time he had a lead and showed up, Kano had vanished. Did he ever exist? Unless he caught up with this Kano soon, Monahan knew he would have to admit desperation and release to the newspapers a composite police sketch. If he saw his mug in the papers, a cockroach like Kano would correctly conclude that the cops were having a very difficult time of it. He could breathe easier. Cops don't tell the public what they're looking for unless they've practically given up—and then what's to lose?

"Matty," Leinau said, slapping Monahan's back. "I'm over there getting the toots' John Henrys, right? Then it hits me. Our Monique Mansfield used to be Sheldon Schwartz."

"Yeah?"

"Sure. If you ever get your eyes off those incredible gozonda nuts of hers and look at the face, you're looking at old Sheldon Schwartz, second-story man."

Monahan walked with Leinau back to the fingerprint desk. Monique daintily wiped her hands.

"Hey, you're right," Monahan said. "Shelly Schwartz. How you been, Shelly? Things aren't what they used to be, eh?"

Monique stuck her tongue out.

"I'm not that Sheldon Schwartz anymore," she said.

Then she put her fingers beneath the straps of her blouse and pulled it down quickly, flashing an enormous pair of white breasts tipped in pink. She thrust herself forward and practically slapped Monahan in the face with her stupendous breasts. Then she covered herself when she saw cops converging on her from every corner of the big Central Booking room.

"Where you living now, Sheldon?" Leinau asked.

"The Upper East Side. Where else? And it's *not* Sheldon, if you please. To you, it's Miss Mansfield."

Monahan whistled. "You must have some angel, Shelly. These operations are pricey."

"I'm living with Johnny Rod."

Monahan looked at Leinau. "That's supposed to be someone we know, Charlie?"

"Big porno star. Got a schlong like a goddamn donkey. So I guess Sheldon here went and did the whole thing for Johnny. Probably even the old slit in the melon."

A noisy crowd of cops surrounded Monique Mansfield, who defended her femininity by flashing her breasts and smiling to the cheering onlookers in blue.

Then the sergeant on duty tapped Monahan on the shoulder.

"You Monahan of the Nineteenth?" he asked.

"Yeah."

"Drop a dime back to your house."

Monahan stepped away to make the call, then hurried back to where Leinau and the others were being entertained by the former Sheldon Schwartz.

"You don't need me, Charlie. I got a line and we may set up for Kano."

"Your torch?"

"Yeah, the guy that did the job on Second Avenue and Ninety-third, killed the family trapped on the fifth floor."

"Get out of here."

Between five o'clock and a quarter before six on most weekday afternoons, the Metropolitan Life Insurance Building on Twenty-third Street disgorges itself of a small army of women office workers. Maybe half this army aspires to standard, straightforward career goals. And maybe the other half hold down jobs temporarily, until an important theatrical producer has sense enough to cast them in a Broadway smash hit. In any event, they need good clothes and accessories. In New York, clothes make the woman, so some women will say.

These office workers are exquisitely dressed, despite their rather low salaries, thanks to a certain breed of entrepreneur who greets them during this crucial forty-five-minute period. Their merchandise is offered from the trunks of cars and is known as "swag stuff," the term "swag" being an acronym for "stolen without a gun." None of the customers has ever been known to ask questions about the impossible bargains.

An evening dress by Halston, ordinarily selling for $800 in a boutique on the Upper East Side, is a quick $50 and no sales tax. A $150 Liz Claiborne denim jump suit for $10; a leather skirt from West Bay, $25 instead of the normal $140; a red mohair and lambswool jacket by Betty Hanson, maybe $200 uptown, just $20 from the fast-talking peddler on Twenty-third Street.

There are many such locations around the city where "swag sales" are held afternoons, all of them having in common large numbers of customers who scramble down into subways and go directly home with their bargains and who can just as quickly forget about the fact that they have purchased the latest harvest of goods boosted from the best shops in the city, those in the Nineteenth Precinct.

For a time, it can go very well indeed for the thieves. If they're smart, they ditch anything they cannot immediately sell. There are smart thieves, and then there are thieves who are not so smart.

The peddlers working Twenty-third Street were doing a land-office business for a time, with no overhead and plenty of satisfied customers. Hundreds of women were able to wink away their suspicions and dress far beyond their budgetary abilities. And there was the very special bonus to this particular gang of peddlers, eight effeminate black men doing a very big "smash and grab" business uptown. They kept the best of what they stole for themselves—truly a gang belonging to the age of specialization.

Ed Smith would soon have their number.

9

Police informers—or, as they're called behind their backs, "stool pigeons," "blabs," "stoolies" or "snitches"—come in three basic stripes: the guy who gives away his stuff for free, for reasons that range from paranoia to the fact that there is no honor whatsoever among thieves; the guy who is savvy enough to know when he's in a position to negotiate the value of uncommon knowledge; and a guy like "Orange Lips," something of a fixture at the Nineteenth Precinct Detective Unit.

Orange Lips is so named for the peculiarly vivid hue of his most prominent facial feature. His mouth looks like the business end of a Day-Glo orange toilet plunger, sliced vertically. Every month or so, he winds up in the Nineteenth PDU for one of two reasons. Either he needs a fast sawbuck for a good night's sleep (coincidentally the very same price for a hit of your bargain smack) and is willing to spill about someone he figures the cops would want on some nickel beef (he wouldn't want to get a colleague in any serious trouble), or else he's sitting in a steel chair connected by handcuffs to the rim of a steel desk bolted to the floor while a detective books him on a nickel beef all his own, something like a purse snatch maybe. Orange Lips tries to slither out of his predicament by trading on some skinny about someone who might be a really important collar and sometimes he helps himself.

He doesn't smell much better than he looks, which is why the cops who book him like to have something burning in an ashtray between them and Orange Lips. And that makes two reasons why black officers make themselves scarce when Orange Lips makes the scene.

Detective West walked into the PDU with Orange Lips. Detective Herbert Charles, seated in a far corner and content with catching up on paperwork, looked up quickly and suddenly decided he needed to go out to dinner. Herb Charles is black and the thought of having to appear in a possible lineup next to Orange Lips is not a favored notion.

Detective Charles would make a call and the word would get around that Orange Lips was in the house. In a few minutes, a lot of black officers would suddenly opt for dinner—outside the house.

For Orange Lips is reserved that most damning insult—the racial slur served up by his own. There has been more than one black officer heard to complain bitterly when roped into lineup with Orange Lips, "that ugly nigger who stinks like some weight lifter's jockstrap."

"See you, Herbie," Detective West said to the black cop walking quickly out the door.

"Yeah, sure." Detective Charles scowled at Orange Lips as he passed.

For the most part, Orange Lips is harmless as a criminal because he is ineffectual. He couldn't hurt anyone for the same reason. And by certain practical measure, he is a rather useful citizen, since he fingers a few losers every month and the city is a better place for his efforts, ignoble as they may be. As the unsightly and unwanted stray cat serves us by making an occasional meal of the even more unsightly rat, so Orange Lips performs his civic obligation by his station as a snitch.

As Detective Matty Monahan wheezed upstairs to the PDU, called back to the house to receive an important call he'd give his left nut to bust open, Detective West, a long-burning cigar assisting him, typed out an arrest card with Orange Lips' name on it. Orange Lips, who kept rubbing his unusually dry mouth with his free hand, was not having it his way.

Monahan spotted Orange Lips and groaned. He looked for the lieutenant, Stein.

"Where's the looey?" Monahan asked.

"Dinner, man," Detective Charles said. " 'Bye."

"They call me out of Central Booking for this? For Orange Lips?" Monahan asked this of anyone, but no one was listening. He flapped his arms a bit and headed toward West and Orange Lips.

"That the dude?" Orange Lips asked when he raised his eyes to Monahan.

Detective West nodded and continued typing.

"He's got something for me?" Monahan asked West.

West nodded. "Maybe, maybe not. He's been a bad boy again, though."

"Shee-it!" Orange Lips said. "You pigs tryin' to mess up my mind. I ain't done nothin' 'cept play chicken a little, man."

"He was the lookout on a boost," West explained.

In his own defense, Orange Lips offered, "Hey, man, they tole me there ain't no law bein' the chicken outside."

Monahan sighed. "You know the drill by now," he said to Orange Lips. He started to walk away, but West got up from his chair and steered him off to a corner of the squad room, out of Orange Lips' earshot.

"He might just have something for you on Kano," West said. "Yeah, I know, he's high tonight. But what he told me sounds really solid and I thought enough of it to get you called back home. This is no shit, Matty. Talk to him yourself when I'm done with the Mickey Mouse, okay?"

Monahan looked over toward Orange Lips.

"Shee-it!" Orange Lips said, frightening a petite woman who walked in with her young son to speak to someone about her "goddamn ex-husband who's going to wind up killing us."

Orange Lips wiped his mouth and giggled. The woman with the boy in tow sat down at Detective Herman's desk. Ray Herman is particularly good at listening down through hysteria to whatever essential facts there might be that would constitute police interest in a complaint walking in off the streets.

"I'll get him a candy bar," Monahan said to West. "Looks like he's in for a very rough night."

Detective Herman smiled through a familiar story told by a spurned woman, this time one named Vicki Balaton. Her husband dumped her for a "two-bit whore from the office" and now that he's living with "the slut" he thinks he has the right to "shove my little boy's face in his degenerate life-style."

Mrs. Balaton's son calmly removed a notebook and some papers from his school book bag. Herman guessed the boy to be in the fourth grade or so and asked him about the school patch on his blue blazer. Mrs. Balaton shut up for five seconds or so.

The boy smiled. "St. Stephen's of Hungary," he said. "I'm in the third grade."

"What's your name?" Detective Herman asked.

"You got a gun on you?"

Herman lifted his sport coat and showed the boy his service revolver, tucked in its belt clip holster.

"Man-o-man!" The boy started writing in his notebook. He looked up, then wrote down what he saw, in notes.

"What's your name?"

"Greg."

Mrs. Balaton wanted to talk some more, so she told her son to stop bothering Detective Herman.

"He's not bothering me, ma'am," Herman said.

"Oh."

"Greg," Herman asked the boy, "what are you writing?"

"I'm going to do a story about this for my paper."

"You have a school paper?"

"Well, not really the official school paper or anything like that." He fished out three copies of an oversized mimeograph sheet, something called "Eye Spy," from his book bag.

"What kind of stories do you write?"

"Oh, me and Anthony—that's my pal—we try to make about twenty pages and we have news and weather and sports stories. Mostly, we write stories about stuff that happens to us. Like now. Like seeing a gun on a policeman's belt like this."

"What do you think about having to carry a gun around like I do?"

"I think it's neat."

"It's not, Greg. It's sort of too bad. Do you understand?"

"Well, I think so."

"Fine. You think about why it's too bad I have to carry around a gun. Listen, what do you do with your paper anyway?"

"Me and Anthony sell it for a dollar."

Herman took a dollar out of his pocket and bought the latest number.

Mrs. Balaton was considerably calmer.

"Do you think your husband is violating visiting rights?" Herman asked her.

"He *is* violating visiting rights," she said. "I don't *think* he is, I *know* he is."

"Yes, I see. But there is criminal law and there is civil law. Understand what—"

"The law is shee-it!" Orange Lips shouted.

Mrs. Balaton jumped.

"What's *he* here for?" Greg asked.

"Look, Mrs. Balaton," Detective Herman said. "See that guy over there?"

She leaned forward and whispered to Herman, "You mean that man with the big orange lips?"

"Yeah, that's the one. We mostly deal with fellows like that. Now, has your husband acted in some criminal way here?"

"Well—"

"I didn't think so. If you think your husband is in violation of the legal points of your divorce decree and the visitation rights spelled out in the legal judgment, then what you're going to have to do is see your attorney about this and make your complaints before the civil court. This just isn't a police case at this point, you see. And I hope for your sake, Mrs. Balaton, that it never is."

She dropped her head and her shoulders started quivering. Herman reached into his back pocket and then gave her his handkerchief.

When she composed herself, Herman said, "Take it easy on everybody, all right? Call me if you think you need us. Really." He gave her his card, then she and the boy got up to leave.

"So long, Greg," Herman said.

" 'Bye, and thanks," he said.

"Yes," Mrs. Balaton added. "Thanks."

Herman rubbed his forehead and then stood up to walk around the squad room a bit. As usual, everyone was involved in a million cases at once and the noise level of the place was the best evidence of that. He strolled over to Detective Lauver's desk.

"How come you didn't catch that one?" Herman asked.

"You're our domestic expert," Lauver said.

"Maybe so. Nice kid she's got there, you know. I hope he doesn't crack up under it all."

"I suppose you'll never know."

Herman shrugged.

Detective West, a telephone receiver cradled between his shoulder and his ear, shouted, "Who's up around here?"

"I'm catching," Lauver answered. "What's the line?"

"Three."

Lauver picked up on it and started writing notes on a pad.

He asked someone on the other end of the line a series of short questions: "Look like she was alone? . . . Windows normal? . . . You talk to the doorman? . . . What about the door locks? . . . Things been thrown around?"

He hung up the phone.

"What do you have?" Herman asked.

"Uniform call from a building on Eighty-first and Third. They got something that doesn't look right. Maybe it's just a lonely one, I don't know."

He went to the PDU duty log book near the sergeant's office to sign himself out. Inside the office were Monahan and Orange Lips. Lauver poked his head inside.

"How you doing with him?" he asked.

"Orange Lips here is about to earn his keep, so he says."

Lauver waved and was gone.

"How do you know about this?" Monahan asked Orange Lips.

"Shee-it, man, I start tellin' you that and I'm out of business, you know?"

"You ever do a job with Kano?"

"Not my kind of people, man."

"So how is it you know about him? The guy's good and he's professional and he's quiet about it. You're out of his league, dirtball. What do you know about him?"

"I tole you, man. I got ears. People got mouths and I got ears, you know? You want me to tell you what I know, or you want to sit here jivin' tonight? Makes no never mind to me."

Monahan figured him for being square on this one. If a small potato like Orange Lips managed to hear something about someone as shrewd and canny as Kano, then it had to be worth something. He decided to bite on it. One more shot at nailing the bastard before turning over the police sketch to the newspapers.

"So spill, Orange Lips."

"Hey, not so fast, my man. Not so fuckin' fast! You know, I got myself in a little jam here and now I got to look out for number one, right?"

"Better stop wasting my time or you're number shit, *my man.*"

Monahan watched the sweat bead up on Orange Lips' forehead and neck and he knew he had the snitch where he wanted him, desperate to get uptown someplace for a hit at a shooting gallery. He reached into his breast coat pocket and pulled out a Hershey chocolate bar. Orange Lips rubbed his mouth and his eyes fell half shut and he trembled visibly. He needed a rush and he needed it fast. A candy bar might hold him for a while.

"What's the matter, Orange Lips? You seem tense."

Orange Lips almost fell out of his chair. He righted himself and he giggled. "You want this firebug dude real, real bad, man. How much you want this bad dude?"

Monahan pushed himself back in the sergeant's swivel chair and unwrapped the chocolate. Orange Lips seemed ready to lunge at him.

"How old are you, Orange Lips? Fifty or so?"

"Huh?"

"You heard me."

"Yeah, that's about it. I don't know. Fifty, I guess."

"Not too much in this life more pathetic than a fifty-year-old junkie snitch, you know?"

Orange Lips was growing weak. "Let's deal here, man."

"You're old enough to remember the good old days of cop hell, right? You know, when we wanted something bad and somebody like you was holding out on us, playing games with us."

"Shee-it!"

Monahan bit off the tip of the chocolate bar and Orange Lips whimpered.

"Picture how it used to be," Monahan said. "Rubber hoses, those nice leather truncheons. I want Kano so bad, I don't mind telling you that I'd like to take you right now to a little museum us old-timers have right here at the precinct house, a little room with no windows where we keep stuff from the good old days. Get the picture?"

"Ah, shee-it. I was just tryin' . . ."

"You know we'll make it right by you, dirtbag. You want out of here on the nickel beef? Talk, *my man.*"

Monahan leaned forward and waved the chocolate bar under Orange Lips' nose.

"I know," Orange Lips gasped, "I know this place he goes regular-like for his gasoline."

Monahan smiled.

"Let's talk," he said. "Then I'll think about giving you this candy bar."

"No, you can't go in. No, you can't take any pictures. Why don't you just go on home now?"

The uniformed officer spoke to a woman in hair rollers with an Instamatic camera slung around her neck. They stood in the fourth-floor corridor of an apartment house on Eighty-first Street a half block east of Third Avenue.

"But I live here!" the woman in the hair rollers shrieked. "She's a friend of mine."

"Why would you want to go and take a picture of her, lady?"

"None of your business, that's why. Who do you think pays your salary, flatfoot?"

Detective Lauver stepped out of the elevator, a Polaroid camera in hand.

"What's he going to do with that?" the woman hollered.

"He's a police detective, ma'am. It's official business."

"What's the problem here?" Lauver asked the uniform.

"The problem is, I'm a friend of hers," the woman said, jabbing her finger into Lauver's chest, "and I want to see what happened to her."

Lauver took out his notebook. "You're a friend of hers? What's your name? I guess we have your address."

"My name?"

"Oh yes. For the record, you know. And maybe for testimony."

"I don't want to get that involved."

"You're a friend of hers, you say?"

"Well, we see each other sometimes."

"What's your name?"

"I have something on the stove."

"You better go attend to that, then."

"Yeah, well . . . maybe I'd just better."

Lauver and the uniform watched as she waddled down the hallway. She turned and looked over her shoulder at them, glaring angrily at the policemen, then turned a corner and headed down a corridor to her own door. The officers listened as she slammed the door behind her.

"The resident ghoul," the uniform said.

"Yeah. I've seen plenty of their kind before. Okay, what do we got here?"

"One dead fat lady, lived alone. Take a deep breath and see for yourself."

Lauver took a handkerchief from his pocket and held it over his nose. The uniform pushed open the door to apartment 4-D. Two more uniforms were inside, stepping around a living room that looked like it had been burglarized every day for years.

Furniture was upended, clothing was strewn everywhere. Papers, books, beer cans and what looked to be several hundred medicine bottles covered the floor. An antique chest in the vestibule leading to the living room was tipped over and one of the drawers broken. Personal correspondence and canceled checks spilled out of the only quality piece in the place.

Copies of *True Confessions* magazine, the *Midnight Globe* and the *National Enquirer* scandal sheets as well as the New York *Post* tabloid daily lay in piles around a sagging couch near a window that looked out on the building's gray air shaft. Some of the magazines and newspapers were more than two years old.

There was a television set opposite the couch, an enormous Mediterranean-style cabinet model, wedged between a pair of tall bookcases laden with paperback romance novels. The books were neatly stacked, the only sign of order in the flat. The television set was on, tuned to the *Merv Griffin* show on New York's WNEW, Channel 5. Merv was busy interviewing a television actress Detective Lauver had never heard of complaining about how she'd been libeled by the *National Enquirer*.

Lauver poked through some of the papers, letters mostly. He learned she had a son upstate and a married daughter living in Connecticut. There was a letter, too, about a month old, from a nurses' association informing her that the check enclosed was the last she would receive and recommending that she seek public assistance.

"Oh God," Lauver said. "Why is it always so much the same?"

He looked at the window ledge, piled with old medicine vials.

"What is all this stuff anyway?" Lauver leaned over and took a look at the labels.

"Antiflatulence. What's that mean?"

"It means the old lady farts so much she can't stand it so she went and got pills for it," one of the uniforms said.

"Jesus Christ."

"Where is she?" Lauver asked.

"In a closet in the bedroom, facedown. We haven't touched her."

"I'll take a look in the kitchen first," Lauver said.

It was just off the living room, a small galley containing new appliances, plenty of cupboards and a long Formica counter. Lauver took a handkerchief from his back pocket and used it to open the cupboards. They were bare. He opened the refrigerator and found a can of unopened beer, six empties, an aged onion and a jar of mustard. The range top showed no signs of ever having been used.

But the long counter was covered with medicine bottles, many of them half full.

"More of these antiflatulence pills," Lauver said. "This gal had a big problem."

He stepped back into the living room and said to one of the uniforms, "All right, let's see her." The cops started walking toward the bedroom. On the way, Lauver poked his head into the bathroom door. Inside, the bathroom was eerily clean, even sweet-smelling.

When he stepped into the bedroom, he choked at the smell. He took his pipe from a side pocket and lit it, filling the air with something to mask the odor of the dead woman.

Like the living room, her bedroom was filthy. Even more so. The bedding was soaked with urine and feces.

Lauver held his breath, took a look in the closet and saw her there on the floor, an obese ball of graying flesh in a thin cotton housedress, her splotched legs tucked up beneath her and her arms outstretched.

He left the room for air, set his Polaroid and then returned, snapping off several pictures of the dead woman in the closet.

"What do we know from the doorman?" Lauver asked a uniform when he'd finished the camera work.

"He said she used to be a nurse at Metropolitan, that she's about fifty-five or so and that she'd been working as a private nurse at a hundred bucks a day."

"Jesus, what a pig. Who'd hire her for anything, let alone as a nurse?"

"The doorman says she's an alky, as if you couldn't tell. Says she has hallucinations all the time and always calls up the super to get rid of wolves that keep coming into her apartment, stuff like that."

"Jesus, you'd think it might be homicide if you didn't know about her, I mean from the looks of the place when I walked in," Lauver said.

"The doorman says the place is always like this. He says the porters come in about every other week or so and pick up everything, at least, and haul off the empties. But it gets right back to the same condition."

"Yeah, okay," Lauver said. "I'll take one more look and then I think we can call the morgue on this one."

Lauver returned to the bedroom closet, his pipe puffing wildly. He used his foot to turn over the dead woman and get a look at her face.

"There's no blood here," he said. "My guess, it's her liver that's all puffed up and oozing poison. That's what happens with them."

He took his foot away and the body fell heavily to the floor of the closet again.

One of the uniforms said, "You know, she had this little cat or dog dish out in the kitchen, but we didn't find any animal."

"Maybe it's under her," Lauver said.

"Hey, then it is homicide!"

Lauver groaned. It was time for him to leave with his Polaroid pictures, which he would attach to the form he would have to type up back at the house, which he would do as fast as he could and then move on to something else. Something else would not necessarily be pleasant; it would just be something else.

What was it that sent so many sick, suicidal people into closets? Lauver asked the question a long time ago, when he was a young officer himself, when he saw his first moldering body in an unkempt apartment with the pall of someone's final, sadly quiet desperation. Someone told him that people regress when they relinquish their instinct for survival, when they submit to death. And often, they seek the safety of hidden confinement in a small, dark place. Like a dog or a cat in unfamiliar surroundings. Often, the suicide victim will creep off into a closet, then lie down with a belly full of poison and die.

Lauver used to wonder about the people who would take their own lives. He used to wonder how many times they crept into closets and wept, why everyone who knew them well—friends and family members—was always surprised to discover all the signs of their lonely agony.

In the car riding back to Sixty-seventh Street, he used his handkerchief to try cleaning his nose of the acrid smell of the dead woman and her apartment. He wasn't successful.

"Lasts for days sometimes," he said. "That's the terrible thing about it, the stink and how it keeps reminding you of what you just saw. It would be all right if you could just walk out the door and forget the sights, but there's that smell that won't go away, sticking there somewhere in your nose hairs.

"That's why the uniforms back there make bad jokes. You have to when things like this become such a damn routine in your life. I mean, if you start thinking about the lives of all these lonely people here in New York—like if you start trying to figure out each time exactly what crazy thing it was that drove them into a closet, for God's sake—then you're going to go nuts yourself pretty quick.

"Those guys back there are waiting for the morgue unit now and they're probably making more jokes. Let me tell you, it's a scary thing walking into someplace where you know you're there to look for the dead body. So can you blame those guys? You have to whistle in a graveyard, you know?"

New York doesn't roll up its sidewalks at night like some cities around the country. Instead, it rolls up its storefronts.

All over the city, beginning about five o'clock in some districts, display windows are covered over with steel gratings of variously ugly design. There are vertical bars, chain-link and solid-steel plates that retract by day. In most neighborhoods, the solid steel is covered over with spray-painted words denoting a host of sexual suggestions or reminders of exactly which youth gang makes claim to that particular block. Uptown and down, with a single exception, every commercial block of Manhattan takes on a sort of Sovietized look—gray and shuttered and depressing. The style, born in the general urban vandalism of the 1960s, is known as "riot Renaissance." It has helped stabilize insurance rates for the shopkeepers and it's probably more humane than keeping German shepherds about.

The exception to the rule is that section of the Nineteenth Precinct with the city's most impressive collection of outrageously beautiful and enormously expensive art and fashion boutiques—from Madison Avenue eastward to Second Avenue, from Sixty-first Street north to Seventy-ninth. There are French designer shops offering Primrose Bordier linens and towels; the tastefully bucolic wares of Laura Ashley—dresses and pinafores, diaries and wallpapers of English bunched floral patterns; stationers that stock old-fashioned cardboard file folders, black with scarlet ribbons, to be used as "cellar books" with sheets for records and wine-tasting notes; a shop specializing in ostrich handbags and briefcases, with ostrich change purses for the budget-conscious at about $3,000; a ladies' wear shop with $800 silk shirtdresses, "slightly *démodé*," it is explained to browsers; galleries crammed full of paintings and sculptures that cost more than most Americans earn in years. This short stretch of a very long avenue contains something of the best to wear and to eat and to hang on one's wall from every corner of the planet—the very best that money can buy with not the slightest hint of a Rodeo Drive sort of elegant vulgarity.

People who have money enough to live in the area enjoy strolling Madison Avenue and the side streets by night, window-shopping for the things they might purchase the next day with American Express Gold Cards. It would not do the shopkeepers well to deny their customers such simple pleasures of an evening's exclusive promenading.

There are others besides the residents of this fabulous neighborhood who enjoy the window-shopping, however. For instance, there was a gang of eight black men anyone would take for eight extremely well-dressed black women.

One early September night, the eight were most particularly struck by the new fall collection on display at a place on East Seventy-ninth called Gussied Up, Ltd. Words like "divine" and "heavenly" escaped the lips of the eight women (men) dressed in gowns, high heels and fur wraps clustered around the glass and looking in with very wide eyes.

Among those who heard those appreciative sounds was a sad-looking man dressed in greasy, ragged cast-offs picked out of street trash containers. His appearance was in such wild contrast with the sleek fashions in the windows, his demeanor so opposite that of the chic neighborhood promenade that absolutely no one looked at him, even though he approached one and all with a filthy, open-palmed hand and breath laced with cheap wine and pleaded for "spare change." The more he thrust himself at the people passing by the windows, the more invisible he became.

It was an easy matter for him to eavesdrop on the eight fashionable, though curiously muscular women in front of Gussied Up. To them, he did not exist. But to him, a man who made a career of studying the movements of anyone who looked even slightly out of place on his beat, the eight women might as well have worn sandwich-board signs advertising the fact that they were thieves.

Ed Smith chuckled to himself, though he could have done so aloud and no one would have noticed. "Drag queens!" he thought. "Who would have suspected?"

Smith walked his practiced unsteady line toward the eight transvestites admiring the window display and after hearing one of them say, "I'm keeping that lace teddy for myself," deliberately bumped into her (him). She (he) said, "ish!" and Smith made an elaborate production of tipping an imaginary hat to her (him).

" 'Scuse me, ma'am," Smith said. "Can you spare any change?"

She (he) made a sniffing sound and returned her (his) gaze to the beautiful frocks in the window.

"Have a wonnerful day, ma'am," Smith said. Then he crossed the street, carrying his filthy wad of newspapers and cardboard with him. He set them down in the doorway of a shop and sat atop them, lit up a cigarette and smiled.

After the eight transvestite thieves had moved along, Smith unwrapped one of his newspapers, inside of which was a radio, his PTP short-wave used to keep in contact with his fellow SCUM patrolers—Sergeant John Hooper and Officers Joseph LaBrie and John Jaroneczwk.

Smith put his mouth to the PTP speaker, pressed the transmission button and said, "Gentlemen, I believe we have our smash-and-grabbers between the crosshairs. Watch for eight black babes dressed to the nines, just leaving Seventy-ninth southbound on Park Avenue. I'm in a doorway for the night opposite number one-five-oh, Seventy-ninth. At the corner of Madison, we have our requisite steel trash basket."

He waited for an answer.

"Ed, it's Hooper. We'll stick by in the car. It's a stake. Over and out."

"Got it. 'Bye."

10

Ed Smith made himself as comfortable as possible, stretching out in the doorway carelessly, one leg dangling over a step into the path of anyone passing by. Passersby avoided the slobbering wino sleeping it off on the street, even a street on the Upper East Side, which tells you just how far gone the city is.

The air was misting up and maybe there would be one of those late summer nighttime electrical storms. The newspapers and the cardboard Smith sat on crackled. He felt good. He felt secure, too, even though Joe always said no sober bum should ever feel safe on the street, what with all the mean folks around who made sport of the homeless sometimes.

Smith lit a cigarette. He didn't smoke, except when staked out on decoy like this. A lit cigarette was a signal to those who might harm him just for kicks that he was wide awake and watching out for himself. The swells like their derelicts red-eyed and looking scared as hell.

Like any experienced cop, Smith's eyes and ears went on a sort of automatic pilot. His eyes would lock in on essential sights as they swept Seventy-ninth Street, missing nothing; his ears filtered out a city throbbing with noise for the faintest summons of a fellow officer over the PTP radio in the crumpled brown paper bag next to him.

Smith smoked and watched and listened. He knew it would be a terribly long night, this hunt. But he was confident. Everything felt right.

Inevitably, he thought about his life, which divided itself into three plateaus all sharing the same end, his bitter loneliness.

Tonight, he thought about hunting and how much he loved it—as a cop and up in the Adirondacks, where he'd be in a few weeks for the opening of the deer season. He loved even his first hunting experience, even though it had been frightening.

He was seven then, which was just about the last time Ed Smith could remember his life being relatively easy. His father had not yet abandoned the family, never to be heard from again, and home was a comfortable bungalow on a good street in Jackson Heights, one of those streets with curb cuts for front driveways, which was the new style of all the proud new postwar frame houses purchased for zero down by all the heroic veterans. Some of those heroes would begin realizing that a mortgage and a housewife and peacetime were nothing after chasing Hitler and Tojo around the world and liberating villages where the slim young women would throw flowers in their jeeps.

For Ed Smith's father, the war's end was a personal tragedy. A much-decorated commando leader, now Smitty was a displaced person living in a dreary, albeit clean, refugee camp called Jackson Heights.

Ed Smith remembered little of his father. Only that he went off to a job somewhere in a factory each morning, always dressed in starched gray twill workman's pants and matching shirt with a black steel lunchbox prepared the night before by his mother; he frequently woke the entire house, all five rooms full of sleeping relatives, with his screaming nightmares; and, of course, Ed remembered the first hunt.

His father had taken his son, alone. Ordinarily, he would drive upstate with a work mate or one of his brothers. But for some reason that made his mother cry, Ed Smith's father prepared the car for himself and his son. And they were off.

They stopped overnight in a little town about halfway and the boy and his father took dinner in a tavern that had sleeping rooms to rent for hunters from the city. The boy was puzzled as to why his father and he sat at a table off from all the others, who made the stopover dinner a loud and fraternal evening. The boy watched his father drink with anger in his face.

The next day they waited for hours in a blind in the mountain forest. When a huge, heavily antlered buck stepped tentatively into the forest clearing ahead of them, the boy froze in a sudden, unexpected terror.

He was unable to pull the trigger of the big, oily rifle that his father had put into his arms.

The boy had shot the thing before. He'd known about hunting from his uncles, from other boys older than he. But he couldn't make his finger pull the trigger.

Behind him, he could feel his father's breath on his neck; he could sense his father's anger and disappointment. He was afraid and ashamed.

"Kill him!" his father hissed.

The buck's nostrils flared and his ears twitched and the animal focused all senses toward the blind, alert to the slightest presence of danger.

"Kill him, you sniveling little bastard!" his father hissed again.

The buck's knees bent, positioned for flight. But the animal, too, was frozen in his fright and the boy sensed that. Then the boy felt a numbness, then fire in his armpit that held the butt of the rifle stock. His hands felt heavy. There was a thudding in his head. Then an explosion.

At first, the boy thought his skull had somehow detonated. Then he saw the thick spray of maroon blood shower the air of the forest clearing beyond the sights of his rifle, the ugly black hole between the buck's crazed eyes; the buck crumpling in death.

Ed Smith, age seven, had killed with a single, clean shot: his first shot and his first blood.

Something had taken the boy through that momentary, stark fear. He felt a deep and primal satisfaction moving swiftly through his body. His skin glowed, his breath came in rushes, his lips pulled back in a triumphant grin. He felt a tingling in his testicles.

He felt his father's approving hand on his shoulder.

"Go cut off his ear, boy," his father said. "You earned it."

His father handed him a bayonet, "taken off a dead Nazi," he said. Ed Smith walked through the forest, the wet, brown, dead leaves sticking to his boots, his legs shaking as he neared the fallen animal.

Before he put the knife to the buck's ear, Ed Smith turned around, just in time to see his father's back, disappearing through the trees. The boy cried, then calmed himself, afraid his father might catch him.

But he was all alone in that woods and the dead animal was a frightening thing to a small boy hundreds of miles from home, his father's footsteps fading away in the vastness.

He sat down and waited, but no one came near. The boy didn't want to stay near the dead animal at night, so as best he could, he back-tracked his way through the forest to the lodge where they had begun that morning.

His father's car was nowhere to be seen. His father was gone. It was the last anyone would see of the man.

The owner of the lodge telephoned the sheriff's department and Ed Smith stayed with a policeman and his wife until an uncle arrived, a day later, to take the boy back home to the city.

Ed and his sister, two years older, managed to live a fairly normal life despite their abandonment. Their mother didn't permit much discussion of it, referring to it as the "family embarrassment." She seemed relieved to have her husband gone, in fact, and it was only when Ed was twenty years old and a student at City University that he learned of his mother's long, secretive love affair with her brother-in-law—the family's secret breadwinner all his years of growing up.

He began immediately to have nightmares of his own, one recurring dream in particular in which his father, in hunting gear, chased his uncle through the Adirondack woods and killed him—killed his own brother, his rival for his own wife. He started looking for his father then, even growing into the habit of searching the faces of vagrants in Bowery hotels in lower Manhattan.

Briefly, he was happily married to an actress he met while a student at City University. Her name was Eve and she lived with a big, well-adjusted, perfectly normal family in an enormous apartment in Washington Heights.

Eve's father found the couple a modest apartment in the neighbor-hood and Ed went to work as a carpenter after dropping out of school while Eve studied drama and voice downtown and auditioned for every-thing that seemed right for her. She came home nights stimulated, Ed arrived home exhausted. He watched television, she wanted to talk and they usually compromised with a fight.

Eve began coming home later and later. Then one night she burst into the apartment with flowers and champagne, her eyes wild with excitement. She had won a part! Of course, it meant going out of town for a while, but it was a real start at her career—at last!

Ed's young wife toured for two months, through the Middle West and the Pacific Northwest. Occasionally, Eve would telephone. She sent letters three times, stuffed with newspaper clippings from towns he couldn't imagine would ever do a young actress any good, mostly just notices that the show would be playing at the local American Legion Hall or someplace like that.

He saw her two more times after the tour. Once, the day she arrived back in New York arm-in-arm with her director to tell her husband face-to-face that these things sometimes happen and if he was any kind of man at all, everyone concerned could still be friends. Ed Smith didn't want to be friends.

He quit his job and hit the road, leaving his little apartment in Washington Heights to Eve and her lover. Before he left town, he retained a lawyer for Eve, who filed an uncontested divorce suit and that was that.

Did he always suspect Eve of something like this? Is that why he squirreled away the money he would live on for the next year, when he didn't pick up day labor jobs along the way, as he hitchhiked through all but ten states? And what in the world did he think he was looking for?

He returned, at last, to New York and was promptly drafted into the army for a hitch in Vietnam. Before he realized it, he became something of a legendary commando. And he began dreaming the dream again of his father running through the woods after his uncle.

After his tour, he was back in New York at square one—a job as a carpenter. Each day he would show up at the union hiring hall, most days win a job and go home with a six-pack of beer and a long evening of television.

He took the police examination finally, and passed with flying colors. He was screened for any psychological problems and passed again. Then he was assigned to the Police Academy, where he excelled in boxing and marksmanship. And where he found a home.

Within his first year as a rookie cop, he met and married a public relations woman who worked at a Manhattan hospital. They tried for two years for a baby, then finally, after medication for her extremely high acid count in her blood system, they at last conceived. Ed Smith, who loved being a cop more than any other work he'd ever known, was lobbied day and night by his wife to take up some safer occupation now that the baby was on the way and all.

Instead, Ed took all the overtime duty he could. He learned he had become a father seven hours after the fact and across town from the hospital. His wife had found her own way there. Ed Smith, off duty, spent an entire afternoon and half the evening talking to Joe in his "home" under the Queensboro Bridge.

His wife rarely failed to remind him of this incident and then began finding new shortcomings on a daily basis, though she had little opportunity to complain since Ed was mostly working or hanging around with his cop buddies or prowling around Bowery saloons and hotels for God-only-knew-what.

When his daughter was old enough to enter nursery school, Ed Smith's wife was hired back in her old public relations position. She said she needed the job "to keep my sanity." Ed got a job he'd long wanted, a job that matched his obsession. He was made a plainclothes officer with the Nineteenth Precinct SCUM patrol. He was proud of the assignment, considered it a great promotion; he was proud of his ability to take the guise of the bum nobody wants to see. His wife loathed all of it, especially Smith's appearance, his practiced gauntness, his hollow-eyed sadness.

Not long into her resumed career, she met a medical salesman who wore good cologne and impeccably tailored clothes and kept his nails well manicured. His name was Darryl, which confused Smith, for it didn't seem to fit.

Dumped for a man named Darryl. Smith didn't know whether to cry or laugh. What he did do, though, was bury himself in his work. His only friends were cops, and not too many of them, and Bowery bums. Lots of them.

He'd been divorced five years now.

He never saw his wife and only rarely spoke to her by telephone, then only to ask about his daughter. He never visited the girl, or so his ex-wife and daughter thought.

Sometimes Ed would wander over to the Brooklyn Heights neighborhood where Darryl and his ex-wife made their new and stylish life. Smith would hang around the playground near the promenade along the East River, just to watch the little girl swing or slide or dig around in the sandboxes with the other children.

Occasionally, Smith would see his ex-wife there, too. Sometimes even old Darryl, togged out in his Ralph Lauren "rough wear," commercially faded jeans and a stone-washed shirt under a pricey leather blazer.

Ed Smith was invisible to them all.

Each time he visited the playground and saw his daughter, sometimes the whole family, he would move a little closer. Still, he was unrecognized. Not only unrecognized, unseen.

. . . In the humid still of the night, crouched in a doorway of Seventy-ninth Street, Ed Smith decided he might be half-cracked at the least. Lonely, half-cracked and a cop. He allowed a vague worry to creep into his mind. He liked his life.

He felt a storm coming on. Smith sat up and leaned out of the doorway, taking a quick look up and down Seventy-ninth. The first big wet drops splattered down onto the street, wetting his face. There was the glow of lightning up over the building across the street, then thunderclaps only seconds later. He moved back inside the doorway and lit a cigarette.

Then he picked up his PTP.

"Hoop," he called softly into the radio microphone concealed inside the paper bag.

"Yeah, Ed. Come on."

"Sure hope you're making out all right safe and sound and dry in that car."

"Thanks for the concern. So what do you think about tonight?"

"I think we stay, Hoop."

"You're that sure of what you saw?"

"I am. This rain will just make it easier for them, by their way of thinking."

"Okay, we're game."

"You're on."

According to the bartender, he wasn't gay, which was how so many of these things seemed to play.

"Besides," the bartender added, "I don't run that sort of place here. Jesus Christ, you guys ought to know that. All these horny stewardesses around here? There ain't a market for fag joints."

He was found at half-past two in the morning, on Third Avenue just south of Seventy-ninth Street, only two and a half blocks from Ed Smith's stakeout.

He was a white male of average height and build, handsome and meticulously dressed, somewhere between twenty-eight and thirty-four years of age, so the detectives on the scene estimated. A professional man of some sort, judging by his hands and clothes. No jewelry, no billfold, nothing in his pockets whatsoever. Either a robbery or made to appear a robbery.

He had been savagely beaten in the back of the head, probably caught by surprise. Knocked to the ground and then repeatedly beaten, most likely with a bat. Blood mixed with the rain-soaked sidewalk, ran over the curb into the gutter. Uniformed officers held umbrellas over the gape-eyed body while detectives took photographs and made notes of what they saw.

There were only three clues: a label inside his blazer from I. Magnin of San Francisco; a laundry marking inside his shirt collar, the initials "McC"; and a middle-aged man, silver-haired and mildly intoxicated, who happened upon the crowd gathered around the body. He nervously told a cop, then Detective Joe Simon, "I saw him, not twenty minutes ago, just down the avenue. He was drinking at the same place I was."

Simon took him aside and questioned him.

"Sort of a talkative guy," the witness said. "People would come in for a drink or two and he'd start up a conversation, then they'd leave and he'd wait for someone else to come along. I was on the other side of the room. Never talked to him myself."

"Did you happen to hear just what he was talking *about* with all these customers?" Simon asked.

The witness thought for a moment. "Nope, can't say I did. I didn't have much reason to pay any sort of attention to something like that anyway." He laughed, even as the stranger on the street oozed blood. "Had my hands full trying to interest a certain young lady in spending a little time with an old fellow. Know what I mean?"

Simon grinned, white teeth flashing under his black moustache. "Did you see anything like an exchange of money?"

"Money? No, nothing like that."

"Okay, thanks a lot." Then Simon took the man's name and address, home and business telephones and said good night. But the witness hung around with the growing crowd, watching the body until the morgue came to take it away.

Next stop would be the bar, where Simon wouldn't learn much more than maybe he wasn't homosexual. It didn't appear to be a drug thing, either, though maybe Simon would know more about that sometime tomorrow after the autopsy. Most people who dealt drugs used them.

The crowd grew so large that automobile traffic began slowing as well. Even in a downpour at two-thirty in the morning, the people came to see sudden, violent death. The officers holding the umbrellas moved aside and four more officers covered the corpse with a tarpaulin.

"Any unit at Second Avenue and Eighty-ninth . . ."

Officers Randall and Finnegan were sitting in a radio car at Second and Eighty-sixth, drinking sharp-tasting coffee from Styrofoam cups and eating doughnuts that made their fingertips sticky. They had been talking about the latest development in the case of Cibella "Naughty Nina" Borges, then stopped to hear the nature of the call just a few blocks from their location.

". . . for a possible DOA."

"We could use that," Randall said. "It's in and out and we need another job before we turn in."

Finnegan took the microphone.

"Special unit Nineteen-A. We'll take it."

"Stand by, S-U Nineteen."

The electrical storm made the static on the radio worse than usual. Several minutes passed before the dispatcher returned to Randall and Finnegan. Calls of higher priority than someone's finding a possible dead body were broadcast.

"That special unit, Nineteen-A," the dispatcher's disembodied voice said.

Finnegan responded. Randall readied pen to pad.

"See about possible DOA, 1170 Second Avenue, Apartment 6R."

"Got it?" Finnegan asked.

"Yeah. We got a long climb ahead of us, partner."

Randall drove the radio car to number 1170, a narrow old tenement building. They locked the car and rang the lobby bell of the apartment on the top floor, rear. It took several rings before someone upstairs buzzed open the door.

They climbed the steep, rickety wooden flights, rising nearer and nearer toward the top, where they saw a frightened man with a mop of thinning black hair leaning over the corridor railing. "Up here," he called to the officers.

Finnegan and Randall took two steps at a time the rest of the way up. They confronted the caller outside an open door to the rear apartment.

He wore pajama bottoms and a soiled terry-cloth robe. The top of his head was bare skin and he had a part on his left side, close to the ear. What seemed to be a foot of black hair shot through with gray hung in strings on the left side, hair that was ordinarily sprayed into place over the top and down the right side.

"I think she's dead, Officers," the man said. "I didn't do nothing. She just died, I think."

As he spoke, he filled the small corridor at the top of the building with the staleness of his brandied breath. The inside of the apartment smelled like a tavern.

Randall and Finnegan followed the man with the stringy hair into the apartment.

It was not much bigger than a cell, with a small convertible sofa extended and a naked, overweight woman slumped between the end of the bed and a refrigerator. The collision of her head with the refrigerator had put a fair-sized dent in the door. Her buttocks were arched high into the air, rising over the edge of the bed, with the rest of her body jammed between bed and refrigerator. She didn't seem to be breathing.

"What happened, sir?" Finnegan asked.

"Well, sir, we were, you know, making love. Yeah. I think she couldn't take it. She just sort of collapsed and then, down she went."

"Are you saying you screwed the lady to death?" Randall asked.

"Oh, no. I didn't do nothing. I didn't kill her, honest, Officer!" The man in the robe with the hair hanging off his shoulder began sobbing.

Meanwhile, the fat lady made a noise.

Finnegan got down on all fours to look at her face, which was mashed against the floor. "You say something?"

There was another noise.

"Give me a hand," Finnegan said to Randall.

Randall squeezed himself over the fat lady's rump and stood between the body and a wall. He grabbed her under her right shoulder while Finnegan hoisted the left. Together, they managed to flip the huge woman up from the floor, onto the bed on her back.

Her face was the color of strawberries with all the blood that had rushed to her head. Her eyes fluttered. Finnegan tossed a sheet over the big, doughy naked body and both he and Randall were mightily relieved.

She made a few gasping sounds. Randall and Finnegan moved away, her fumes making them nauseous.

"You two been doing a little drinking here, huh?" Randall asked the horrified man in the robe.

Before answering, a very relieved man who thought for several agonizing minutes that his girl friend had died on him in coitus, sat down on a wooden chair and reached unsteadily for a bottle of Four Roses and a glass on a little table overloaded with liquor.

"We weren't hurting nothing," the man said.

"She's all right," Randall told him, "but one of these days the two of you are going to overdose on this stuff. It happens, you know."

"So I hear," the man said. He put back the bottle of Four Roses and swallowed hard.

"You live here, or does she?" Finnegan asked. He started writing up the call in his notebook.

"It's my dump. And Flo there, she's no hooker, I want you to know."

Flo snored.

Smith was not quite dozing when he heard the sound he'd waited for, the slightest scraping of steel against concrete. It came from the corner of Madison Avenue. He couldn't look yet. They would be coming his way. He listened.

When he judged that they were walking quickly, he slowly sat up, keeping his legs straight, dangled out in front of him into the street. The smallest movement could alert them.

He waited until they entered his field of vision. He would not use the radio until they used the big steel trash container they carried, until the sound of the container smashing through the plate-glass display window of the boutique would provide him the cover he needed to alert Hooper and the others.

Three of them hefted the trash container. There were two others in the cab section of a van that moved slowly alongside them on the street. Smith could make out most of the New Jersey license plate fixed to the front of the van. He didn't move a muscle.

The driver of the van looked directly into Smith's doorway. Smith watched him through slitted eyes. Then the driver looked away, not thinking what he saw was of any importance.

He watched as the trash basket was raised up over the shoulders of the three black men who had carried it from the corner. And though his entire body was tingling, he didn't move, waiting until the basket would crash through the window and monopolize their attention for the vital few seconds he would need to radio the van's license plate number to Hooper, who would relay it to General Dispatch.

He took a deep breath to calm himself. The steel trash basket was thrown in an arc. At the moment it hit the plate-glass window, Smith grabbed his PTP. Nothing moved but his arm and his mouth.

"Hooper . . . Hooper!"

"Go."

"It's a hit. Three on the smash and two more in a van for the grab. Maybe more in the van. Jersey plate number Harry Apple Two-Three-Six-Seven. Repeat."

"Jersey, Harry Apple Two-Three-Six-Seven."

"Three just jumped out the side of the van," Smith said. "Doors open. They're loading up."

"How many perps is that?"

"Three on the smash . . . two in the cab, three more."

"Eight. Okay. I'll set up uniforms at the corners and relay the plate," Hooper said. "La Brie's on foot now, on his way from Madison. Jaroneczwk's rounding in from Park. When you see my unmarked pull up and light up like a cherry, we're going to make us a nice bunch of collars, check?"

"Right. Out."

Smith let himself smile.

Maybe a minute passed, plenty of time, even with the silent alarm any professional thief knows he's tripped. They worked efficiently, smoothly, moving the display-window items—furs, beaded evening gowns and jewelry accessories—from mannequins to the van. The three men who had tossed the heavy trash basket through the window were somewhere inside the store, removing garments from the racks. The two men in the van's cab stayed put.

Smith didn't move until he saw La Brie, just a movement in the shadows, coming from the right. He sat up slightly and then saw Jaroneczwk on his left. La Brie and Jaroneczwk stopped, both of them maybe forty feet away from the boutique.

Then the gray-blue Chevrolet, the unmarked car driven by Hooper, moved in from Park Avenue, traveling at a normal speed. Hooper hit the brakes hard when he got alongside the van. The light he'd attached to the roof lit up, making circles of red spin around in the street.

Smith leapt up from his doorway and reached behind him for his .38, pulled it out of the holster at the back of his belt with his right hand and lifted the police shield out from the top of his shirt, letting it fall over his chest on the chain.

He heard Hooper shouting, "Police! Freeze!"

Hooper stood, both hands holding his revolver, just in front of the van and the startled driver.

The driver lurched the van forward. Hooper stepped out of the way to avoid being hit. He fired his revolver into the air and shouted again, "Police! Freeze!"

The van stopped.

The thief in the passenger side of the van ripped open his door and started running wildly toward Park Avenue. He slipped in the glass shards on the sidewalk and screamed as an arm slashed open and he bled.

Three more jumped out of the display window, their arms crammed with gowns and furs and coats. They scattered. Two ran toward Madison Avenue and La Brie, who took a firing-range stance with his revolver and commanded them to halt, the other across the street past Hooper directly into Smith's arms.

Smith held his revolver in the air and used his chest and belly to knock into the thief with arms overflowing. He fell back and landed on his back in the street, the clothes spilling into the rain-soaked street.

"You're busted, drag queen!" Smith snarled. He stood over his man, the thief's eyes wild with fear; Smith lowered the gun and aimed at the heart. "What's the matter, your panties filling up?"

Suddenly, the whole street was alive with the invasion of squad cars. Windows in apartments flew open, heads popped out over the sills.

La Brie knocked down one of the two thieves who came his way and a uniform cuffed him while La Brie chased after the other. Hooper manacled the driver of the van and ran toward Jaroneczwk, who tackled a man who came his way.

Uniforms moved in toward the shop and nailed the rest. One by one, the thieves were lined up against the window of the shop next to Gussied Up, Ltd., hands up against the glass, legs spread. Uniforms ran their hands down their sides, around their waists and between their legs. No guns were taken.

Smith's man lay on his stomach in the middle of Seventy-ninth

Street while the cop who looked like a wino cuffed him up and patted him down for weapons.

"You have the right to remain silent . . ." Smith began in a monotone. "Anything you say may be used against you in a court of law—"

"I heard that shit before," the thief said, dresses and women's sportswear scattered around him.

"Good, queenie," Smith said. "Then let's say it together, shall we? From the top? You have the right to remain silent . . ."

11

The celebration took place in a saloon near Grand Central Station, down in the Seventeenth Precinct. Inspector Short sticks pretty close by the book when it comes to the rule about off-duty get-togethers. It's a simple and sensible rule and it applies city-wide. You drink with your buddies from the precinct anywhere but *in* the precinct. If there's trouble, God forbid, then at least it won't have happened where you have to work the next day. And that avoids a lot of potential compromises.

Sergeant Hooper and Officers La Brie and Jaroneczwk—and, if he were there, Ed Smith—couldn't buy a drink. Their money was no good on this day after their big bust. That was the custom when the collars were as important as this one. Hooper figured that the gang might take the fall for better than two dozen break-ins. It was the most significant piece of work since the formation of the Nineteenth Anticrime Unit and good, solid collars more than anything else secured a command like Hooper's.

"A thing of beauty," Inspector Short had proclaimed it.

The block had been sealed off with backup squads, the stakeout was well figured and completely undetected, cops would be able to testify as to being eyewitnesses to the crime and there was physical evidence all over the place. The thieves couldn't bear to run away without the garments, couldn't part with them even though they might have had a chance of escape if they hadn't been so encumbered.

Smith, Hooper, Jaroneczwk and La Brie had no trouble hauling the gang off to the lockup, but they needed lots of help picking up after them. Dresses and shoes, costume jewelry, sportswear, intimate wear, sweaters and hosiery from everywhere on Seventy-ninth Street.

Jack Clark, from the burglary detail, wandered into the bar and ordered up a green devil for the men of the hour.

"Where's Smith?" he asked Hooper.

"Well, you know, he doesn't go in for this sort of thing."

Clark shook his head and pulled off his hat, this one a red beret with a black tassel, one of a large collection of headgear. "The guy gets weirder by the day."

"You ever heard of a perfectly sane cop, Jack?"

"I never heard of anyone who was perfectly sane, let alone cops. You ever read Karl Menninger?"

Hooper and the other officers who heard Clark groaned, which was something that always urged Clark on to ever greater recitations of ever more obscure esoterica. Properly inspired, Clark could hold forth on subjects ranging from Bert Convy pictures to the metaphors of *La Grande Illusion,* from Brooklyn cheese cake to *carré d'agneau au miel, caramelisé* as served in his favorite bistro in Casablanca's French quarter, from Spike Jones to Erik Satie and his rebellious young followers, Les Six. Now the topic was cop neuroses, and Clark being Clark, there would be no stopping him from delivering an absolute filibuster.

"Menninger, in the event you men have never heard of the guy, is a shrink who croaked some years back. He remains the only shrink who didn't belong in a straitjacket," Clark explained.

"He had this really intense interest in veterans and how war fucks us over, which applies to everybody in this bar today, I would guess just offhand—"

"Is there no shuttin' him the fuck up?" a cop at the bar asked.

Tony Ciffo, next to him, said, "We ought to listen to Clark every so often. He's a half-smart guy in a mostly stupid world."

"—As I was saying," Clark said, clearing his throat, "this guy Menninger talked about everybody being a little nuts sometimes. I'm quoting from memory now: 'We know that in the unconscious we are all mad, all capable of a madness which threatens constantly to emerge— sometimes does emerge, only to be tucked away again out of sight, if possible.'"

Clark waited for some reaction, but instead saw a lot of faces fall asleep. He would not be deterred, though.

"Well," Clark said, "that sure sounds like a lot of cops I know, right?"

"All I got to say," said Sergeant John Laffey, who clapped an arm over Clark's shoulder, "is that when they do Jack Clark's autopsy someday, I want to be there with a chain saw to start cutting into his head to see what oozes out."

"Ah well, then," Clark said, "shall we all continue in the grandest tradition of human folly? Shall we separate ourselves on the basis of who is smart enough to learn abstractly and those who won't understand diddley-squat unless they step in it up to their knees?"

Laffey clapped him on the shoulder again and said, "Jack, even you should be able to notice that no one's listening to you."

"And so you are right, mine sergeant. We shall ignore our brother Smith in his obvious hour of lonely peril."

"Is that what this was all about?"

Clark sighed. "It's what it's always about. I'm my brother's keeper, you see."

"You know where he is?"

"I think he's with the people who know him better than we do even, down where we can tell he's gone full circle as a cop. I'd like to tell you my theories on that point, sergeant. Have you got a minute perhaps?"

"Jesus, Clark. What, are you wired or something? Got a little Peruvian flake out of the property room?"

"I'm high on life, mine Sergeant. Sometimes I'm down on life, tonight I'm high on life. Let us repair to a table in the corner and I'll press on."

"Oh God, make it brief."

They sat down and ordered a pair of Moose Heads.

"So, what's eating you now, Clark?"

"I've been trying to think like Smith lately, trying to figure what might happen to a guy like that in, say, a year."

"Anything could happen, like anything could happen to us."

"Not so. You and I have a root or two in our lives. Smith? He's more likely your time bomb than you or me."

"It's just as likely me as him," Laffey said.

"Oh, is that so? Maybe I should have a little talk with your wife about those new sergeant's death benefits then?"

"Get serious."

"Of course. How quickly you change your mind. I shall return to being serious. What do you think's going to happen to Smith?"

"I don't know."

"The way I figure it," Clark said, "he's more advanced than the average cop. It takes a long time for a cop to figure out what Smith has."

"What's that?"

"Okay. You grow up like we did, right? Average guys, sort of middle to your lower middle class. Sunnyside, Queens, sort of guys, right? You have your share of troubles as a kid, even with the cops in your neighborhood. And maybe those cops even hit you once in a while when you deserved it. That's the way it was.

"You do a couple of things you don't want anyone to know about, to this day. You got some worst thing you never told and never will tell, maybe both. But basically, you come out of everything all right. At least you're not talking to yourself on street corners or sitting in a closet nights drinking warm beer and making telephone calls. At least as far as the world is concerned, you're normal.

"So one day you become a cop.

"You go through the academy and all that stuff and the mayor shakes your hand and you put on the .38 and for the rest of your life, probably, you're going to feel naked without that piece.

"You're told a lot of stuff and you see a lot of people you've never really paid much attention to before. But the academy doesn't really teach anything besides the fact that you're about to learn so fast and furious it's going to scare you pretty bad sometimes. If the academy can make you understand that and if you think you can cope with it, then you'll be all right. Maybe.

"So then you're put out on the street. Smith and you and I all went through that first time out there.

"I was assigned uptown in the Twenty-eighth and I also was called in to work the Columbia campus in Morningside when all those kids took it over. The war was still on and I was a veteran and I knew better than any of those kids what bugfuckery the war was. And the kids spit in our faces, remember? And they tossed shit over us, literally. Remember?

"You know what I mean when I tell you how much that part of it hurt."

"I know," Laffey said.

"Yeah. But you keep right on going on. That's what you're supposed to do when you're a cop. You're supposed to be the good soldier and you're supposed to do your job even though they're doing all that stuff to your head.

"But every day you keep seeing things that make you sick in the gut. You start just naturally hating all these people you have to deal with. God, I'd just once like to see somebody besides cops spend a day dealing with what we see.

"Well, I mean you have to believe that it does something to you when you go out on a call and you don't know what the hell kind of sickness you're going to find. Maybe some guy who just made a bloody pulp out of his wife. Maybe a little baby with cigarette burns all over its body because mama couldn't put up with the noise.

"I've seen little boys with big guns killing other little boys. And girls, maybe twelve, pregnant. Babies having babies. You got your junkies and their needle nightmares, and coke heads and people who don't know anything about misery making jokes about it.

"And worst of all, you have those pimps. Always the pimps out there, laughing at us all.

"Like I say, you get to hate a lot. Things and people. Then one day, something happens. It happens in different ways with different cops, but for me, what happened was that I started seeing where these people came from. I started feeling their hatred instead of mine. You're on this one side of the line pretty much your whole life, then with what you get to see on this job, you cross over that line.

"You go right through this series of stages as a cop, right through a circle you make for yourself, like I said. It's quite a ride, boy."

"So I've heard."

Ignoring the response, Clark went on. "First, you get out there on the streets and you want to save everybody from all the bad guys, just like you believed a cop could do back when you were a kid and just the way it seems like it's going to be when you're still in academy and you can't wait to get on with it.

"Next, you start hating a lot of the people you're supposed to be helping, which is pretty easy when half of them are spitting in your face and the other half are figuring up ways of blowing you away.

"But then a funny thing happens. You start thinking like some of them. You start actually empathizing with the bad guys."

"That's where Smith is?"

That's where Ed Smith was. And his circle was about to swallow him up.

There were three of them and they were doing just about everything in their power to attract the sort of trouble that makes a lot of people who live quiet lives west of the Hudson River believe that Manhattan is an island madhouse.

Two were blond and the other redheaded and they all had big blue eyes and lived in suburban Indianapolis, where they were studying to be fashion designers at a community college not widely known for producing innovators in *haute couture.* Midway through their two-year course of studies, they decided to throw in together on a trip to the Big Apple and a look at the fashion capital of the United States, where they were certain their futures lay.

They wandered aimlessly around Times Square on the night in question, gape-jawed and high-heeled with the sort of neon-sign tourist expression of simultaneous fear and fascination that reads money in the bank to entrepreneurs of the Great White Way, legitimate and otherwise. They would learn in very short order that New York isn't very much like *My Sister Eileen* would have it; they would learn that New York doesn't always issue tender embraces to its visitors, not even fair-haired, blue-eyed flowers of Indiana maidenhood. But the possible danger of the place, much as they had discussed it back home, was the furthest thing from their uncautious minds; the promise of something unexpected in their lives, for once, even if it was dangerous, was fatally glamorous that night. And who knew when they might return next to this Emerald City?

There was nothing at all like Times Square back home, of course. Nothing remotely so chaotic, so squalid, so oddly beautiful, so uniquely illusory and alluring. Certainly nothing so outrageously sexy.

Cheap hotels, blazing billboards that turn night into mazda day, record shops that blare their audio wares into the streets around the clock, smut parlors, informal pharmaceutical trade at every other step ("Pass me by, you don't get high!" whispers the reed-thin young black man in the shadows), morose prostitutes sizing up their clientele from among the passing parade of convivial conventioneers and motorists gliding slowly by with New Jersey and Connecticut license plates fastened to their station wagons, impresarios of dubious physical culture studios ("C'mon, rubberneck! Sex for dinner! Live boy-girl acts! It's showtime!") and gaunt men and women staring dumbly and dead-eyed from the doorways of a hundred dives, their ulcerated junkie ankles bulging out the tops of their ragged shoes from all the times they smacked up down there when the veins in their arms and necks and the backs of their papery hands couldn't rope up tight enough for the fix.

All that and Broadway, too. Rehearsal halls and prop shops, costume lofts, photo studios, producers' suites, theatrical pubs full of loud singing, press agents' offices, wigmakers and flymen and the ghosts of a thousand shows, fat dowagers waddling beneath tentlike mink stoles, angular young women in flowing evening gowns with sequins glittering in all the right places, tall dark men in tuxedoes with bright red boutonnières and silvery temples, Cadillac and Mercedes-Benz limousines and long-hooded Rolls-Royces and chauffeurs with black-brimmed caps, hansom cabs driven by raw-faced actors temporarily between engagements dressed up in top hats and tails and patched denim jeans, street-corner violinists with tin cups and high hopes of recitals one day at Alice Tully Hall, policemen in gleaming leather riding boots up on horseback and clopping over the night pavement—and the magnificent old theaters and opera houses, a string of pearls in the tenderloin of Times Square, the place Diamond Jim Brady said was lit by a midnight sun.

They were three ingénues, blind to the fact that New York is not the movie set it seems at first gasp, blind to the curly-haired man with the tight smile following about a half block behind in the Lincoln, waiting for his chance.

Any cop in New York could have seen it coming. The setup was routine and low-risk, as easy for a creep like Angelo as swiping a hot apple pie set out to cool on a windowsill in Indiana.

Since the shots were fired somewhere in the vicinity of Third Avenue and East Sixty-ninth Street, the case ultimately wound up for disposition at the Nineteenth Precinct PDU. Specifically, it landed on Detective Lauver's cluttered desk, since he was catching.

There they sat beside his desk, embarrassed and sobbing now and then; Lauver riffled through the notes he'd made on the case and spent an equal amount of time in another useless task, which was trying to keep his pipe lit. The facts of the case, such as they were, had been distilled from telephone calls Lauver had made, most of them futile, and nearly an hour of his time dealing with three semihysterical out-of-towners with mascara and tears streaming, like the Niagara, down their wised-up faces.

In his time, Lauver has seen just about every kind of truth and every kind of lie and most every instance of the irresistible attraction of these two opposites.

Detectives and certain others—priests, tax examiners, bill collectors, buyers of used cars—learn by experience that truth is rarely a pure commodity. Everyone lies a little bit and sometimes a lot when they talk to cops. Facts are hard to come by when they have to be picked out of the shade. That's why some cops seem awfully slow. It takes a long while sometimes to separate the facts from the not so factual.

So Lauver listened and sometimes took down a note, but not too many because he didn't feel right about what he was hearing. There wasn't anything very scientific about his listening methods, or the way he watched the women, searching them for signs of something that might read more substantial than the story they choked out. Under such circumstances, there isn't much place for anything so neat and tidy as scientific process. Or time.

In the absence of time, especially, all a cop has to work with is instinct as best he can temper it. And that's what Lauver was dealt with now because these three were in some big hurry to get back home to Indiana.

Frenchy, Bandana Bill and Whispering Ed shared a quart bottle of rye and a good-sized joint on a traffic island in the middle of Houston Street at First Avenue on the Lower East Side of Manhattan. They sat in a row on a blue and gray pinstriped mattress with half its stuffing eaten away by rodents. Every once in a while, Bandana Bill would laugh, a crazed sort of merry sound, and say, "I wonder what the rich people are doing tonight."

The rye came courtesy of Whispering Ed, and the marijuana, an even rarer treat for the three, was Bandana Bill's contribution. Frenchy took off his leg and rubbed his stump and wondered if the fat lady on the eastbound side of Houston would cross over for the westbound bus stop. She looked like she might have money and some spare pity and maybe Frenchy could snag a few coins so he wouldn't feel so much the freeloader.

Whispering Ed told Bandana Bill that he smelled worse than usual and Bill laughed. Frenchy elbowed Ed and pointed to the fat lady crossing the street.

"Here comes my swell," Frenchy said.

Unusual, thought Whispering Ed, since it was nearing nine o'clock. But there she was, big and lively and wearing brand-new leather boots and a good coat, eyes trained squarely on three dirtbags sitting in a row on a mangy old mattress. Whispering Ed didn't much trust straight folks who looked into bums' eyes. He stuffed the rye bottle into a brown paper bag and held it between his legs.

"Watch out you don't get that bottle mixed up with your dork," Bandana Bill said to him.

"Shhh!" said Frenchy.

Frenchy waved his wooden leg a little bit to make sure the fat lady saw it. The leather straps made dull smacking sounds against pine shaped like a man's thigh. Frenchy stuck out his free hand and grunted as sorrowfully as he could muster, which was considerable.

The fat lady smiled and said nothing. Then she reached into a big leather handbag and rummaged around a second or two and pulled something out. She stooped in front of Frenchy and her face turned red. Then she stuffed whatever it was in her plump hand into Frenchy's grimy paw, stood up straight and walked off to the bus stop on the westbound side.

Frenchy looked dumbly at his hand, not quite believing his good fortune. He held a crisp green one-dollar bill.

He looked up and just stared at the retreating broad back of the fat lady and his voice cracked as he called out to her. She didn't turn around.

"Oh my God!" Frenchy yelled, his words muffled in the mist-filled air. "A dollar! Oh, thank you, lady, please. Oh, thank you!"

Bandana Bill and Whispering Ed were shown the prize. Ed whistled and Bill started laughing, a little more crazy than usual.

"I wonder—"

"Yeah, we know," Whispering Ed interrupted him.

Then Bill laughed very loudly and stuck out his hand. Frenchy, his partner, gave him the dollar so that Bill could stash it away in his blue and red bandana for safekeeping. He wore it wrapped three times, tightly, around his skinny neck. In the folds were the necessities of life —tobacco, matches, coins, toothpicks, bread, handbills passed out on street corners by out-of-work actors, good for sizable discounts on franchise hamburgers.

"I'm all right?" Frenchy asked him.

"Yeah, you're all right," Bandana Bill said.

Their sometime companion, Whispering Ed, said after a while, "Looks like our kind of night. We got us a bottle of real stuff, a joint and a real live buck."

"Where'd you say you got the whisky?" Bill asked Ed.

"Didn't say."

Bandana Bill had his suspicions about everybody except Frenchy, whose brain was so wrecked he couldn't harm anyone if he wanted to. He'd named Ed "Whispering Ed" one day just that summer because, he said, "You're like some sort of whisper in a crowded room. Like we know you're here with us, but you don't make yourself plain." Ed liked the moniker so much he used it whenever he was in the company of what he called his friends with "real names that mean something, that tell a story." Like Frenchy, who lost a leg in the Normandy invasion, then stayed on and married a local girl and lived with her in her village until she died on day in childbirth and he went gently mad with grief.

"You done this once before," Bandana Bill pressed. "You play Lotto or what?" He laughed and his nose dribbled. He cleaned himself with the hardened fabric of his coat sleeve.

"I didn't ask where you got the dope, did I?"

Bill thought about this for a moment, then laughed.

"I'm all right?" Whispering Ed asked.

"Yeah, you're all right."

Ed passed the bottle and Bill took a long pull of it, then gave it to his partner.

"I'm just celebrating," Ed volunteered.

"You're all right," Frenchy told him.

They conserved the rye over the next two hours, drinking the way the homeless drink, small swallows at a time to keep numb and warm without getting drunk and careless. The alcohol is used to insulate, not to libate. Sometimes the end result is the same, though, and a bum falls too deeply asleep, too numb to the threats around him.

And then there was the dope. It made them happy and if you're living on the street, happiness is dangerous because it makes you trust too many people.

They shouldn't have let Frenchy strap on his leg and go off with his dollar and some coins Bandana Bill gave him for that pint of Mad Dog 20/20. They should have saved it. Bill should have kept it against his neck.

The redheaded one spoke when Lauver asked the girls to take it from the top, one more time.

"Well, we wanted to go over to one of those restaurants on the Upper East Side because we hear that's where you can meet some nice men and it's where all the singles are and everything. And it's safe.

"We didn't know where to go or anything, but we figured we'd just get over there and we'd walk around and we'd see something we liked and that's how we'd do it . . ."

One of the blondes put in, "Besides, it was looking really icky where we were. There were only these big black guys around and we were scared and everything, you know?"

"Yes, I guess so," Lauver said.

"So anyway," the redhead continued, "the guy came by in his limousine and he stopped and got out and talked to us. He said his name was Angelo and he said he was worried about us walking around where we were because a lot of ugly things happen to women from out of town."

"Weren't you suspicious of *him?*"

"Well, a little. But he seemed so nice and everything. Anyway, he said he'd just dropped off his boss at a restaurant and was looking around for a place to sit with the limo for three hours and saw us while he was driving around.

"He said he could take us somewhere nice if we'd like, right in the limo, and he didn't have to worry about being out of contact because his boss could always just telephone the car and if he was outside the car, his beeper would beep and he'd be in contact with his boss in just a few minutes anyway."

"I said it was pretty strange that he'd just offer to take us around town," the other blonde said.

"No you didn't," the redhead said.

"Yes I did. Didn't you hear me?"

Lauver said, "Let's just hear the story again, okay?"

The redhead said something under her breath to the blonde and continued talking.

"Well, this Angelo said something like, 'If you feel better about it, you can pay me for the ride like you'd pay a taxi driver. Or we could just go places and you could pay my way, you know?'

"I guess that did make us feel better about him—"

"Like I said," the blonde interrupted.

"Anyway," the redhead said loudly, "we got in and he just drove us around and showed us things and was like a sort of tour guide. It was real nice."

"And the telephone in the limo never rang?"

"No. We just drove around. He took us up to the Rainbow Grill and we had a drink there, then we drove around some more and we went by the United Nations and this little piano bar at the top of a hotel near there and that was really nice because we seemed like we were right up among the buildings instead of on top of them like at the Rainbow. Just a different way of looking at it all."

"Anyway," Lauver said. He looked at his wristwatch and tried lighting his pipe again.

"Yeah, anyway, we started going to a few of the places on First and Second and Third avenues on the Upper East Side and they were really something. I really liked Maxwell's Plum the most.

"So everyplace we were, everybody kept asking us if we were from out of town and what we did, you know? And most of the time, guys would ask us if we'd like to take a line of coke, but we said no to that.

"We were getting hungry, so Angelo suggested we could go to this place he knew where a whole lot of celebrities always came in to eat. And he was nice about it, at first. He said we didn't have to buy him a whole dinner and maybe he'd have to get back to work anyway.

"But then, I don't know, he changed. His mood changed or something and he started talking different, like he was mean."

Lauver had heard the play before. A guy like Angelo knew he'd reached his now-or-never point and he had nothing to lose.

The redhead shivered and started crying again. She managed to stop herself and then she continued after she'd wiped her eyes.

"He said, well . . . he said, 'You girls into rough fucking?'

"We didn't say anything at all. I guess we didn't want to know what he meant. And then he started driving real slow and it looked like he was going to park the car up against the curb somewhere. God, I was never so scared in all my life.

"So he manages to get the big limo double-parked for a while and we hear all the door locks click shut on us and there we were, all of us in the back of that limo and we couldn't get out or anything. Angelo turns around and starts talking to us.

"He starts telling us that if we do what he wants, he'll get us any drugs we want and we can meet a lot of important people and that we'll all have a lot of fun anyway because he knows just how to please three . . . well, he called us 'cunts.' He said he knew just how to please three of us, all at once.

"I started thinking maybe he had a gun or something. So I screamed, or maybe I just thought I did . . ."

"You screamed, all right," one of the blondes said.

"Well, Angelo pushed a button up front and the doors opened and he said, 'What do you think, I'm going to rape you?' And he had this look on his face like he was real mad at us for thinking something like that of him.

"We moved pretty fast then. We just got out the limo door on the street and thank God there was a taxicab coming along. The taxi stopped for us and we got in.

"So we just started crying and the taxi driver didn't know what to do and we just told him to get out of there, fast. So he was driving along when all of a sudden we could see Angelo and his limousine pull up alongside of us in that taxicab.

"He was in his limo, driving along, and he was laughing at us and he had this gun."

"It was Third Avenue and what?"

"Third and Sixty-ninth."

"Two blocks from the station house."

"Yeah, just around the corner."

"How many shots?"

"I don't know. Three maybe. We had the windows open. The shots went right through."

"From one end to the other?"

"Clear through, except once and a window was cracked."

"And I've got the cabby's hack number and the limo license plate number?" Lauver looked at the notes on his desk.

He had them.

"So that's what happened. Then this Angelo just drove off and we didn't see him again and we came here in the taxi."

"How come the driver didn't come in with you?"

The redhead shrugged her shoulders.

"Well, thanks a million," Lauver said. "I have your local number?"

He did.

It was as good a place as any to sack out the night. Until sometime around the second week of January, when the air gets dry enough to really hold the cold, a man can sleep without freezing himself right out on the streets of New York. If he's lucky, he can find a grating that has some good warm steam shooting up from below, or even a steam tunnel like Joe finds for himself. He'll be all right if he's got a little alcohol in him. Another way of keeping warm is to sleep alongside your partner for some extra heat.

Bandana Bill, Frenchy and Whispering Ed bunched up together on the mattress after finishing off the Mad Dog 20/20 and nodded off amid the noise of motor traffic on both sides. Nothing to stop for on Houston Street at First, so it seemed safe enough. Frenchy kept his leg strapped on tight. He had enough of his brain left to know someone might steal it from him, just to be mean.

Whispering Ed dreamed about hunting up in the Adirondack Mountains again, and he dreamed something about a Sam Shepard play and a song about V-8 engines in that play.

And then he heard screams.

Whispering Ed opened his eyes and he saw flames.

Frenchy was screaming, struggling to get up onto his foot and his wooden leg. And he was flapping his arms against his pants legs, which burned orange and smoked and smelled of gasoline.

Ed's cuffs blazed, too, and he screamed and jumped up to his feet, then went back down and rolled around on the cement and managed to douse the fire.

Bandana Bill was okay, and for just a moment, Ed thought he might have done it.

But then he heard running feet and laughter more crazy than he'd ever heard from Bandana Bill.

He could just make out the sight of three or maybe four young men, probably no more than eighteen years old and maybe younger because they all wore high school varsity jackets from someplace. They ran up the traffic island and one of them carried a can that sloshed with gasoline. They jumped into a car.

Whispering Ed pushed Frenchy down to the pavement and Frenchy hurt himself with the fall, but he wouldn't know about that for a while because he was screaming in pain from the fire that licked up and down his pants.

Bandana Bill jumped on his partner, putting out some of the fire by pressing his body against Frenchy's good leg and his wooden one. He got it under control. Now there was only the sickening smoke from what was left of Frenchy's pants, and the smell of burned wood and the shrillness of Frenchy's screams.

Whispering Ed started running for the car.

The car lurched away with a ripping squeal of tires and all that Ed saw was the color green and a license plate from Jersey. If he'd had his service revolver with him, he could have stopped the car maybe. Then maybe he would have killed the punks.

12

"He's over there."

Orange Lips the stoolie pointed with a long, bony index finger through the window of the unmarked Chevrolet. Monahan peered through the gray cloud of cigarette smoke that Orange Lips had made across a vacant lot at the corner of East Ninety-sixth Street that was strewn with used condoms and broken glass. There was a thin young black man in a knit cap in the distance. He was smoking, too. Monahan could see the circle of orange at the tip of a cigarette in the darkness of the morning. He looked as nervous as Monahan felt.

"We'll walk it," Monahan said. "Get out."

"Shee-it!"

"Let's go."

Monahan slipped quietly out the driver's door, shut it lightly. Orange Lips made a slamming fuss on his side. Monahan walked around the front of the car and grabbed Orange Lips by the back of his neck. He dug his thick fingers deep into Orange Lips' skin, then pressed hard against his collarbone. He used his other hand to cover Orange Lips' mouth.

"You don't come along with me on this nice and quiet, pal, you're going to get a little cop hell. You know what I mean, don't you, Orange Lips?"

Monahan released him. He wouldn't have any more trouble.

The two men walked across the lot, in the direction of the nervous thin man in the distance, the ASPCA Building looming behind him.

The air was damp and a little chilly. Monahan hadn't slept all night, not with Orange Lips to watch and not with the idea that he might have Kano collared in the morning.

The thin man spat the cigarette out of his lips and stepped on it when it hit the ground. Orange Lips spoke.

"This is the detective dude, man," he said to the thin black man. To Monahan, "This is Moses."

Neither man offered a hand.

"What do you got for me, Moses?" Monahan asked.

"Hey, Mick, you tell Moses what you got for *him*, understand?"

"For you, maybe I got criminal association. You know Orange Lips here and you're violating your parole just by talking to him and I know you did because here we all are, right? So that's enough for me to crack you on a nickel beef. You got me up out of my warm bed on this cold morning, away from my nice warm lady and standing around here with two pieces of the ugliest shit walking the streets and I'm mad, see, so maybe I'll just do the nickel beef. What do you say?"

"Motherfuck—"

"Not a bad idea, slimeball. Where's your mama, anyway?"

Moses cocked an arm and swung at Monahan, but Monahan knew what he was doing, knew the punch was coming, and blocked it with his right forearm. At the same time, he raised a knee into Moses' crotch and made a dull, painful contact.

Moses fell to his knees, both hands between his legs.

"Get up," Monahan said. He turned to Orange Lips. "You get him up, pal, or you get the same and then I'll run you both in to that little museum we talked about."

Orange Lips stuck out his hand and Moses used it to right himself.

"Okay, toilet cake," Monahan said. "Let's get it straight and short because I can't take much more of your stink." He reached into his breast coat pocket and pulled out a fifty-dollar bill, then slapped it into Moses' hand. "Give it to me."

Moses told him quick about the all-night filling station uptown, told him how Kano used it twice a week, just where he drove into the place, how long it took to fill up the Lincoln and which direction he took leaving.

"Ever anybody with him?" Monahan asked.

"Just puss."

"All the time or some of the time?"

"Puss sometime, sometime a bimbo. You know, white-bread shit. He most always with puss one kind or another."

"One, two? More?"

"Sometime two pusses. Least one all the time."

"And that's all?"

"Kano be the only cannon, if that's what you're sayin'. He do what he do all by his lonesome, man. He run with the players sometime, 'cause he can't keep his hands off that white shit, but he don't run with nobody like him."

Monahan liked it. It sounded right, like Moses wasn't hiding anything, like he knew just what he knew and no more. Monahan almost felt sorry about kneeing Moses in the balls. He put his hands behind his back, clasped them, looked around to see if Moses had any friends nearby. Not so far as he could tell.

"How's the family jewels?" he asked Moses.

"Fuckin' poe-lice brutality, man!" Moses turned his head and spat on the ground defiantly. He would have spit in the cop's face if he could and then he would have cut him and thought nothing about it. Under the circumstances, though, it was best to complain about police brutality.

"Sometimes I wonder if a turd like you could have thought up that phrase all by himself," Monahan said.

Moses looked at Orange Lips, his eyes flashing. "This poe-lice a case, man. He makin' me awful hot."

"Now I want you two to come along with me," Monahan said.

"Hey, I ain't goin' nowheres with no nutjob pig, man!" Moses said.

"Come on, brother. We goin' be okay if we just get the hell out of here, right?" With that, Orange Lips put a friendly grip on his pal Moses' shoulder.

Monahan almost could have kissed Orange Lips. Almost.

He grinned at his two snitches. "Now look how good it can be when the law-abiding members of the community cooperate with their local law enforcement agents. I tell you fellows, America is a wonderful place."

"Motherfucker's a fuckin' case, man!" Moses said to Orange Lips."

Dominick Salvato awoke with the usual nightmare. He sat up in bed and drew his knees up to his chest and clasped them with his arms. He trembled a little less that way. There was a roaring sound in his head, something like a subway express train barreling around a curve, somewhere beyond visibility.

It hadn't come in a while, the nightmare. For two days, he didn't sleep. Every time he shut his eyes, he saw it. Then everybody worked on him—Inspector Short, a psychological counselor for the department, the department lawyer, his family, his fellow officers at the Nineteenth.

It's not your fault. . . . The guy was a creep, a rapist creep who took aim at you. . . . You did what you had to do. . . . He was nothing and all the people he was victimizing, including your partners, had to be protected. . . . You helped the innocent and the weak against this creep, this racist, this scum of the earth.

For a few hours at a time, sometimes only a few minutes, it all helped. But then Salvato could only seem to see this nobody kid, a good-looking Puerto Rican kid who no one claimed at the morgue, this kid who was buried now under the earth somewhere out on Hart Island, the Potter's Field of New York. He saw that handsome kid, dark-eyed and wavy-haired, his face so eerily peaceful in death, lying there in the blood on the street. It was Salvato himself who first noticed that the weapon aimed at him was a pellet gun.

Dominick Salvato had gone to his priest:

It's not a question of right or wrong, son. . . . There isn't anything I can tell you that will take away your pain. . . . But try to understand how life-affirming your own pain is, son; it shows you're humane and compassionate, it shows you reverence life if you feel so responsible for the death of even one of the least of us. . . . Don't you see? . . . Given the facts at hand, you were the man who happened to have had to do what was inevitable. . . . We can only work to your grace now; you and I can pray for the soul of this Miguel. . . .

The priest's words helped Salvato more than he thought they would. "Everybody says that," the priest told him. "We're not so bad, you know, even though our mothers dressed us funny."

The priest's humor helped, too. But even that, along with his wisdom, was enough. Salvato began to learn what most every other cop in the same situation learns, that the power he holds is more awesome than he ever imagined—and the consequences of that power as well.

A thought popped into his head as he sat up in bed, as he pulled at his legs to keep them from shaking: Maybe I'll go up there to Hart Island someday, to Miguel's grave . . .

He learned, too, to take comfort in the occasional nightmare as the closest thing to knowing an understanding source, a friend who had gone through precisely the same experience. The nightmares, though they hurt his head, also did their part to make Salvato understand that what had happened under those streetlamps was a tragedy, not an evil.

Yet for a time, Salvato had thought his burden might be lighter if someone could find that *he* had been wrong, that somehow he shot the wrong person, shot when something short of deadly force would have done the job of stopping a thief. Something! Some way that punishment could be visited on *him*, some way that he might be made to feel he could pay for what happened.

But no one had anything for him on that order. Everyone comforted him. Salvato didn't even have the accusation of police brutality leveled against him. If someone had told him he would have welcomed such a charge, he would have denied it. Yet he did wish he could feel punishment coming. The priest said it was his "Catholic guilt" working against him and laughed.

Everyone felt sorry for Dominick Salvato, the cop who killed the "creep," the "rapist creep."

Children who lived on his street in the Woodhaven section of the Bronx looked at him oddly. Salvato was the big guy who killed somebody. *Watch out for Officer Salvato! Hey, Officer Salvato, are you going to shoot me?*

Salvato shut his eyes. He opened them and looked toward his bedroom window, saw his reflection and didn't recognize it. He shook again.

Then a thought hammered into his head. It came to mind like some half-forgotten old tune:

Too much power . . . too much power for any one man . . . maybe too much power for me. . . .

Later, after another hour of lying awake in his bed, Officer Dominick Salvato arose, dressed and took the subway train into Manhattan. He walked through the big, dreary lobby of the Nineteenth Precinct station and past a wall he refused to look at.

On a section of wall just outside Inspector Short's office was a plaque proclaiming Dominick Salvato "Cop of the Month."

Detective Joe Simon had the identification by early afternoon. "McC" was Paul McRae and was a forty-four-year-old city manager of a suburb of San Francisco, unmarried. It was easy enough. He put out the only clues he had to his counterparts in San Francisco, who in turn made the information known via California's LEIN—Law Enforcement Information Network. Missing persons reports were checked and up popped the name Paul McRae, who never returned home from attending a wedding in New York City.

Simon got hold of the bridegroom in New York, who turned out to be a longtime friend of McRae's who broke his pal's heart by marrying a woman. The bridegroom gave Simon the preliminary identification he would need to put some money out on the street to anybody with a special knowledge of murky goings-on among the more discreet homosexuals living in the Nineteenth Precinct.

But he didn't hope for much.

A few more clues had popped up in the meantime. McRae stayed on in New York for at least three days longer than he had planned, without notifying his parents back in California; he'd stayed in New York for the initially scheduled two days at the Hotel Wyndham on West Fifty-eighth Street and kept to himself, so far as anyone at the hotel knew; his lodgings were unknown after that; in New York, he knew only his old friend, no one else; he had disappeared from the site of the wedding reception without saying farewell to his friend or his friend's bride.

There were loose ends all over the place and Simon knew it and knew there was nothing he could do about it. Just then, anyway. No detective enjoys that. It seems disrespectful and it isn't anything like the cop television shows, shipshape little dramas that insist on the image of a cop with lots of wavy blow-combed hair with the luxury of being able to drop everything in the way of a case load when someone decides to kill someone else.

Joe Simon has a bald head and gravity has a grip on his belly and he smokes too many cigarettes. A lot of the time, especially on homicide cases, he wishes he were that TV dick. Things would be so much simpler.

She hadn't the slightest idea who was feeding the material to the top brass, but she had always feared the worst and now her fears had come to pass. Officer Cibella Borges sat at the kitchen table of her mother's apartment on the Lower East Side, dropped her head into her arms and sobbed. In the other room, her mother was sleeping, her mother who had been praying for days.

How would she tell her mother?

Beaver was not the only magazine for which Cibella Borges—the tabloid "Naughty Nina"—had posed. Her lawyer had telephoned.

"They've got the others," he said.

He didn't need to mention them.

She was guilty twice more. "Guilty?" she asked herself. "Guilty of what? I've broken no laws!"

What she had broken was the hard-line rule that no female cop in New York can break. Perhaps no other city in the country is more conservative in the matter, oddly enough. Cibella Borges had broken the rule.

She had posed nude in two erotic lesbian scenes for *Pub* magazine, which was selling briskly with its replated cover featuring "Naughty Nina like you've never seen her before," and a crudely done lesbian skin magazine, *Girls on Girls*.

Cibella Borges knew she was alone. Very alone.

He had to have them paged in the lobby of the Milford Plaza, the big new Times Square hotel that advertises enormously in out-of-town magazines appealing to people from places like suburban Indianapolis who want to give their regards to Broadway by staying in a hotel that looks just like a hotel on some suburban Indianapolis freeway strip, but he got them all right. He recognized the voice of the redhead.

"Detective Lauver, Nineteenth Precinct," he said.

"Yes?"

"I've reached Angelo. He's supposed to come in at four o'clock this afternoon, with his lawyer. Could you come by then for the identification?"

"Identification?"

"Don't worry. We'll do it through a two-way window. He won't be able to see you."

"Well . . . well, we—"

"What is it?"

"We're leaving."

"I see."

"Well, I'm sorry."

"You've leveled some pretty serious charges, you've taken up my time. What is this?"

Lauver thought he heard her crying.

"Why don't you postpone your flight home?" he asked.

"Oh, no. Not now. We just couldn't. Look, I'm sorry. It . . . Can't we identify him from pictures or something? From back home?"

"Won't stand up in court."

"Oh."

"You sure you want to leave?"

She cried, then said yes and hung up.

Lauver figured as much. Something very fishy about this one, although he didn't trouble to figure why. Maybe some of it happened, just like they said; maybe Angelo held some threat for them still, something they weren't telling; maybe a lot of things. One thing was for sure, though. None of it was police business, no matter that Angelo was rattled enough to have taken off somewhere. Lauver had reached his brother, his partner in the small limousine business he operated, and his brother had arranged for the lawyer to call the cops. The lawyer knew Angelo's whereabouts but wasn't volunteering. Lauver wasn't asking, anyway.

The taxi driver said he sure would have remembered any shots that might have gone whizzing through his cab—if it had happened like the girls said. He had a vague recollection of a black limousine that drove parallel to his cab at one point in the evening, but he paid no particular attention to it. Yes, there was a crack in one of the rear windows in his cab, but it had been there for months. He promised Lauver to have it repaired.

Angelo's lawyer asked about the presence of the girls. Lauver didn't answer, exactly. It didn't take a genius lawyer to figure out that three scared girls from Indiana wanted nothing more to do with his client and it didn't matter what had happened.

Angelo was about as likely to show up at the Nineteenth Precinct PDU for questioning and identification by complainants as the Vatican was ready to announce the Pope's engagement.

"It's a trap and he knows it and he'll never show up," Lauver said.

He stuffed all his little notes into a manila folder and shuffled it off to the side of his desk.

"That'll be that," Lauver said. "A million stories, like they say, and this has been one that falls apart. It happens."

Whatever he did, Angelo got himself a gift of time. More than likely, he knew it.

Monahan sat in the unmarked Chevy with LaGravanese beside him, taking up most of the seat, what with his newspapers and his books, the "Racing Form," a plastic bag full of cookies and apples, a crossword puzzle magazine and a thermos of coffee. LaGravanese wore a light topcoat and a hat over a shiny suit. It made him look like a man of 1948, with all the dash and taste of a man who'd spent half a career in postal management.

While LaGravanese spent the hours occupied with his food and other diversions, Monahan mostly spent the time thinking how much he hated the guy.

The hatred was an immediate thing. LaGravanese shook his hand, said hello and then the very next thing out of his mouth was an insult.

"Too bad you fucked up the first time, Monahan . . ."

Monahan had put out a fifty to a couple of stoolies and it didn't pan out. That's all. It happens.

But territory is territory, boys will be boys and cops will be cops and LaGravanese, when he heard about Monahan's early morning stakeout and how it didn't yield Kano, was mad as hell that he wasn't called in on the job. LaGravanese had been gunning for a guy called Kano from East Harlem for a year.

". . . But look, leave us cooperate on this venture and maybe we can get somewhere together, eh?" LaGravanese smiled and made noise about it and his chins shook. Monahan didn't have any choice in the matter. His lieutenant, like any lieutenant, liked to cooperate with the city-wide units because one day maybe he'd command one of those city-wide units because he'd cooperated so beautifully.

So Monahan and LaGravanese had picked up Moses the snitch and his pal Orange Lips, too, and sweated the two. But Moses stuck to his story and Monahan felt a little better about the situation when LaGravanese gave an approving nod later on when they were alone.

"I tole you what I know and you pay me the fifty and that's that, man. I ain't bargainin' for no trouble and I don't want your damn money, neither," Moses said.

"Shee-it, he's bein' square, man," Orange Lips said.

"So how come he didn't show like you said?" Monahan asked.

"How the hell do I know? I'm just a no-count nigger, man, far's you're concerned. Hell, maybe your man knows somethin'."

"If he knows you took a tip, Moses, we'll bust you for being an accomplice."

"Think I don't know that?"

There was no point to questioning Moses further. He was dead certain that Kano used the filling station in question and seemed genuinely surprised that he hadn't shown, since his past behavior had been so regular.

Kano was a smart son of a bitch, Monahan thought. He pays attention to the details. He uses a filling station so long as everything goes right. One thing is out of place—like the fact that Moses isn't working there anymore—and he changes his patterns.

"All is not lost," LaGravanese told him when they left Moses' dump over the fish shop on East 117th Street. "I think he's telling us straight. I believe him, just like you."

"So what do we do?" Monahan asked.

"We stake him out again. I want this guy bad."

They were agreed.

And now they waited. LaGravanese got on Monahan's nerves.

"Know what a three-letter word for Guido's high note is?" he asked Monahan. He held the stub of a pencil over his crossword magazine.

"Don't ask me that stuff."

"You don't know, do you?"

"You asking or telling?"

"I'm telling. You never know when you might want to take this up as a hobby, like me."

"Why don't you shut the fuck up?"

"No need to get tense, Monahan. How's about a joke?"

"You married?"

"No."

"No kidding."

"So there's two guys, sort of like us. Best friends, but they split up. Mike, he goes upstate and buys a little farm. And George, he stays back in the city, right?"

Monahan stared out the windshield and noticed for the four thousandth time or so that the gasoline vapors trapped between two of the pumps shimmered in purple and yellow when the light was just right.

"Years pass and Mike and George just don't get around to seeing one another. Just Christmas cards, that sort of thing. And then one day, George decides to go on up into the country to see his old pal and how he's made out with the farm and his wife and kids and all . . ."

"Is this going to take long?" Monahan asked.

"Shut the fuck up yourself. As I was saying, George decides to go upstate. So, he rents himself a car down in the city and one fine morning bright and early he takes off.

"He drives all day and into the early part of the evening, but he makes it to Mike's farm and Mike's just happy as hell to see him and the two old friends spend a great night in a big old country kitchen drinking and telling stories and catching up on old times, that sort of thing.

"The next morning, Mike's wife has fixed them a big meal of sausages and eggs and potatoes and George is as happy as a guy with a foot-long rod in a convent. So Mike says to him, 'How's about I show you around the spread this morning?' And George says, 'Yeah, I'd sure like that.'

"So off they go out from the house. Mike loans George a pair of his spare boots and they're wandering around the barnyard and Mike's giving him the big guided tour, like his farm's some damn Disneyland attraction.

"Then George notices this very peculiar thing coming at him. It's a huge pig with a wooden leg."

LaGravanese waited to see if he'd hooked Monahan yet.

"A pig with a wooden leg?" Monahan asked.

"Yeah, you heard me. So, naturally, George can't take his eyes off this pig with the wooden leg, partly because the pig's standing right beside him looking up at him. George starts to say something, but Mike interrupts him.

" 'Hey, pal,' Mike says. And he's pretty stern when he says this. 'One thing you don't do around here is make fun of my pig, got it? That pig has saved my life, twice. So you don't make fun of it, okay?'

"And George says, 'The pig saved your life? How?'

" 'Yeah, he saved my life twice,' Mike tells him. 'The first time, I was out on the tractor plowing up the south forty out there and what I didn't know is that some of the bolts were coming loose under the seat, what with the strain of all that jolting up and down and pulling this big old combine hooked up to the tractor. Anyway, the seat gave way and I spilled off and as I fell down I lost control and hit the gear shift the wrong way and the tractor keels over with me. I was trapped there on the ground, in a big rut in the soil and I was half buried and my leg was broken and I could barely move and those big combine blades were coming at me and I thought it was curtains, boy.'

" 'But I'm here to tell you, my pig back in the barnyard sensed danger. Don't ask me how, but he did. So he comes running out onto the field from the barnyard and he right away sees what sort of terrible trouble I'm in and he burrows into the soil with his snout and makes a sort of tunnel for me to crawl up, and he even helps me by standing there so I can grab onto his shoulders and pull myself to safety—just in the nick of time!'

"George says, 'And then he saved your life a second time?'

"And Mike says, 'He sure did. It happened not long ago, in fact. We were all sound asleep, it was the middle of the night and the pig saved me and my wife and the kids. Trouble was, something was left burning on the stove and the curtains caught fire in the kitchen, and the fire just spread through the house, with the smoke and all. The pig sensed danger again and he ran to the house and he started banging his snout against the bedroom window where the wife and I were sleeping. Well, we didn't know it then, but we were pretty overcome by smoke, so the pig had to work really hard to wake us, but he kept at it until he did.

" 'Well, he got us up and we managed to get the kids out, then the volunteer fire department came and we managed to get the fire stopped and we saved most of our things.'

"Mike is just standing there in the barnyard looking down lovingly at his pig with the wooden leg—"

Monahan stopped him by slamming an arm across his wide chest. "Hey! He's coming!"

Across the street from where Monahan and LaGravanese were staked, a white Lincoln Continental driven by a dark-skinned Hispanic pulled into the filling station. There was a woman in the passenger side of the car.

Monahan's shoulder dipped as he reached for the ignition key to start up the Chevy. LaGravanese reached for the radio mike.

The two cops had barely moved. But Kano saw it and was alerted. He saw it and he made them.

The Lincoln's huge back tires bit down hard into the pavement as Kano floored the accelerator. The big car roared out of the filling-station apron like a fighter jet leaving the deck of an aircraft carrier.

"Some machine," Monahan shouted. "Jesus Christ, how in hell are we going to nail him?"

He jerked the Chevrolet into gear, stalled it and restarted it. Slamming a fist into the dashboard, Monahan cursed at the top of his lungs, bouncing up and down on the seat as the police Chevy sped after Kano's Lincoln.

LaGravanese picked up the battery-powered cherry top flasher and rolled down a window to fasten the magnetic plate to the top of the Chevy. Then he picked up the microphone and held it to his face for several seconds, before turning to Monahan, red-faced and still cursing.

"I keep forgetting the damn Ten code!" LaGravanese said.

"Never mind the fucking code!" Monahan sped past a taxicab and the driver shouted an unintelligible curse at him, waving his fist. "Just say what you mean!"

"Okay," LaGravanese said.

"Go ahead, Special Unit Five-Nineteen," the dispatcher's voice said.

"We're in hot pursuit of a white Lincoln Continental, New York plates, no numbers available, east from Lexington Avenue on 118th Street in the Two-Three, out of sight. Request uniform backup, all eyes of anticrime units. Over."

The Lincoln had fully three blocks' lead distance on the unmarked Chevy with the flashing red light. Kano was some smart operator, Monahan muttered. He knew full well he wouldn't have to move fast beyond a quick exit from the filling station. He knew he could rely on the fact that at some time in the recent past, New York City motorists became largely unconcerned about the matter of emergency vehicles, blithely ignoring sirens that signaled them to pull off to the side of the street so that a squad car in hot pursuit—or even a fire truck—could travel at maximum speed through a crowded city.

If a guy like Kano, who knew he had to be careful in his travels, simply did a little minimal planning in terms of sticking to efficient routes, he could proceed calmly through traffic without arousing anyone's attention.

Of course, it was supposed to be the other way around. A police car with a flashing red light once upon a time parted traffic like a hot knife through butter. No longer. Private cars simply don't bother yielding and precious seconds are lost this way.

Monahan was pushing the Chevy hard and it was sometimes all he could do to keep the front wheels under control as the car slammed over potholes up First Avenue. The sweat was pouring off Monahan's brow as he stayed with the patch of white he tried to keep in view, way up the avenue. He said about a hundred Hail Marys as he alternately pumped the gas pedal, then the brakes, hoping to God he wouldn't cut down some innocent pedestrian or slam into another car.

A couple of blue-and-whites, lights flashing and sirens screaming, appeared nearby and Monahan's grip tightened on the wheel. The marked cars would run the interference for him. He had a real chance.

"There he is!" Monahan shouted.

About four blocks up the avenue, the flash of white made a fast, squealing turn onto an eastbound side street. Monahan jumped up and down on the seat and ground his foot into the accelerator. His head hit the ceiling of the Chevy. "We got him!" he shouted. "He's got nowhere but the river to hit from here!"

Monahan weaved his way through the sparse traffic of First Avenue in the 130s, infuriated by drivers of private cars who wouldn't move fast enough—or at all. It seemed like hours before he reached the corner where he thought he spotted Kano turn, though it was only a few minutes.

Then the flash of white again as Monahan turned.

The front of a car nosed past a parked mail truck, screeched to a halt as the Chevrolet roared toward it. Monahan very nearly smashed the Chevy into the fender of a white Plymouth.

"Damn!" Monahan shouted.

He looked into the rearview mirror. Four blue-and-whites were behind him, all of them doing the best they could to keep from colliding with parked vehicles and curbside piles of garbage as they skidded to a halt.

Monahan pounded the dashboard with both fists. Then he wheeled the Chevy around and headed back out to First Avenue and sped further uptown, knowing full well he'd lost Kano again.

Kano and the Lincoln had simply disappeared. Somehow, Kano had found a way.

No doubt, Kano would have the Lincoln repainted and replated and he would start using a different filling station. And no one in whatever blocks Kano had managed to pull off his miraculous escape would have seen anything.

Monahan and LaGravanese both pounded the dashboard. Both knew what it would have meant if they'd been able to run down Kano. Commendation. Promotion. Maybe a command of their own just before they put in for retirement.

They headed back downtown, below the Ninety-sixth Street line between the Twenty-third and Nineteenth precincts, immersed in the blackest cop gloom. They'd had their man in sight, they lost him and that was that for now; they'd done all they could. So why did they feel like a couple of flatfeet in a Mack Sennett movie?

LaGravanese grunted and started chewing an apple. "This fucking frustration gets to be as familiar as your Jockey shorts after a while, you know?"

Monahan knew. He had to get LaGravanese off that noisy apple or he'd go a little nuts. "Say, what about the end of the joke?"

"Oh yeah," LaGravanese said. "Where were we?"

"The pig with the wooden leg had just saved the guy with the place in the country for the second time."

"Yeah, that's right. So anyway, there they are, the two friends standing in the barnyard with that pig that had the wooden leg. So George, the guy from the city says, 'Look, I wasn't going to insult your pig or anything. And I certainly never would, now that I know about the incredible things he's done for you. I was just curious, that's all, about why he has that wooden leg.'

"Well, Mike just stands there with sort of a dumb look on his face like his friend George is supposed to understand. He says to George, 'Well, a great pig like that—you don't want to eat him all at once.'"

Jimmy O'Brien drove his car everywhere. He didn't used to, but now he was afraid to leave it out on the street near his home in Eastchester, the Bronx. He hadn't made payments on it in six months and the bank was telephoning his wife every day and threatening letters from an attorney came every week without fail.

A city marshal had come by the house one day to impound the car, but O'Brien had enough cash on hand to make a bargain and he kept the car. Long enough, that is, to get it over to a shop in Bayonne, New

Jersey, where he'd had it painted red and where he'd managed to buy license plates from Illinois with counterfeit stickers.

Jimmy O'Brien felt safe enough to ignore several more payments. He kept the car parked in a different neighborhood, just to make sure.

The phone calls and the lawyer's letters started up again. And O'Brien had lately seen the city marshal snooping around his neighborhood.

Both men knew how the game was played now. O'Brien had to keep the car out of sight. The marshal had to find it, wherever it was, impound it and return it to the bank's lawyer to collect his fee.

The marshal was a small black man with a nasty mouth and an authoritarian personality. He was a man who seemed to enjoy rooting about in people's private troubles. Every day, he saw the raw anxieties that so many people try so hard to hide; every day, he, Marshal Royal Billings, dealt with tenants being evicted by their landlords and people like Jim O'Brien.

The more a guy like O'Brien resisted, the more Royal Billings enjoyed the challenge of his job, which was taking away the things people needed but couldn't afford and returning them to big banks and landlords for fairly brisk fees. Royal Billings was doing the right thing, of course, and it was a nasty job.

But the way he did it made otherwise gentle folks listen to their more violent angels.

Jimmy O'Brien sat in a saloon on Lexington Avenue near East Eighty-fourth Street, the only bar on the Upper East Side that serves shots and beers and the only bar in the Nineteenth Precinct where every last customer seems to be wearing a twill work shirt with his first name embroidered on the pocket.

O'Brien looked out the window. His car was safe and sound, good for the next hour at the meter just outside.

He downed a second shot and then started on a second Budweiser chaser. O'Brien shut his eyes for a moment and listened to the sounds of Crystal Gayle singing about cheating on the juke, the voices of the other men in the bar—most of them white and Southern or border state, just like him—and he breathed deeply of the muzzy beer smell of the place.

For one brief second of longing, Jimmy O'Brien was transported back home. To a simpler place and time, when no white man had to take any lip from some uppity coon.

"That nigger's going to get his," O'Brien said aloud.

PART II

13

"I sort of hate to say it," Tony Ciffo was saying, "but I try my best not to get involved. Doesn't sound so good, does it? Especially me being a cop. Well, maybe it's best. I don't know. What I do know for sure is that you can always count on the weirdest thing in the world happening once a day, at least.

"Did I ever tell you why I bought the car and started driving in from Brooklyn to work?

"Oh boy!" Ciffo slapped his head as he drove, up Park Avenue to where he would cross over at Eighty-sixth, aimlessly eastward, keeping an ear cocked for the radio calls.

"All the time, I used to take the subway. I took the D train, which is the line that the Guardian Angels call 'The Zoo.' Well, I used to ride at night a lot and the zoo was in full bloom then, I'll tell you.

"One night, I'm going back home after eleven and after we cross over the bridge into Brooklyn, I'm one of three people in a car. There's me at one end minding my own business. I'm in my street clothes. And down at the other end of the car are a skinny white woman and sitting across from her a big, beefy black guy who's sort of growling or something.

"So I'm watching these two. And I know that sooner or later, unless the black guy is just a psycho who likes to make strange noises, I'm probably going to have to get involved. God, I'm groaning to myself, you know? Why in hell am I riding the subway? There's no way I can be just a plain innocent bystander. I'm a cop and so I'm always on duty.

That's the law. I can't just ignore something or *I'm* up on charges by Internal, see.

"Anyway, pretty soon the big guy gets up and stands in front of the woman and he starts yelling at her. Now I know what I have to do.

"So I get up and I walk over there and while I'm walking, the guy starts putting his hands on her shoulders and she's really scared.

"I shout at him and he turns around and goes for something in his coat, which later turns out to be a knife. I took out my shield real quick and identified myself as a cop and told him to just relax and everything would be all right. I don't like to get these guys any more tense than they already are.

"So then I do what you're supposed to do, which is to put yourself physically in between the people in a situation like this. I'm standing now with my back to the woman, who is scared out of her mind, and this guy with a knife in his coat. Again, I tell the guy to just lay off, maybe come down to the other end of the car with me and talk about whatever's on his mind. I'm real friendly with him, which usually sort of catches them off guard and works to the cop's advantage.

"But this time, it's no go. He starts swinging at me and I took a few pretty good shots. Thank God he didn't use the knife. Well, he was a lot taller than me, but his swings were pretty wild and I missed most of them, so I figured I could do what had to be done.

"I start hitting back, which just infuriates the guy and so I had to sort of pound him pretty good. The guy is lying on the floor of the train against a door and pretty soon someone's punching me in the back.

"It's the woman! She's screaming at me, 'How dare you hurt my husband? How dare you hurt him!' Jesus, I never figured for a minute they were together.

"That's a true story. I swear. And that's why I don't take the subway in. No more, man. I just don't want to know what's going on sometimes."

His partner, Jean Truta, reached across the front seat of the car and poked him in the ribs.

"What's that for?"

"I don't believe you," she said.

"What?"

"I don't mean about the D train. God, anything could happen and does. I mean, I don't believe you when you say you don't want to get involved. What a lie that is! You forget, I see you in action."

Something white and wet hit the windshield.

"First snow of the season!" Ciffo said. "Christmas is coming. Oh boy, watch out!"

Jack Clark ended his tour at four, showered in the basement locker room and then walked from the precinct house over to Madison Avenue where a certain shop sold a piece of Moroccan art he figured on buying for his wife that Christmas, if he could nick the price down a bit.

It was a clammy, windy sort of early winter day in New York, the sort of raw weather guaranteed to bring on influenza. You bundle up against the cold air and the dank humidity makes you sweat, so you open up a bit and then start shivering when the cold gets you again.

The outdoor air is bad enough, but coming as it does at the beginning of the Christmas shopping season, it is particularly bad in combination with the routinely overheated shops. The jostling crowds are not what make New Yorkers tense and quarrelsome at this jolly season so much as the schizophrenic atmospheres of hot, dry stores and frigid mugginess outside.

For thousands, it is an intolerable season in New York, a city which does its absolute best to remind everyone that if you're alone for the holidays you might as well dig yourself a nice little hole in the ground and say good-bye. Festive announcements ring everywhere—East Side, West Side and all around the town. It's a wondrous time, a gorgeous plum-pudding sort of time, if you have money in your pocket and maybe a little in the bank, if you have the love of some good people, a safe harbor of a home, if you have reasonable hopes, if you can live most of your days without fear. That eliminates several million New Yorkers in one way or another.

There is a side of the New York Christmas orgy that cops begin to dread on the day after Thanksgiving. While millions of brightly colored greeting cards float through the post office swearing peace and goodwill, while happy skaters at the Rockefeller Center picture-postcard rink glide rosy-cheeked past the gilded statue of Prometheus and the giant pine tree glittering with thousands of green and red and gold lights, there is an agony about to explode with grim repetition—the holiday blues, so-called.

Wives with long-standing grievances court danger when they nag their husbands; burglaries, the special concern of Jack Clark and his colleagues, will inevitably rise as single professional apartment dwellers spend less and less time in their flats, more time drinking, more time shopping; those who cannot cope with the disparity between television plenty and their own mean poverty begin staring sullenly at people on the streets, especially those with the brimming shopping bags, and they grow angrier as Christmas Day nears; the unemployed middle class nurse their shame, or bitterness if it's been a while; the hungry are required to be grateful for the seasonal charity when encountered by newspaper reporters who specialize in what are called "human interest" stories; the lonely, who are legion, are ignored a little less than usual, but it doesn't help much. Some of them can't or won't take it anymore.

It is the time of year when every cop in the city figures he'll sooner or later see something nobody wants to hear about because as far as everyone seems to be concerned, the whole world is supposed to be wrapped up in ribbon and foil and candy canes.

Jack Clark calls it the time of year "when cops try to get in and out of the job without everything getting to them, which it can at Christmas; the time you have to keep thinking about whatever it is you have of a life outside the job, when you just want to do what you have to do at work and then get the hell home as fast as possible afterward."

As Clark rounded the corner at Madison Avenue, an old woman he didn't know, would never hear of, stood at a lace-festooned window four floors over an apartment house rear court that was clean and pleasant when she first came to America with her young husband.

She lived in the East Eighties, in a big old squat building in Yorkville, one of the first houses to become solid German during the big immigration of the 1920s. She used to grow roses in one spot down in the courtyard that drew a half-day's sun. Children used to play down there, they used to sing songs in English, songs they learned in the American schools, and their German-speaking mothers would beam with pride.

The courtyard was a filthy place now. The old woman stared down at it through her windows, covered by an accordionlike web of rusted steel grating, with padlocks so big and heavy that she had trouble dealing with them on those rare days she was brave enough to open up and pretend she wasn't living in a prison of sorts.

There was glass and rubbish all over the ground below, filth the super didn't bother picking up because there was no use to his labors. The trash would return in a matter of hours. One day last week, she opened a rubbish can and a rat jumped out at her. She fell and cut her knee and it hurt her to walk back upstairs, write a note of warning for the back door and then walk all the way back up to her apartment. She noticed the day after that her note had been spray-painted with an obscenity.

Children were often in the courtyard these days, but they were not young children. They were teenagers, most of them less than sixteen. All of them smoked marijuana and played loud radios and cussed like the thugs they would become. On summer nights, the marijuana smoke would float up and through her windows and make her sick.

As she looked on this cold gray day down into her courtyard, one of the super's two Doberman pinschers barked insanely, the beast's breath crystallizing in the air. The dog barked on the exact spot where she and her late husband, Franz, had once taken coffee and crullers with the Sunday newspapers in the two wicker chairs they thought nothing of leaving outside for their use, just as everybody else in the building did. Last week, for the fourth time that year, her mailbox in the lobby had been pried open.

Well, it hadn't much mattered. Long ago, she had had her Social Security check and her husband's pension check mailed directly to her bank account. Only bills came now, and a dwindling number of letters from old friends at Christmastime. Her children knew only the telephone and none of them lived in New York and long distance was so expensive they would complain.

The day her mailbox was broken again was the day she tried to kill herself.

She drew a good full tub of hot water and put some oil into it and eased herself in after stopping up the drain and the overflow slot. Her intention was to fall asleep and sink down into the water and she would drown in the warmth. But when the tenant down below, someone with a loud and thumping stereo that played from the moment he rose until well after midnight, complained about water seeping into his bathroom, the super was at the door. He marched right into the bathroom and shut off the water, then took hold of her arms and yanked her out of the tub all naked and wet and humiliated.

You can't kill yourself if it means inconveniencing someone.

The dog had barked now for an hour, steadily, madly. The old woman walked slowly to her kitchen and took down a tin from on top of the refrigerator, inside of which was a key.

She walked back to the window, slid it open and shivered, then fitted the key inside the padlocks. It took her several minutes to twist them free. She pushed open the grates and a wet, nasty wind filled her apartment.

With more agility than she'd been able to summon in the past dozen years, the old woman stepped up onto a chair, then to the sill. Below was the degraded courtyard. Behind her was a spotlessly clean house. She'd used scouring powder to scrub the bathroom fixtures earlier that day. The dishes had been washed and dried and stacked. Fresh flowers were in a vase on top of an old upright piano.

No one knew what she thought as she stood on that sill, nor how long she remained there, although detectives from the Nineteenth PDU guessed it was long enough to take stock of her decision—several times over. It appeared she had shifted her weight from foot to foot, indicating that she had remained there on the sill for some time, maybe as long as half an hour.

It was easy enough to guess her motives, though, once her children were interviewed by the police. Her son said, "Mother told me, the last time I saw her, which was three months ago, that she got so lonely sometimes she thought about killing herself."

Her son hadn't known of the bathtub incident.

"I was making plans to come visit her," he told police.

But he hadn't telephoned his mother. It was to be her surprise.

She left no note, no word and no inconvenience this time. She simply jumped, silently, to her immediate death.

Jack Clark had never seen her before. A short, heavy woman with thick white hair and yellowed skin. Her eyes were bad, one of them bouncing around out of control, the other filmed with cataracts. She had a man's torn brown topcoat on and a rag around her neck to keep out the chill air. And she had only one mitten, which she wore alternately, one hand and then the other.

She was chanting something. Clark couldn't hear the words yet over the traffic noise and the chatter of holiday shoppers like himself who crowded Madison Avenue in the upper Sixties. The thing that was unmistakably pathetic about her was that she knelt, knees pressed against the cold, hard pavement, with a brass cup full of pencils thrust out in whichever hand wore the mitten.

He was a half block away when he noticed her, when she turned her head and he saw that face, the injured eyes and the constantly moving mouth, set in a smile that didn't belong. He stopped for a moment, then started again.

Clark walked slowly toward her. Others, he noticed, walked quickly by. A few stopped to inspect the pencils, some of them dropped a coin into the cigar box on the pavement in front of her knees.

She kept right on chanting. As he got closer, Clark heard the words "Merry Christmas to us, one and all . . . Merry Christmas to us, one and all . . . Merry Christmas . . ."

New Yorkers are confronted every day with a huge assortment of grotesqueries on the streets, everything ranging from the simply objectionable to the horribly pitiful to the deranged screamers and mumblers. Even this latter group knows enough to stay away from the tonier districts of the Upper East Side. But every so often, someone like the white-haired woman on her knees with a brass cup set up on a corner like Madison and Sixty-eighth and everyone just tried to cope with it as best they could. It was inconvenient, but one couldn't escape everything in the city, after all.

As if in a trance, Clark found himself walking straight past the woman on her knees, like the overwhelming majority of holiday shoppers. Nobody would fault him for ignoring her. Certainly *she* wouldn't; she couldn't even see him. Besides, she wished everyone a merry Christmas, whether they bought her pencils or no.

Now he was almost a block past her and he couldn't remember taking the steps. In another block, he'd be at the shop dickering over the price of a Moroccan *objet d'art.* Morocco! He thought of the exotic little back streets of Casablanca, full of cafés and beggars and forbidden pleasures. In the tourist districts, there was a popular wisdom about beggars: You shouldn't put a single *dirham* in even one grimy hand because then the whole mob of them would follow you around. It occurred to Clark in Morocco that that was pretty ugly nonsense and so he defied it. He would travel the little back streets and make a habit of putting a little something into every beggar's hand or cup. And he was always thanked for his generosity.

All it cost him now to turn around and start walking back to the old woman on her knees wishing peace and goodwill with no guarantee of even simple civility was a momentary wave of embarrassment. It proved a false embarrassment at that, anyway. No one cared that Jack Clark went back to the blind woman and dropped a fiver into her cup any more than they cared he had passed her up the first time.

He felt better than he had in days.

"It doesn't hurt us to take the attitude once in a while, 'Hey, I've got it and this guy doesn't, so I'll give him something,' " Clark reasoned.

For a change, he'd done something about someone's misery that didn't involve busting anyone. For a change, he'd come across someone who had found the way. Too often, especially at Christmas time, he had to deal with people who lost their way, like the lonely old woman on the sill.

The 10-19 came over the radio in the last hour of their tour. Officer Ciffo pulled the squad car over to the corner of Park Avenue and Seventy-eighth.

The district radio dispatcher often cannot afford the time necessary to broadcast assignments requiring lots of detail. In those nonemergency cases, a 10-19 is issued, meaning the squad is requested to telephone the precinct desk at the very earliest opportunity.

"Got a dime?" Ciffo asked as Officer Truta gathered up her pad and opened the passenger door.

"Yeah, but give me one of yours anyway," she said. "I'm always coming out on the short end of these things."

"Here's a quarter, kiddo. Knock yourself out."

Ciffo watched her dial the station-house number in the phone booth, knowing what they were likely to face in a few minutes. She made some notes and returned to the car.

"So we've got a DOA possible, right?"

"Yeah," Truta said, closing the door. She read the address of a high rise on East Seventy-second Street between Second and First avenues.

"Jesus H. Christ, what did I tell you?" Ciffo said. "It's starting, all right. 'Tis the season to be jolly and all that. What's with this one?"

"She's sixty-eight, lives alone, had heart surgery a few months ago. Her son up in Albany has been trying to call her for the last three hours and all he gets is a busy signal and he's out of his mind with worry. He even had the super go up to her apartment and knock on the door and call him back. The super said he didn't hear anything. He asked him to go into the apartment and he said he couldn't do that without the police—"

"So here we go."

"—so here we go. We're supposed to call him collect up in Albany the minute we get inside that apartment and find out what's what."

The snow fell heavier, pelting the windshield of the squad car. Tony Ciffo, thirty-five years old, thought about the day not far off when his own mother would die.

At the apartment building, the staff was waiting for the police. The super, two porters, the doorman, a security guard. There were also several tenants.

"A good building," Truta said. "The people stick together here."

Ciffo got out of the car, heavily, like he weighed twice what he did. He worked himself up into a smile.

"Hi, how are you doing?" he said to the doorman who let him and Truta in.

The tenants who had gathered started twittering. Ciffo took his hat off and said, "Listen, folks, we'll let you all know, okay? Right now, we have to get up there quick, so why don't you wait right here and when we come down, we'll let you know. Help us out, okay?"

Then to the super, "Let's go."

Ciffo smiled at the small group of worried people in the lobby as the elevator doors shut and the super pressed the button to the eleventh floor.

"Mrs. Rotare was the nicest lady I ever had in this building and that's the truth," the super said. His name was Freddy. "All the time, she's got something nice to say to you, even when it's a big problem in her apartment I got to take care of.

"She had her little weird points, like everyone does. You get to see a lot of weird things about people when you're a super." Freddy thought a second, then added, "When you're a cop, too, right?"

"Right," Ciffo said. He looked at his watch.

"Like every time she tossed her daily stuff down the hatch," Freddy went on, "it was mostly wine bottles and astrology magazines. Who knows? She never hurt anybody anyway, not like some people I could mention live here in the building.

"Jeez, I'm going to miss old Mrs. Rotare. Who knows what'll move in after her. Some of these people who get in here, man-oh-man, I'm telling you . . ."

Freddy let the image fade away as the elevator door, at long last, opened to the eleventh-floor corridor. Ciffo stepped out of the car, followed by Truta, who still wore her hat. A woman somewhere in her thirties carrying a black plastic garbage bag and dressed in a powder-blue terry-cloth robe and slippers let out a little scream when she saw the officers.

The woman in the robe dropped the garbage bag, spilling egg shells and coffee grinds and unidentifiable bits of tissue paper all over the carpeted floor. Something liquid and milky splashed on her ankles.

"What's wrong?" she whispered loudly. "Who are you coming after?"

"You been behaving yourself?" Ciffo asked her.

She blinked. "Me?"

"Yeah, we're the heat."

"Don't pay any attention to him," Truta said to her. "You'll just encourage him."

Freddy didn't know what to think. "You always take this stuff so light?"

"We're not taking anything light," Ciffo said. "We're trying to keep our heads straight. You'd know how it is if you've been on this kind of call more than once."

They stopped in front of the last apartment door at the east end of the corridor.

Ciffo knocked. Nothing.

"Okay," he said to Freddy, "open it up."

The super took out his passkey and slid it into the lock, then stepped back, like he expected something to leap out the door at him.

Ciffo and Truta took deep breaths and proceeded slowly through the door.

"I smell bread," Ciffo said.

"Yeah," Truta agreed.

There was a small kitchen off the vestibule. Ciffo poked his head around the corner. The aroma of cinnamon and raisins filled the vestibule. Truta looked over his shoulder. They both stared at a sweet-faced, white-haired woman about five feet tall. She had square wire-rimmed eyeglasses, a violet and yellow flower-patterned apron around her ample waist and a quizzical look in her bright brown eyes.

"Yes?" she said.

Ciffo and Truta blinked.

"Um, are you all right?" Truta asked the old woman.

"Speak up," Mrs. Rotare said.

"She says," Ciffo asked, walking into the kitchen like he was visiting his mother's house, "are you feeling all right, sweetheart?"

"Well, I'm just fine," she said to Ciffo. "How are you, son?"

"Couldn't be better. Do you know why we're here?"

"No," she said. "But I don't suppose you're going to hurt me, are you?"

"Naw, don't you worry, darling," Ciffo said. He draped an arm around her shoulders and she giggled. "Listen, tell me something, will you? Your son up in Albany has been trying to reach you on the telephone for hours. Something wrong with the phone?"

"Oh, I don't think so," Mrs. Rotare said.

"Well, let's just go and look, okay?"

"Certainly, Officer."

Ciffo and Truta followed her to a living room running wild with chintz and doilies. There was an aqua-colored telephone on a stand near an enormous Queen Anne chair, one of the models the New York Telephone Company calls a "designer phone." The designer was French, apparently, with a fascination for ersatz brass curlicues.

"Oh look at that," Mrs. Rotare said. "I see the problem right there. Look, the cord is unplugged. See that?"

"Listen, darling, why don't you sit down and call up your son?" Ciffo said.

"Speak up, won't you?" Mrs. Rotare said.

Ciffo raised his voice. "I said, why don't you call up your son? He's waiting to hear from you."

"Oh, he was calling for me? Yes, you said that. You'll forgive me, but I'm a little surprised." Mrs. Rotare touched at her hair in several places and sat down on the chair next to the telephone. "He always gets nervous if I'm not right here when he calls, but I can't always be sitting next to this thing waiting, can I?"

"No, of course not."

"Well, I am, half the time anyway."

"Mrs. Rotare," Officer Truta asked, "the super knocked on your door and you didn't answer. Are you all right?"

"I'm fine. I was either sleeping or I was in the kitchen and couldn't hear."

"Well, I'm glad you're all right," Truta said.

"Thanks, honey."

"Well, maybe we'd better go now," Ciffo said.

"Do you have to?" Mrs. Rotare sat with her hands folded in her lap. "I just made some bread, you know. You could have some. Would you like that?"

"Well, we have a great big city out there, you know. Lots of bad guys." Ciffo laughed and so did Mrs. Rotare.

"Yes, well. Maybe another time?"

"Sure. Meanwhile, give me your telephone number," Ciffo said, taking his pad out of his pocket. "I'm going to call you up once in a while and see how you're doing."

"Oh! Oh, I'd like that." She gave him the number and he left, with Truta following him into the hallway.

Mrs. Rotare caught Truta by the sleeve. Out of Ciffo's earshot, she asked her, "Will he really call me?"

"He really will, yes."

Ciffo was through for the night and, as was his custom after a safe tour, he looked up at the sky and said a little thank-you when he hit Sixty-seventh Street in an off-duty status. He tightened his collar and walked west, to where his Renault Fuego was parked, next to a pile of construction materials in the next block.

The snow had stopped, leaving a fresh white dusting that made the streets slippery. Good and clean, though. Streetlamps made amber pools of light on white sidewalks. It was a good night to be grateful that all was right in the world, at least for yourself; it was a good night to be on your way home.

There was a silver Ford Grenada parked just behind Ciffo's Fuego. It was Keenan's car. And inside it, there was Keenan, more white-faced than usual, shivering, alone and, Ciffo guessed, probably drunk.

Ciffo groaned. "Jesus H. Christ, you can't win. I stop taking the subway and I buy a car and now this."

He rapped on the window. Though his eyes were wide open, Keenan jumped like he'd just been awakened.

Keenan fumbled with the window knob, managed to crack open a slit and said, "Hiya, Tony. How was the tour, pal?"

"How long you been sitting there?"

"I don't know."

"What tour did you work today?"

"The middle."

"So you were off at eight. What, you visit the dolly or something?" Keenan didn't respond.

"How long you been sitting in a cold car there?"

"I don't know."

Ciffo groaned again. "Come out of there," he said.

"Yeah, all right," Keenan said. "I get it. You think I'm stinking drunk, right?"

"I know you're stinking drunk."

"So what the hell?"

"So you live in Riverdale, that's what. You don't think you're going to drive up there, do you?"

"Of course not." Keenan slammed his shoulder against the inside of the driver's door, a difficult way to open up a car. It then occurred to him to try the catch and the door opened. He stepped out onto the street, somewhat indignantly. "There, now here I am, a fine upstanding citizen indeed. And I'm knowing that drinking and driving don't mix, Officer."

Keenan belched softly. "Oh hell, Tony, I was waiting here anyway to get myself straight. I was planning on either sobering up, falling asleep or freezing to death, whichever came first."

"Give me your damn keys."

Keenan obeyed and Ciffo locked up the Ford.

"Let's go," Ciffo said, taking Keenan's elbow and steering him around to the passenger side of his own car. "You need some straightening up, all right. What'll it be, your place or mine?"

"What do you take me for? That's a filthy suggestion. Besides, you're not my type."

"Jesus H. Christ, just get in the car."

14

Sometimes there dawns the day when being a cop is something approaching triumphant satisfaction, namely when one of life's little injustices can be countered by the simple fact of career.

Such a day was had one gray Wednesday in December by Billy McBride and Carl Altner, neighbors out in suburban Suffolk County who, like suburbanites the world over, car pool it to work—which in their case happens to be the plainclothes burglary detail under the command of Sergeant John Laffey, Nineteenth Precinct, Manhattan.

It was shortly after nine o'clock when they slipped onto the Long Island Expressway, McBride at the wheel. The morning rush was another memory and there was now plenty of time to cruise into the city by ten o'clock for another day's round of mostly walking the streets of the Upper East Side on the lookout for shifty-eyed nervous types who didn't quite belong on the scene, especially the ones carrying large canvas bags that were just the ticket for hauling off other people's property. If they were lucky at this unending game, which Altner and McBride sometimes were, they might wind up the day with a good solid red-handed collar on which they might also hang up a lot of backlog.

All of which they talked about just as they passed over the Nassau County line and entered slightly heavier traffic. A very impatient eighteen-wheel semitrailer truck loomed in McBride's rearview mirror, though he heard the behemoth before seeing it, actually.

The trucker blasted his diesel whistle over and over again, apparently urging the two plainclothes cops in the nondescript car in front of him to get going beyond the fifty-five miles per hour that McBride had set on his cruise control. McBride ran up to sixty, but the trucker was still agitated, all the more so since he was unable to pass at the moment.

McBride had no choice but to run up to sixty-five miles per hour. Otherwise, the truck threatened to bash into the rear end of his car.

Then the truck did bump the back end of McBride's car. Once, then again, then again.

McBride floored the accelerator pedal and cleared up a space in the adjacent lane for the giant truck to pass around a slower-moving vehicle. All the while, the trucker kept blasting his diesel whistle.

Finally, when the trucker passed by McBride's car, Altner leaned out and caught the eye of the trucker.

"I show him my tin," Altner told Sergeant Laffey later that morning, when he finally got into the station house, "and you know what the idiot did? He gave me the finger! Can you believe it? He sees I'm a cop and he just gives me the finger."

"So what did you do?" Laffey asked.

"I tried not to do my usual wild-man routine and then we chased him, that's what."

The trucker, when it apparently occurred to him that he could be in big trouble, veered off the freeway at the nearest exit ramp, his cargo nearly spilling over by the weight of centrifugal force.

The huge vehicle careened around the ramp curves, with McBride and Altner in very hot pursuit, knowing that an eighteen-wheel truck had to stop somewhere very soon, as it would simply not be sufficiently agile to outmaneuver a speeding car. Luckily for all concerned that morning, there happened to be lurking in a speed trap on a particular bend of that ramp a squad car belonging to the Nassau County Sheriff's Department.

And now, just like in the movies, there was a high-speed parade of a chase—the berserk trucker, the suburban commuter and the sheriff's deputy, who was immediately on the radio for reinforcements.

It was all over in a few miles. The truck pulled over to the side of the road. Actually, one of its tires blew and the trucker was forced over. He jumped out of the truck, snarling at McBride and Altner, who rushed him, and the uniformed deputy, who had no idea how in the world it was that the fellows in sweaters and jeans in the car happened to have handcuffs and manacles. For all he knew, he had three speeding citations to write, along with a reckless-driving collar on the trucker.

"All in all, slapping a guy in the bracelets on the way to work is a pretty good way to start off a day," Altner said.

"Listen up, Sleeping Beauty!"

It was Ciffo's third attempt to rouse Keenan from a deathlike slumber in the convertible sofa in the living room of his flat in Brooklyn. Keenan lay on his back, arms thrust out from his sides and palms up, his legs straight and still. His mouth was open and his breathing shallow, nearly nonexistent, eyes half open but rolled back and looking like a pair of eggs left outdoors all winter. The fumes from the man were enough to call out a city health inspector.

Ciffo put his foot to the side of the couch and rocked it back and forth roughly. "Up and at 'em! Let's roll out!"

Gradually, he succeeded in winning Keenan's attention.

The eyes fluttered and a hand moved, to ward off the invasion of sunlight.

"Oh my God, I've died and gone to hell and Lucifer turns out to be an Italian cop," Keenan said.

"So you're all right, Paddy? You can make with the jokes after the night you had. Unbelievable, the Celtic constitution, I'm telling you."

"Maybe not so much as you'd think," Keenan said. And as he spoke, his meaning became clear. He looked anything but the picture of a man capable of keeping inside him the contents of the previous night's excesses.

Ciffo gave him a hand and pulled him to his feet. The bed Keenan left behind was awash with perspiration.

"Go say your morning offerings, knight of Gotham's constabulary," Ciffo said. He pointed in the direction of a bathroom in the hallway. "Go pray to the porcelain god."

Keenan put a hand over his mouth and turned his head halfway around. His eyes slitted in pain and his lips began rumbling, as if they held back a ghastly sea of sickness.

"The can's that way," Ciffo said, pushing him hard in the correct direction.

In a half hour, Keenan emerged, sadder and maybe wiser. He was reasonably presentable, though his eyes were traced with red lines and he had to be careful to grip things for support as he moved through Ciffo's bachelor apartment, wending his way to a little eat-in kitchen where Ciffo manned a coffee percolator.

"I have," Keenan announced, though he did not go so far as to point a finger in the air, "performed my morning *toilette*. And I apologize for my inconvenience, trusting that this shall remain a confidence between discreet gentlemen."

"You call your wife, Tommy? She have any idea where the fuck you are?"

Keenan didn't say anything for a few seconds. His wife knew where the best dishes were, the ones that came out whenever the Irish came calling from the other side; she knew where the aerosol furniture dusting wax was; she knew where the half-dozen cans of Comet cleanser that she bought on special at the Riverdale Pathmark were; she knew where to lay her hands on some paperback novel about times that never were and circumstances beyond all likelihood. But no, she did not know where her husband was at this moment.

"That my whereabouts matters is debatable, Tony my friend . . . highly debatable. Take it from me."

"For now. Sit down and drink this, you hump. What's your tour today?"

"Noon-eight."

"That's what I thought. You haven't got much time."

"Time's a crook and a thief, some say. But time's all we've got as well."

"Save the philosophy for the cups," Ciffo said. "You have to be a cop in a few hours."

Keenan sat. He let the steam rise from a cup of coffee and work through his nostrils, still sharp-smelling from his session in the bathroom.

There was a small radio on the table, which Ciffo turned to the 1010 frequency, WINS-AM, the all-news station. The police officers learned —in addition to the fact that the day would be perfect for suicide, gray, cold and clammy—that a Bronx mother had turned around for a few critical seconds in a shopping mall and had her young son snatched off the face of the earth; housing cops in lower Manhattan were treated at Bellevue after being bitten by an apartment full of Haitian illegals who were incensed by their raid, coming as it did right in the middle of a "solemn religious ceremony," so the lawyer called it, involving the sacrifice of twelve chickens and a goat; a bag lady died of the overnight cold, her blue-skinned, swollen body discovered by a Chelsea news vendor beneath a pile of cardboard scraps on the corner of Twenty-ninth Street and Tenth Avenue; a pair of bright-eyed New York City cops ran down a startled, albeit berserk and allegedly drug-ridden truck driver on the L.I.E. in Nassau County on their way to work; and there were six shopping days until Christmas.

"Ever hate New York, Tony?"

"The thought crosses my mind sometime every day."

"Life's a goddamn crock." Keenan rubbed his head, which hurt like hell. It would be the first day of his long period of punishment on bow-and-arrow duty that he would be delighted with the stress-free make-work assignment.

"Life might be a crock, pal, but there aren't too damn many volunteers for early exit that I know of. Except maybe you."

Keenan rubbed his head again and moaned.

"I'll take a wild guess about what happened to you last night," Ciffo said. "Her name was Dory."

"Tony, now that we have covered our mutual dissatisfaction with New York and life in general, shall we turn to the subject of women?"

"Jesus H. Christ."

"Oh well, you may invoke the name of our Lord and Savior. Many have at times such as these. But it hasn't ever done much good. I'm afraid there is no help from the heavens in the battle between the sexes. It's God's joke, you know."

"Do I have to listen to this? You're sounding like Clark more and more every day."

"God, as I was saying, has been having a lifelong joke watching us men and women." Keenan sneezed once, then again. "He is an ironist. He created us with totally opposing sensibilities and yet placed us in a system requiring that we be intimate with each other."

"For a drunk, you talk pretty, Keenan."

"I have said it before and I'll say it again. Sometimes, my friend, drinking is the answer."

Ciffo looked at his wristwatch and wanted Keenan to know he was impatient, that he'd had enough of this. Ciffo was the sort of man who could tolerate all sorts of human foibles, but he never saw much percentage in coddling a whiner one inch beyond his purpose, which in this case was to expose Tommy Keenan to Tommy Keenan and hope it would light some sort of fire under his seat.

"Tommy, you sound like a case for I.A.D. if you don't start getting hold of yourself," Ciffo said. "You're how many months on restricted duty now? You going to make some sort of career out of going to the corner deli for your sergeant's damn coffee? The whole damn station house knows you're tapping into a dolly on the side. Where the hell do you think you are, you dumb hump? We're the cops. We're not exactly what you'd call libertines, in case you haven't noticed."

"You're going to call the I.A.D.?" Keenan looked at Ciffo and blinked.

"I don't think I have to, man. You might as well be wearing a sandwich sign that says 'Please Put Me on Conduct Trial' and parading up and down in front of the division boys on your goddamn lunch hour."

Keenan bolted up out of his chair and the coffee he'd started to drink fell to the floor. "Where the hell do you get off talking to me like that, Tony?"

Ciffo stood. He was a half head shorter than Keenan, but Keenan and everyone else knew about Ciffo and how height bore no relationship to the prowess and sweep of his left hook. Keenan thought about taking a swing at Ciffo, but not for long.

Keenan doubled his right hand into a fist and made threatening gestures with it and Ciffo laughed at him.

"Look at you, Tommy. You got that real smart mouth, but you got nothing to back it up, nothing but dumb."

Keenan sank back into his chair.

"That's the trouble with lots of people, Tony." He looked at the splinters of china all over Ciffo's kitchen floor, the streams of black coffee he'd spilled. Mairead would have been horrified. "Sorry about making more mess than you found last night, pal."

"Sorry's not enough. You're a cop in trouble with himself, which makes it bad for all of us."

Ciffo picked up the broken bits of china with his fingers.

"Now get the hell out, Tommy. Fix your head and do us all a big favor."

Sergeant John Laffey sat down at his gray steel desk after he'd cluttered up the surface with the things he would need for the long day ahead of him: a PTP radio, which he'd tested for battery strength first thing when he walked through the door of the Penthouse; a .22-caliber pistol with small belt clip; the New York *Times* and the *Daily News,* which carried a piece about Nicky Barnes and how he'd probably sing to the feds about heroin wars in Harlem in hopes of a pardon from President Reagan; a large, well-thumbed spiral notebook indexed for three academic subjects; two textbooks with protective dust jackets bearing the logo for the John Jay College of Criminal Justice; a bulletproof vest, one of two he owned, this one covered in a white duck fabric textured like pimpled thermal underwear; and a brown paper bag, which, when empty, would shield the PTP radio from sight as he walked around the city on the prowl for burglars.

Laffey enjoyed the work of being a cop well enough; he gloried in measuring his professional role against all the other segments of American society. He looked the very modern model of the ordinary New York cop dancing along the edge of middle age, but civilians usually revealed interesting prejudices when they talked to Laffey and then told other civilians that he was "pretty damned articulate—and a cop, too." This is what interested Laffey about himself and others—those who were not police officers, those who did not come up quite the way he had. It is what gave his conversation its philosophical tone.

Laffey started his adult life as a construction worker, then went to college and quit after two years when he got sick of it. He went back into construction, a chancy business. He took the police civil service examination and hoped for the best, which came along in 1969, a year of massive new hiring in New York's police department. John Laffey was called and told to report to the Police Academy and he was a happy man, as he'd just gotten married and by his lights that meant he was required to bring to the deal a solid, steady job.

The job gave him more. Laffey was forced to see everyday life in an entirely new light, just as everyone saw him largely by the color of his uniform. For some cops, the world is diminished in the professional process; for others, like Laffey, the world becomes a much larger and infinitely more fascinating place, sometimes as a defense against the forces that circumscribe the lives of those who not only look ordinary, like Laffey, but who are ordinary.

The coffee steamed up Laffey's glasses, so he took them off and put them on the desk next to his pistol. He dipped the edge of his bagel into the coffee, shrugged his shoulders and then resigned himself to a bite.

"I keep eating this stuff every day like I do and pretty soon I'm not going to be able to make it up here to the Penthouse," he said to Valentine from Community Affairs, who sat in a molded plastic chair, winded after the climb to the very top of the Nineteenth Precinct station house.

There was plenty of room here for Laffey's small command, which was the plainclothes burglary detail. Elsewhere in the house, things were terribly cramped, though there was the sense of being near the center of things. The price of spaciousness, which everyone talked about but which no one really wanted, was a long climb up five steep flights of dingy stairs and an unnerving echo to everything you said and did once you reached the summit, where you wouldn't be perched for long anyway, since the work of the detail was mostly walking around the streets.

Laffey's position at the exterior of things, as it were, denoted the low seniority of his command. The burglary detail was a relatively new one, created by Inspector Short as evidence of his commitment to the theory of preventive police work, and its clout in the precinct pecking order had yet to be firmly established. In fact, there was some threat to its continued existence once Short retired, which would be within the year; already, there was some administrative carping as to how the burglary detail duplicated the work of Sergeant Hooper's anticrime unit.

Laffey liked to talk about the downward trend of the large graph lines superimposed over a map of the Nineteenth Precinct, which was the only thing covering the government-green walls besides a collection of photographs and wanted posters of various antisocial specimens. Fewer and fewer burglaries occurred as the months passed and Laffey was particularly proud of pointing out how only a few arrests could reduce a whole lot of incidence. This sort of thing was emphasized in red print on his graph, insets in lined sectors of the Nineteenth Precinct map broken down into quadrants.

The trouble, and Laffey knew it well, was that a commander isn't so dramatically commanding when he has to make his case for survival with charts and graphs. Collars is the name of the game when you're vying for more desirable squad-room space, for instance, especially in as highly visible a precinct as the Nineteenth.

Toward the effort, Laffey had personally assembled his crew—Jack Clark, Kathy Waters, Carl Trani, Billy McBride and Carl Altner. Five officers, Valentine suggested, who were pretty good examples of what he and Laffey had been talking about down in the lobby where they met, a conversation that continued up in the Penthouse as they waited for the squad to assemble for the midday tour that was being run this week. The subject of the talk was the difference in outlook, it seemed to Valentine, between cops back in the 1960s and cops today.

"I hear all kinds of things about that," Laffey said. "And I listen to the theories whenever they come up.

"The one that seems to be stylish now is that cops are different today because they are more sensitive to the things the rest of society started being sensitive about back in the sixties.

"Then there's the theory that since most of us cops now are from that postwar baby boom that we're more in tune with all the struggles of the sixties, which were fought by everybody in the postwar baby boom. So we're supposed to be sympatico, you know?

"Well, I respectfully suggest that there isn't any particular difference between cops back in the sixties and cops today. And I think I know what I'm talking about, since I'm thirty-six years old and I'm from that postwar baby boom and my decade of coming into adulthood was the sixties."

Laffey took another bite of his bagel, happy to have put Valentine quite off balance.

"Trouble with the sixties was that the constant attacks against the cops were *personal*. Like at Columbia, when cops were taunted hour after hour. Most of us were in Vietnam and we came back and there we were on duty at Columbia and we saw these college kids urinating on the flag. I mean, what do you think most cops are going to be thinking when they see that?

"You had cops standing out there, day after day, with no duty rotation. Cops being taunted until they had to react. Of course they did, just like any other human being would.

"We're supposed to rise above being spit at, being stoned, having shit flung at us, having the flag pissed on in front of us. But a human being can take only so much of that. And until someone invents robot cops, we're stuck with human beings for cops.

"I think society has changed, not the cops. The cops are pretty much the same breed today as they were back then.

"Maybe it's all been an aberration, though, and both society and the cops are the same, with certain improvements all round.

"I mean, remember those kids back in the sixties? The ones who got all the press? The ones who made all the noise and all the trouble for the cops, among others? They grew up in Dr. Spock homes. The theory was that you weren't supposed to upset the poor darlings.

"Well, maybe they should have been upset at an earlier age. Maybe they should have learned that there was a world out there beyond Ozzie and Harriet and the suburbs.

"They got to be eighteen and nineteen and all of a sudden they left the golden nest and discovered there were things out in the real world like poverty and racism and cops who sometimes beat up on people. Well, fine.

"But before they got to be eighteen and nineteen and so damn wise and concerned about everything wrong with the big, bad world, their own little worlds were pretty damn good.

"They had fathers who worked as vice-presidents at places like Chase Manhattan, for God's sake, and they lived up in Scarsdale and it never occurred to them that maybe the reason there was poverty and racism out there beyond Scarsdale was because there were places like Scarsdale in this world.

"Me, I grew up in three rooms over a flower shop with five people. I think I know something about poverty they didn't know for a long time and never will in a practical sense anyway. And I saw racism a long time before they ever saw a black face, I'll bet. And I've been cracked over the head with a nightstick and I didn't like it then and now I'll do something about it when I hear of some cop doing the same.

"So how come all there was was yelling?

"Things were getting better and things are getting better now. I knew that in the sixties. Hell, back in the twenties, they were lynching blacks down South. I'd say we've made at least some measurable progress, wouldn't you?"

Valentine nodded his agreement.

"So, anyway, the kids in the sixties like you saw at Columbia were supposed to be the cutting edge of the decade. Every opportunity in the world handed to them on silver platters and somehow or other they get all steamed up in some blind rage which, as far as I can see, didn't change all that much.

"I'm not saying they didn't accomplish something. But I would say it was largely useless. Where did the rage get us? Where did it get them to taunt the cops like they did when they were supposed to be struggling for things for 'the people,' as they called us? Who did they think 'the people' were, anyway?

"They were supposed to be smart kids, kids who had lots of time to read books. Me, I go to college now at the age of thirty-six, right? What I wouldn't have given to have stuck at the books when I was eighteen. I had to work. They were supposed to be smarter than Irish mugs like me, but they weren't even smart enough to be courteous, were they?

"How come they didn't talk to me? How come they looked at me in a blue uniform and saw nothing but that blue? That's smart?"

Laffey shook his head.

"They should have paid more attention to their books. Books tell you that human nature doesn't change a single bit—and human nature includes cops, doesn't it?

"That's the lesson of literature. It's what makes literature so great. You can read Shakespeare today, for instance, and he talks about the same things involving human nature we all know about today that everyone knew about when they were enjoying his plays the first time they were performed.

"Ever read 'Hell hath no fury like a woman scorned'? It was true when it was written and it's true today and it'll be true tomorrow. Right?

"I wish Shakespeare would have written about cops. If Shakespeare would have written about New York cops, he would have written how they were polite and calm and how they care. That's true today and it was true in the sixties.

"The only difference is in the way we're seeing it all. People see the cop and they see that what he does is business, that the cop isn't the enemy. They don't make it personal, not like they did for a while there."

15

Just five blocks from the Nineteenth Precinct station house, where Sergeant Laffey's able crew straggled one by one to work and where Detective Leinau claimed his favored desk under the Muzak speaker in the second-floor PDU and started talking up the idea of a summer "cruise to nowhere" off Long Island Sound, Mrs. William W. Whitson removed her diamond rings and set them down on the butcher block in the center of her elegant kitchen so she might begin her morning task of arranging red and yellow roses in eight identical cut-glass vases.

The other detectives generally tuned out Leinau's pitch on the cruise deal for the very good reasons that it was only Christmas now and everyone was tapped out and the prospect of three or four days confined on a boat with Leinau did not conjure up anyone's visions of Shangri-la. The officers of the burglary detail tried but failed, as usual, to tune out Jack Clark and his morning pep talk.

Today, Clark pounced on the opportunity to address unjaded ears. He approached the sergeant's visitor, Valentine, and wheezed in a very exaggerated fashion, placed his hand over his heart and rolled his eyes back toward the landing of the long stairway he had just climbed en route to the Penthouse.

"God, what a privilege it is to enter this precinct house day after day," he said. "A landmark building, rich in the heritage of this great crossroads of the world, making us ever mindful of our special mission. This building, where men and women have spent their lives vouchsafing the city for democracy!"

Clark pointed a finger at Valentine. "And you! You probably think of this place as just another dirty old building!"

In the Whitson kitchen, one of twelve rooms in a genuine penthouse apartment, Mrs. Whitson listened carefully to Maria, her Puerto Rican maid, bubble on about her husband Juan's latest project—guaranteed to make him a millionaire, if only he could find some way of raising the necessary start-up capital. Mrs. Whitson understood about half of Maria's words, the Puerto Rican vernacular being only faintly related to the Castilian dialect she had learned at Sarah Lawrence in order to help her father in his Canary Island fish cannery enterprises, which hadn't helped her there either.

Juan's newest scheme had something to do with running a yacht around Manhattan, up the East River from the Thirty-fourth Street helipad landing past the United Nations and the grand perched apartment houses of Beekman and Sutton Place and River House, past Coogan's Bluff and around the Harlem River bend and through the Columbia University boat house and Spuyten Duyvil Creek, down the broad Hudson and under the George Washington Bridge, finally around the Battery and back again to the East Side at Thirty-fourth Street. All during the slow evening sail, there would be music and dancing and even a gourmet dinner served.

That was Juan's dream. This time.

The last time, it involved purchasing alternate use rights in dormant cemeteries, as it were, from the families of the long-deceased with an eye toward garden apartment complexes in the outer boroughs.

She hadn't ever met Juan, a baker by trade, and Mrs. Whitson doubted she ever would, when she thought about it at all. She and her husband had each shrugged off subtle and not so subtle requests for capital investment. Tuning out such requests was a knack that came with breeding.

And so Mrs. Whitson listened attentively for the purpose of accustoming herself to Maria's Spanish. She had only just hired her six months ago and communication was very difficult still at times. Mrs. Whitson remembered fondly the late 1940s and early 1950s when it was still possible to get an English girl, so happy they were to leave the bomb-devastated London for a new life in the States.

She asked Maria a few questions about any experience Juan might have that would qualify him to oversee such a complicated business as a floating restaurant that would cater to the moneyed set, since such a dinner setting would surely be costly. Her question was meant to keep the conversation going, it wasn't really asked in genuine interest.

Maria chattered on, encouraged by Mrs. Whitson's inquiries.

"We'll see," Mrs. Whitson said finally, ending the conversation. Her flowers were finished and she picked up her diamonds and began slipping them back on her fingers. Maria watched, her dark eyes shining brightly, as three sparkling rings were set back in place.

Mrs. Whitson smiled at her.

"My husband will be entertaining at half-past five, you know," she said.

Yes, Maria remembered from yesterday. She would have the room readied. Not to worry.

"All right then, I'll just do what I have to do now in the way of errands—"

Maria turned her head at the sound of an urgent knocking at the kitchen door, which led to a service area, elevator and stairway. Along with the knocking was the super's voice, a man named Mickey.

Mrs. Whitson stopped herself. "What can that be? If it's Mickey, he usually calls up on the intercom."

Maria stepped to the door.

"Mickey?" she asked.

"Yeah. Can you open up?"

Something didn't sound quite right in his voice, but before Mrs. Whitson could register any objection, Maria opened the kitchen door.

Both Maria and Mrs. Whitson shrieked when Mickey was thrown headlong into the kitchen. His body slid across the glossy terrazzo floor, landing painfully against the butcher block. One of the vases full of water and roses was jarred and fell off the edge, the blossoms and the water covering Mickey's head and the glass shattering on the floor.

Two men had shoved Mickey and both wore knit ski masks, only their hot eyes and their lips visible. They wore leather gloves and tight-fitting pants and jackets. And both aimed guns at Mrs. Whitson and Maria.

"This is a holdup!" one of them shouted. He held his weapon in both hands and crouched, as if he thought someone might bolt from the kitchen.

Mrs. Whitson thought the man was black by hearing his voice. She stared at him, tried to see what she could of him. Yes, she thought, he was black.

The other man spoke to Maria, who was crying. She was upset and couldn't possibly understand English at that moment. So he asked her in Spanish where the plastic garbage bags were kept. Maria showed him while the black man asked Mrs. Whitson if she had any rope in the house.

"Certainly not!" she said, not certain why his question offended her.

Mickey tried sitting up, but the black man pointed his gun at him and yelled something Mrs. Whitson didn't quite hear. Then he asked Mrs. Whitson, "Your husband have plenty of neckties, does he? Good. Let's go get 'em."

She and the black man with the gun pointed at her back walked from the kitchen through a pantry, a dining room, a music chamber, an anteroom and the living room before reaching the corridor that led to the master bedroom and the wardrobe alcove where William W. Whitson housed his clothing and accessories. The gunman helped himself to an armful of foulards, which he carried back to the kitchen and used to bind up Mickey the super.

The other gunman, meanwhile, had been given a box of green plastic garbage bags. "Let's go," he said to his partner.

"Okay," the black man said. He turned to Mrs. Whitson and said, "Lady, you and the maid here are going to give us all the jewelry and then we're going to be on our way nice and happy and you're going to stay here, safe and sound if everything goes just fine. Understand?"

"Quite," Mrs. Whitson said.

The black man looked at Mickey, his arms tied behind him and lashed to one leg of the butcher block, a huge piece that would prevent his moving from the kitchen to any other room.

"You sure he'll be all right?" the other gunman, the one who spoke Spanish, asked.

Mickey twisted around and tried to get a good look at the two gunmen in the ski masks.

The black man brought a foot down heavily on Mickey's head, mashing his face to the floor. Mrs. Whitson winced at the sound of bone against floor. Poor Mickey. He'd been the super for eight years now. And such a capable man. How did he allow this to happen?

"Let's move!" said the black man, clearly the robber in charge.

Maria held Mrs. Whitson's arm as the two women were marched at gunpoint from the kitchen and along the route Mrs. Whitson had taken before. This time, the black man had said, they would clean out jewelry and valuable clothing.

Mrs. Whitson led the men directly to the dresser that contained her best jewels. She sighed. Never had she and her husband even considered keeping the pieces in a bank vault. Now she handed over gem-encrusted rings, necklaces, pendants, bracelets and brooches.

"I'm not going to part with this," she said. She pointed to her gold wedding band, an ancient ring that had belonged to her husband's grandmother and had become hers some thirty-five years ago. "It's a family heirloom and I'm going to keep it. You're getting enough as it is."

Maria trembled. The black man seemed stunned. He didn't answer her, speaking instead to his partner:

"Look through the closets, man."

His partner crammed two plastic garbage bags with a full-length mink, a lynx wrap and the jewelry.

"Get some more of her old man's ties from the other room there," the black man told his partner. He waved his gun in the general direction of Mr. Whitson's wardrobe area.

"Come on now. We're going to make our exit, ladies."

Mrs. Whitson and Maria were tied up with more of the Whitson neckties and, like Mickey the super, lashed to legs of the kitchen butcher block.

The two gunmen in ski masks fled the kitchen, into the service corridor and down the long stairway to the street.

Mickey managed to slip loose just as they disappeared into the corridor. He ran out after them.

He would later tell Detective Leinau that he stayed "at a distance, so they wouldn't spot me" and that he saw them flag down a taxicab going uptown on Park Avenue.

"I got so mad at what they'd done that I picked up a trash can off the corner and just about threw it at them," Mickey would say.

Tony Currin sat in the hearing room at Police Headquarters in lower Manhattan wearing light-sensitive aviator glasses, which made him look pretty much in character. Cibella Borges sat opposite Currin, next to her lawyer. She wore a high-collar sweater and a plaid skirt and looked like a teenager who attended an all-girls high school.

Deputy Police Commissioner Jaime Rios was the judge. The prosecuting officer, Captain Henry Harrison, handed Rios a number of photographs of the defendant in the sweater and plaid skirt. They were poses of considerably different tone than those that had appeared in magazines Rios mentioned in passing that he'd never before encountered—*Beaver, Pub* and *Girls on Girls.*

Rios looked at the photographs. "Objections?" he asked Cibella Borges' lawyer.

"No objections."

Rios couldn't look at Cibella Borges, though he must have wondered at the contrast he faced. Indeed, the photographs Captain Harrison presented seemed to support the claim of "posing for licentious photographs . . . simulating sodomy and/or masturbation." The question Rios had to decide, of course, was whether such poses brought discredit to the department, apart from the question of how in the Sam Hill this petite suspended cop before him today could possibly be taken seriously as a vice officer.

"Now I'll call Mr. Currin," Captain Harrison said.

Duly sworn, Tony Currin told Deputy Commissioner Rios on questioning by Captain Harrison that he had taken something approaching a quarter million photographs of nude women. Then he testified as to how Officer Cibella Borges became one of the pantheon:

"I just came up to her on the street and told her she would be a perfect centerfold, that she was pretty and had a woman's body and the face of a child.

"She said she was interested and was glad that she had met me."

That was in April of 1980, he said. Cibella Borges, then a civilian clerk working for the New York City Police Department, first auditioned for the publisher of *Beaver* by stripping off her clothes in his office to "make sure she had no disfiguring marks," according to Currin.

Then there were two photo sessions. Cibella Borges earned $150 each time.

Currin completed his testimony, cool as could be, and then left the hearing room. Except for the inconvenience of a long subway ride downtown from his Upper West Side studio, a man like Tony Currin was able to walk out a door, simple as that, and resume his life and pursuit of happiness.

Officer Borges felt chilled. It was a common discomfort for her lately, since she'd lost five pounds. She could ill afford the loss. Now she weighed eighty-five. Dark lines grew deeper by the day beneath her eyes and they burned now because, try as she might, she couldn't draw tears.

Jimmy O'Brien's mistake, apart from the whole matter of stubborn pride in hanging onto the automobile he believed he needed, was in not varying his patterns. Anyone who made the simplest effort at surveillance of his Eastchester home would know that Jimmy O'Brien rose each workday about six o'clock, left his house by seven after the usual argument with his wife and took a bus to the Fordham section of the Bronx to pick up his altered car.

He would drive the car to his job at the warehouse on upper Madison Avenue, then drive down to the bar on Lexington and Eighty-fourth Street for the usual two or three drinks before the trip home to Eastchester, via bus from whatever spot he found to park the car in Fordham.

Royal Billings, the intrepid city marshal, figured out the routine after a while. He'd tried a few times to get into the car and duly impound the camouflaged property of the bank, but he couldn't handle it by himself, what with all the sophisticated antitheft deterrents O'Brien had purchased for it.

Marshal Billings' mistake was to become angered. Impounding someone's car was just a job, not a crusade for righteousness. Besides, it was advisable policy to take it easy while taking it and Billings let that basic rule go by the wayside in this case.

Billings compounded his mistake by trusting in the sense of textbook right and wrong on the part of someone who stood to lose a car.

Billings thought he would be smart and bring along two of his buddies, both of them black, one Friday late afternoon when he knew the car he was after would be parked outside a certain bar on Lexington Avenue in the Eighties.

Just like clockwork, Jimmy O'Brien and his pals were drinking inside the bar—a bit more freely than usual, as it was Friday and payday.

Every so often, as was his habit, O'Brien looked out the window to check on his car.

At one checking period, O'Brien's beer-soaked eyes took in the view of a small black man with an incongruous five-pointed star of a badge on his shirt standing in front of his car while two younger black men worked levers and wires down between the window cracks and into the slits under the hood in order to open up the car, start it and presumably steal it.

"Holy shit! There's a bunch of niggers stealing my car!" O'Brien hollered.

The clientele of the bar was electrified. A dozen and a half men, happy to be given the opportunity to work out a little racial hostility, marched through the door to the street behind the red-faced O'Brien, who had a large knife in hand.

O'Brien and the others from the bar made some primitive noises in the general direction of Billings and his assistants. Billings made sure everyone saw his handsome badge, then began taking a few steps back when he realized this display seemed to heat up the situation.

A man in a red beret, a leather bomber jacket and gloves, faded jeans and construction boots bounded across Lexington and seemed to be talking into a paper bag.

The man in the beret acted out of what seemed to be pure instinct. He positioned himself between O'Brien and his knife and Marshal Billings, who was unsteadily unbuttoning a coat pocket to go for the pistol he was duly authorized to carry in a concealed fashion, even though he should never have any use for it if he had a brain the size of a walnut.

"All right, gentlemen," the man in the beret said. "Let me introduce myself."

Slowly, he reached into his jacket and pulled out a metal chain, which secured his NYPD badge.

He looked first at Marshal Billings. "Okay, Marshal Dippity-Do, I'm the real item. Jack Clark's the name. Stay cool now, or there's going to be a lot of real trouble here."

The crowd behind O'Brien started hollering. Clark smiled at them and held up his hands. Meanwhile, Clark's fellow burglary detail cops —Sergeant Laffey and Carl Trani, along with four uniformed officers on foot patrol who received the call as well—backed up his street mediations by gently moving Billings and his two friends with the levers a block away from the barful of workmen, who missed out on the chance to tear them apart.

"Gentlemen," Clark said to O'Brien and the others, "we have today struck a blow for civilization. You have all done yourselves proud. I thank you and my children thank you."

The men went back into the bar, most of them confused.

Clark chuckled and crooked a finger at O'Brien, who obeyed the summons.

"Got yourself trouble, eh pal? Listen, I understand. Sorry as hell, but if that guy's straight and he's a marshal and all, there's not a whole lot you and I can do about his taking your car, you know," Clark said.

He put an arm around O'Brien's shoulders. "You know what just happened here, though?"

O'Brien shook his head no.

"I just saved your ass from a really big problem. If you'd have knifed that guy, you'd be sitting up in the cage at the Nineteenth Precinct station house on your way to Riker's booked for attempted murder."

O'Brien let out a whoosh of air and began trembling.

"So look at it this way, pal. You lose your car today, but on the other hand, it's the luckiest day of your life I happened to walk by and catch all this about to come down."

"Well, maybe—"

"Maybe nothing, pal. I saved your ass. Now come along with me like a friendly guy, okay?"

O'Brien walked meekly alongside Clark as they made their way toward the subdued Marshal Billings, in the company of John Laffey and Carl Trani.

Billings' papers were inspected. They seemed in order.

Clark took O'Brien's car keys and walked back down the block toward the bar, waved to the fellows inside, then opened the car and drove it back to the marshal.

Nobody was hurt. O'Brien had not been humiliated too badly. And most people in the neighborhood were unaware that something heroic had taken place that Friday afternoon.

Clark was a little shaky when it was all over, but his recovery was, as usual, rapid.

He first telephoned Dory and reached her Sanyo.

"Hello," said the machine. "This is Dory Smith . . ."

"No it isn't," Keenan said, wondering where she was in the apartment as she listened to her messages come in, screening out calls from people she wasn't receiving. That included him, of course.

". . . I'm not here right now . . ."

"Yeah, no shit."

". . . But if you leave your name, the time of your call and a number where I can reach you—"

Keenan slammed down the telephone. He started to dial his number up in Riverdale, but was interrupted. Under the circumstances, he was happy for it.

A man in a heavily stained overcoat stood in front of him. There was a line of drool sliding down one side of his mouth. But other than that, and the condition of his coat, he looked all right. His hair was combed and he held a hat in his hand. He was clean-shaven and his teeth were good.

"They sent me in to see you, Officer," he said.

"Oh did they now? Sit right down and let me get to your concerns," Keenan said.

The drooling man sat down on a cracked plastic chair, an orange-colored thing that might have been at home in a cheap Cantonese restaurant. Keenan stood up and poked his head around a corner. The desk sergeant on duty rolled his eyes.

"I thought so," Keenan said to no one but himself.

He sighed and returned to his desk. The drooling man was drawing a swastika on a corner of the desk top with a dull pencil. Keenan ignored it and sat down.

"What's your name, sir?" Keenan asked.

The drooling man covered up his art work with an elbow. "Let's just keep this confidential."

"Suit yourself. What can I do for you besides try and guess your name?"

"I'm here to help you."

"Rumplestiltskin!"

"What?"

"That's it, isn't it? Your name is Rumplestiltskin?"

"No." The drooler looked very confused.

"Tom, Dick? Harry?"

The drooler brightened. "Yeah, it's Harry. How did you know?"

"Hey, I'm a cop. What do you think? It's my business to know these things."

"Of course. Forgive me. I should have known that."

"But there's one thing, Harry. I don't know what you're doing here. It's got to be pretty important, or you wouldn't be wasting valuable police time. Am I right?"

"I assure you I am here on a vital mission." The drooler crossed his legs.

"Are you going to tell me what it is?"

"I need first to look at all your mug shots."

"The mug shots. Why, Harry?"

Why fight it? Keenan dialed up to the PDU. Leinau answered. After telling Leinau what he had sitting in front of him, including the business of the swastika drawn on the desk top, Keenan held the telephone receiver a few inches away from his head in order to protect his eardrums.

In a few seconds, Leinau was downstairs in the little public reception room off the lobby where Keenan sat with the mysterious drooler. He crooked his finger at Keenan.

"Excuse me, Harry. You wait here while I discuss this with a colleague."

Harry grinned and went back to work on the desk top with his pencil.

"That the nutjob?" Leinau asked, jutting his jaw toward Harry, who was hunched over Keenan's desk.

"That's him."

"He come with anything? Like a bag or something?"

"Just the opposite. He came in missing something. About three or four million brain cells, I'd say."

"These guys are easy to laugh at," Leinau said. "But sometimes they're not really so damn funny."

"Well, he seems all right."

"Yeah, all of them do at first," Leinau said.

Leinau was there in 1973:

A slightly built Puerto Rican walked into the lobby of the Nineteenth Precinct, carrying a brown paper grocery bag.

"Yes sir?" the desk sergeant asked.

"Um, I want—"

Those were the only words anyone heard him speak. The Puerto Rican, a man of about thirty years and perhaps 120 pounds, pulled a .38 revolver from his belt and calmly aimed it at the sergeant, cocked the hammer and squeezed off a single shot which opened a gaping red hole in the sergeant's throat. The bullet ripped through the back of the sergeant's neck and slammed into the plaster wall behind the big desk.

The Puerto Rican dropped the weapon and screamed something in Spanish, something even the Spanish-speaking officers standing about in the lobby didn't understand, and hoisted himself up to the rail of the desk. He began scrambling over the top as the sergeant fell backward, both his hands clasped over the hole in his throat, blood oozing through his fingers.

An officer named Gonzalez waited for the madman to make it clear over the top, then pulled at his arms and got him down onto the floor behind the desk and tried restraining him. Two other officers came running and now three of them, all big men, tried to contain the flailing Puerto Rican.

The little man on the bottom was throttled in the face and chest and stomach and still he could not be held down. One by one, he threw off the big cops. Then he rose and came out from behind the desk to a lobby full of cops with guns drawn.

His eyes were drawn to a lieutenant standing near the desk, his service revolver aimed at his face. "Freeze!" the lieutenant shouted.

The Puerto Rican rushed him, grabbed the lieutenant's revolver as it fired, a bullet sinking into his chest. Blood rushed from the hole, but the little man kept coming.

The little man wrestled the lieutenant's gun away from him and now he started firing the gun into the air, wild shots as he screamed in some insane emotional release. He began lowering the gun. Maybe there were two shots left. It was no time for calm counting.

A dozen police specials started firing in his direction, round after round of fire whizzing past the Puerto Rican. Incredibly, only one slug ripped through an arm. The rest of them, scores of bullets, peppered the wall behind the desk.

The inspector rushed from his office and placed his revolver against the Puerto Rican's ribs. He emptied the gun into the Puerto Rican's belly and still he struggled, still he had the strength to fight off the dozens of arms trying to pull at him, trying to subdue him.

The inspector withdrew the revolver, and the Puerto Rican, an eerie laugh exploding from his mouth, stumbled around the lobby in the direction of the complaint room. Several officers put a few more shots into his body, now striped red with blood and doubled over.

Finally, the Puerto Rican fell to the floor.

"Like a damn sack of potatoes," Leinau told Keenan. "He fell right about where you're standing now."

Keenan looked back at Harry. His shoulders were moving to the task of writing obscene words on the desk top.

"After it was all over, they counted up the number of slugs the little guy took. Twenty-one in all. The sergeant lived, believe it or not.

"And somebody thought to take a look at what the little maniac brought with him in the bag. He had enough Molotov cocktails in there to blow this house to Jersey."

Keenan thought for a minute. "There's a big flag behind the desk now," he finally said.

"Covers a lot of sins."

"Yeah, I guess so," Keenan said. "So what'll I do with Harry in there?"

"I'd ask him very politely to leave if I were you. Me, I got my own troubles. Some rabbi's upstairs with a letter from a nutjob down in Texas who says he's on his way to New York. The rabbi used to have a congregation in Texas, in the town where the letter's postmarked."

"What's the letter say?"

"Oh, it's a real statement of brotherhood, boy. It says this Hanukkah the rabbi's going to 'drink the blood of the malignancy in your womb.' "

"Doesn't make any sense," Keenan said.

"Neither did the Puerto Rican. Nobody ever did find out what his gripe was. So what's Harry's beef in there?"

"No beef. He says he's here to help us."

"Just what we need. Got to go now, Keenan."

Keenan returned to the complaint room.

"Harry, what the hell have you been doing to my desk?"

The drooler looked up. He'd covered fully one third of Keenan's desk with obscene words and drawings and dozens of little swastikas. "What?"

"Harry, I'm only going to tell you this once. I haven't got time to repeat myself, so listen carefully. I need your help."

"What is it, Officer?"

"My colleagues have informed me that they're after you."

"Oh?"

"You'd better get out while the gettin' is good, if you know what I mean."

"Who's after me?"

"No time to chat, Harry. You better get out of here. Run, Harry. Run, don't walk."

Harry drew himself up, imperiously. "You're nuts. I will not deal with psychopaths. Good day!" Then he turned and strutted through the lobby of the precinct house. He turned around and looked at Keenan before he went through the door to the street and scowled. "Nut!"

"Well, he's right," Keenan said softly. He sat down behind his desk again and stared at the green telephone in front of him. Then he steeled himself and dialed home.

Every year at Christmastime, for all five seasons Ed Smith had been divorced from his second wife, he cleaned up. The effect was stunning. Ed Smith would shed his Bowery-bum ensemble and, like the metamorphosis of a butterfly, he became a man who looked as if he might have strolled in from Harvard Yard.

The tip-off to all concerned in the Nineteenth Precinct locker room was Smith's use of the showers. That cleaning was in preparation for his visit to a men's hair stylist on Madison Avenue, which was then followed by Smith's visit to a Turkish bath on the Lower East Side, one of a handful in the city that wasn't yet a homosexual xanadu.

There in the Turkish bath, Smith would spend the late afternoon and early evening getting clean down to the very last pore of all the street grime he'd built up during the year.

When he was through, he would take out clothing he wore at no other time from the suitcase he'd taken off the shelf of a closet in his tiny apartment. Pleated olive corduroy slacks, a red- and white-checked tattersall shirt, a navy-blue oiled-wool sweater, cordovan tassel loafers, a loden stadium coat, red woolen muffler and a gray tweed cap.

He wore a wristwatch, too, a Baume and Mercier. It was the gift his wife had given him on their wedding day.

When he left the Turkish bath, he felt like walking in the crisp wintery air. Besides, he had the usual thinking to do.

He walked down Third Avenue and stopped at a place called Phebe's at Fourth Street. A mildly trendy place popular, due to its prices, with actors and writers and others of uncertain incomes. Smith sipped an Old Parr scotch, neat, for nearly an hour. The perfect gentleman. He enjoyed the private joke of it and more than one attractive woman in the place found his appearance and the attitude he exuded quite worth watching.

He left without speaking to anyone, though. And then he walked through a more familiar terrain. In less than a block, Third Avenue became the Bowery, and even though he looked the way he did, Ed Smith felt relaxed.

"Bathroom for Customers Only" was the sign in every window of every cheap all-night spoon and every dump reeking of malt that served a watery shot of whiskey for a quarter and a forty-cent mug of beer for a chaser. The other men who walked about—not men, really, so much as dark shadows that moved—carried pale green flat bottles of Thunderbird in their pockets and asked him for spare change, which he gave over.

There was a Salvation Army chorus standing beneath a streetlamp, red-faced and ragged and howling a rendition of "Silent Night." Smith dropped a dollar into the red kettle hanging from a tripod and the soprano of the group smiled at him and nodded her head in thanks.

He saw a familiar face loitering outside the Sunshine Hotel, beds for two and a half dollars in advance. He was a tall, skinny man of perhaps forty. He and Smith had gotten drunk together one summer afternoon that year and stood outside the Sunshine punching well-dressed shoppers who had to walk by the hotel on their way to the shops that carried expensive lamps and housewares at discount prices.

Smith waved to him. The wino growled and spit at him.

Next to the Sunshine was the Bowery Mission. The 7:30 P.M. service was in full swing. The door was open and Smith could hear a nasal voice from up in the pulpit saying, "For what shall it profit a man, if he shall gain the whole world and lose his soul?"

Smith moved on. He didn't have any particular quarrel with the religious, he just didn't have much use for the type. At Grand Street, he flagged down a taxicab.

The driver looked him over carefully before stopping and admitting him into the back door.

"Don't usually pick up many fares down here," the driver said. "What the hell's a guy like you doing hanging around here anyway?"

Smith could have guessed the next question.

"Say, ah . . . you lookin' for some really good-quality stuff, pal? I got your Christmas trees now, you know? Little greenies that'll put you on another planet."

Smith didn't say anything. He reached into the breast pocket of his stadium coat and opened his billfold for the driver. His NYPD shield had the effect of a crucifix on a vampire.

"Since it's the holiday and all," Smith said, "I'll just pretend like I didn't hear you."

"I'll take you wherever you want, no charge."

"You'll take me to Brooklyn Heights and if you high-flag it, I'll make a complaint to the Taxi and Limousine Commission. Got it?"

"Yes, sir."

Smith gave him an address in Pineapple Street and sank back against the seat.

All the way over, he wondered if this would be the year he would actually knock on the door. Or would he get to the top of the stoop, enjoy the aroma of the wreath she always put out and then skulk away?

It wasn't that he wanted to cause any trouble for her, or her husband. He wanted to see his daughter, sure. But that wasn't the important thing, either.

"It'll be a good excuse, though," he'd told his friend Joe the other day when the two of them shared a cigarette under the Queensboro Bridge.

"What the hell's it all about, then?" Joe had asked.

Smith didn't know then, he didn't know now as the taxi crossed over the Brooklyn Bridge.

Ten minutes later, he was paying the driver, and as he stepped out into Pineapple Street, which looked like the Hollywood set used for the filming of *Arsenic and Old Lace*, he was no closer to the answer he'd sought for five years.

He walked up the stoop and there was the wreath. Smith raised his hand. Maybe he wouldn't have knocked that year, either, but a car backfired in the next block and his hand fell against the wood reflexively. As long as he'd made contact, Smith reasoned, he'd give it an honest knocking.

It was quiet at night in Brooklyn. Smith always noticed that. And the Heights was perfect for his wife. But not for him. Smith didn't approve of Brooklyn Heights any more than he approved of suburban towns. To him, it was a synthetic place, a place where people distanced themselves from reality, from any sign of how most of the people of the world lived. Here, the people wanted boutiques and designer ice-cream shops and Belgian waffle stands and news dealers who carried *Paris Match*. It seemed worse to Ed Smith than most of what he saw on the Upper East Side.

Smith heard footsteps from inside the house. A small light flicked on in a foyer and he saw a woman's face peering out at him from a square of glass that ran alongside the door.

His wife! He didn't recognize her at first. For years, he'd seen her only at a distance. Ruth looked more beautiful than the first time he'd seen her. The years washed away and Smith felt wobbly in the legs. And afraid.

The door swung open.

"Ed, my God! You look fantastic!" she said.

The two of them stood there staring at each other.

"Come in." Ruth pulled him through the door, into the home she and her husband, Darryl, had made. She shut the door and Smith was as nervous as a cornered rat.

"Is Eve here?" he said. It was the only thing he could think of to say, his first words to this woman in years.

"No, not tonight. I'm sorry. You should have called."

"Okay. Well, I can go—"

"No, stay. Come in with me. Sit with me for a minute."

"Your husband."

She laughed and took him by the arm. They walked through the foyer into the living room.

"Sit down," she said. "And let me tell you something."

Smith took a leather club chair, wondered if it was Darryl's favorite. If the man had any sense, it would be.

"Eve's visiting Darryl tonight, okay? He has his own apartment now."

Smith's face was full of a very stupid expression.

"Get it? It's not working out with us any more."

16

Sergeant John Laffey and Officer Jack Clark, along with Valentine, sat crowded around a small plastic table on swivel chairs bolted to the floor. They had three plastic trays in front of them, two orange and one yellow, piled up with paper containers of pathetic little hamburgers and limp deep-fried potatoes glistening with salt.

"God, we're in the shadow of La Grenouille and look at us!" Clark said.

All three men wore jeans of variously faded hue. Clark wore boots and a woolen cap with a ball on top and a heavily scarred leather bomber jacket. Laffey and Valentine wore navy pea jackets and running shoes.

"Every time I find myself in a McDonald's," Clark said, "all I can think about is that movie, *Soylent Green*. Ever see it? Charlton Heston, Leigh Taylor-Young, Chuck Connors, Joseph Cotten, Brock Peters, Paula Kelly, Edward G. Robinson, directed by Richard Fleischer, 1973 I'm pretty sure and Robinson's final film."

"Jesus, the trivia! It's amazing," Laffey said. "If the guy knew anything useful, he might be frightening."

"Everybody ate this stuff the government gave them to eat and the standard fare was a green thing about the size of a piece of that flat bubble gum that comes with baseball cards, only it was green instead of pink.

"So the payoff of the movie is discovering the connection between the government death factories, where people volunteered to go off themselves because the world was such a goddamn pain in the ass and the factory was a palace, and the food supply. Turns out everybody who ate soylent green, which was the whole population of New York City, was eating processed people."

"Thanks a lot, Jack," Laffey said. He pushed his tray away. "I'm not going to be able to eat this slop now."

"You're better off," Clark said. He crammed half a burger into his mouth.

Laffey opened his coffee container.

"Can you see our mope?" Clark asked him.

Laffey stole a glance from the corner of his eye in the direction of a young man on the other side of the restaurant, their "mope," meaning that he'd been moping about a neighborhood where Laffey and Clark knew by instinct and some other fairly obvious clues he didn't belong.

"Sure, I can see him," Laffey said. "He's sitting there in the corner with two quarter-pounders and three cartons of fries and he's got a cigarette going while he's eating."

"What a pig."

Laffey and Clark had been following the mope for half the morning. They picked him up at Carl Shurz Park, where they spotted him sitting on a bench, smoking and tapping his feet, a canvas bag at his side. Running shoes, warm gloves, jeans and a coat long enough to have lots of inside pockets handy for carrying burglary tools. He was a stocky Hispanic man in his mid-twenties.

The mope got up from the park bench and started scoping out the buildings nearby, ducking into lobbies and then reappearing in the street. He worked his way down from the park into the far East Sixties, westerly toward Third Avenue. Several times, he would spend enough time in a lobby to test a door. Then, for whatever reason, he would dash out into the street and walk around the block, seeming to be in some deep thought.

"He looks real good," Laffey had said when he started his scoping near the park, in the Eighties. "We'll stay on his ass awhile."

And so they had.

Laffey would follow him a block or two, then take over in the car that Clark drove. Clark would follow for a while on foot. Then maybe Carl Trani would pick up the mope for a time, or Kathy Waters, who worked with him that day.

About noon, he headed for the McDonald's. Laffey and Clark decided to follow him on in.

Laffey talked to Valentine, keeping an eye on the mope in the corner.

"So this is how it is a lot of the time. We're waiting for a mope to make his move and we try to get a good look at him making that move, then we can bust him and make it stand up. These guys can be pretty cagey sometimes, though, and they'll keep us on the walk for a whole day and we end up with nothing.

"Of course, I don't look at what we're doing as 'nothing' just because we might not come home with a collar. I mean, even if the mope makes us and acts like a wise guy with us, he's prevented from committing a burglary, isn't he?

"And next to rape, burglary is the thing that bothers people the most. Rape and burglary ought to be special concerns for cops. We ought to work at preventing the crime, see?

"People don't want to live with the fear of rape. And it's pretty much the same thing with burglary, if you've ever experienced it. Your home is violated and you're never quite the same afterward.

"I'm talking about your home, your privacy. The guy who's had his apartment burglarized thinks, 'My home is where I live my life, it's where I raise my kids, it's where I make love to my wife. And some creep just waltzes in and rips it all off.' "

Laffey stopped talking for a moment. The mope in the corner started to get up. Then he sat down and lit another cigarette.

"This guy's looking worse and worse," Clark said. "I don't think he's going to get up the balls for it today."

"It's only been a couple hours," Laffey said. "Some guys take that long."

The mope got up again. He dumped the wrappers from his tray into a trash container and walked past the table where Laffey and Clark sat.

Laffey picked up his PTP radio and talked to Trani, outside the McDonald's in a plain green car.

"What's he doing now?" Laffey asked.

There was no answer.

"Carl!"

Trani whispered. "Stand by."

"Shit. Two hours and—"

Trani was back on the radio, which interrupted Clark.

"Your mope walked right up to the car and gave me a big smile, Sarge. He made us all."

Laffey and Clark walked quickly out the door of the restaurant. The mope was at the corner. He waved to the two officers who had watched him eat his meal.

"Oh man, I thought we'd have one for sure there," Clark said. He and Laffey walked dejectedly across the street and got into the car with Trani.

They weren't in the car long before the 10-19 call came over the radio. Laffey called in from the booth just outside the car, then rushed back and told Trani to get to East Sixtieth and Second Avenue "quick and quiet."

"What do we got?" Clark asked.

"Silent alarm in the building."

"Lot of nothing sometimes," Clark said.

"Sometimes."

Trani pulled up in front of the building and Laffey and Clark, pulling the shields they wore attached to chains around their necks, jumped out of the car and showed them to the confused doorman. "What's going on?" he asked.

"Just got a call to help out, that's all," Laffey said. "Look, in case we don't get back down here to the lobby in a few minutes, do me a favor, okay?"

"Of course."

"There's an officer out there, waiting in a car. See him?"

Trani waved from the car to the doorman.

"He's with us. I want to leave him there and I want to leave you here so you can make sure nobody leaves the building for a little while. Keep them right here. Shouldn't be too long. You have any trouble with that request, there's a cop right there for you and you let him know. Okay?"

The doorman looked like he might faint at any moment.

Laffey and Clark took the elevator to the top floor, the twelfth, and took a walk through the corridor, inspecting the doors for signs of forced entry. They split up at either end of the corridor, each man taking a separate stairway down to the next floor, crossing paths through the corridor and taking the stairs to the next point of search.

On the ninth floor, Clark came across a man waiting for the down elevator.

"You live here?" Clark asked. The man waiting seemed frightened by the question from the cop in the jeans and bomber jacket. Clark showed him his tin and relief spread across his face.

"Yes. Can I help you, Officer?" He wore a blue cashmere overcoat, a pinstriped suit and carried an attaché case. "Was it this floor?"

"Can't tell," Clark said. "We're looking at everything."

Clark saw paint chips on the floor below the doorknob near the elevator.

"What do you have in the attaché, friendly?"

"I beg your pardon?" The elevator made some clanking sounds and the man in the cashmere coat buttoned up.

"What's in the case?"

Laffey opened the door from the stairwell and walked toward the elevator. Clark raised a hand and Laffey stayed where he was, as backup.

"Look, Officer—"

"Just open up the case, please."

"I haven't got the time!" the suspect said. The elevator stopped at the ninth floor and opened.

"Sure you do," Clark said. "If we hold you up unnecessarily, I promise to get you where you're going faster than you could make it there on your own anyway. You'll get a police escort, okay?"

The suspect looked over his shoulder at Laffey, who was talking to Trani on the PTP.

The suspect smiled. "Nice work," he said. "How'd you make me?"

"Just a guess," Clark said. "The paint chips there." He pointed to the flecks on the corridor's carpeting.

"I'll have to be a little neater."

"Open up now like a good fellow."

Laffey moved in as the suspect opened the attaché, inside of which were pry bars, skeleton keys, a box of business calling cards, loose cash, cloth bags full of other people's jewelry and glassine packets of what appeared to be cocaine.

"Where'd the flake come from?" Clark asked him.

"From the fine, upstanding solid citizens of Apartment 9-E," the suspect said.

Clark had a good laugh. The suspect held out his wrists while Laffey cuffed him up for the ride to the lockup and booking.

"Ever have one of those days?" the suspect asked Laffey.

"Everybody does."

Keenan had taken a sick day, but it was his wife who needed the time off. He arranged for the girls to stay after school at a friend's home and even talked the doctor into making a house call.

She slept now as the doctor spoke to Keenan.

"Have the two of you been fighting?" he asked Keenan. "And I mean something beyond ordinary tiffs that couples have."

"Not fighting, exactly. More a case of not caring. Maybe that's the worst sort of a fight."

"Maybe, yes."

"How is she now, really?"

The doctor made bag-packing motions. "She very nearly lost the baby," he said. "And there's no reason for that to be the case with her other than psychological stress and strain. She's a healthy woman, there has never been the slightest problem with her pregnancies in the past."

"There was the—"

"You had a baby die, that's true. But that has nothing to do with her health, you see. No, what I'm telling you is that there are cases where women lose their babies—abort—that are entirely psychological in nature."

Keenan's face drained of color. "The baby she's carrying. Is it all right?"

"I think so. The body and the brain, too, are remarkable creations for their restorative powers."

Keenan read a book once, or maybe it was an article. The title of it played through his mind. *My Enemy Grows Older.* It was a story of modern marriage.

And he thought of his wife's sensibilities, how terribly vulnerable she must be since she spent such considerable effort at presenting a controlled face to the world. Most people Keenan knew, unless they bordered on the moronic, were masses of irony when it came to determining their personalities. Most people were anything but candid. How many times had he asked his wife "What's wrong?" when he sensed trouble. How many times had he believed her when she said "Nothing at all." Of course that's what she would say.

"Doctor, I suppose Mairead thinks her whole world is caving in because her whole world revolves around me and, well, I've had a lot of troubles lately."

The doctor clucked. "What you say makes sense. If your wife wasn't pregnant, maybe there wouldn't be any way for us to receive the signals we're getting. Pregnancy makes a woman's senses more acute than they ordinarily are. Ordinarily, they're just as dumb as us men, I'd say."

"What can I do? I don't want her to lose this baby. I think that would kill her."

"From what I know of her, I would agree," the doctor said. "Now I'm going to tell you something and I don't want you to take it as a doctor's advice. Hell, Tommy, you must know that medicine is an art, not a science. That's why I want you to take my advice as something coming from a concerned friend of the family. I don't make house calls otherwise, you know."

The doctor stood up and prepared to unload himself of the weight of friendly advice. Keenan stood up, too, though everyone says you're supposed to sit down at such times.

The two men walked to the door, Keenan following the doctor.

"Well?" Keenan asked when the doctor started turning the knob.

"It's this. You're going to have to decide whether the problems you're having outside this house are greater than the ones you're having inside it. You're a good-looking young man and you have the sort of charm women like, you're a good talker. I can guess what your problems are. What I'm telling you is that you're in a situation, son, where you're going to have to make absolute choices. It's either Mairead, or it's the other woman."

"What about the kids?"

"Kids take care of themselves, surprisingly enough. It's the grown-ups who find these things such a torment. Look around you and see if you don't agree with me."

The doctor pulled open the door, but he didn't step out into the hall. "Napoleon used to say, 'If you're going to take Vienna, then *take* Vienna!' You can't very easily have a part-time affair, not if you're a man with the sorts of principles that have been hammered into you. It has to be all or nothing and that goes for your wife."

"I have to choose . . . between Mairead and . . ."

"The name's not important. But the choice is. Yes, you have to choose. This is hardly a medical observation, like I said, but I think Mairead's going to be sick until you make up your mind."

"God." Keenan cried.

"You don't have to feel you have to choose Mairead, son. I'm just here telling you that you have to choose *one* of them. The thing you're doing, and I suspect it's just as bad for the other woman, is you're putting lives on hold. You're not letting Mairead live, except around the edges of your indecision. Do you see?"

Keenan nodded his head. "I don't think I should tell her anything while she's pregnant, though. She—"

"Aren't you listening to me, boy?" The doctor was angry. It's not an easy thing to confront someone and it's more difficult still when you encounter deafness. "This is the worst possible time to keep her wondering, to keep her on the string. Can't you see that? Or maybe you're the most completely selfish man alive."

"But the pregnancy."

"Listen again. A woman's senses are never more heightened than when she's pregnant. She's never weaker, she's never stronger. She's never more capable of handling herself, no matter what happens. If it was up to me, I'd have a nine-month presidency in this country and vote for a pregnant woman."

Keenan put out his hand. "Thanks, Doctor."

"Let me know, will you?"

Leinau agreed to meet William W. Whitson at his office, which was atop the headquarters building of a small but highly influential investments and securities firm that did a worldwide business. The building was within the Nineteenth, as it happened, and an easy walk from the precinct house.

Besides, Leinau always enjoyed glimpses into the working life of tycoons. While he himself wore polyester suits that tended toward colors like salmon, he could enjoy being near the good taste of others.

Whitson had him wait alone in his massive office for a few minutes and Leinau didn't mind at all. He sat with his legs outstretched in a butter-soft black leather chair near one of the three window walls, and he helped himself to the contents of a Moroccan-bound humidor on a marble side table.

Leinau freed a crisply wrapped Individualé, which he estimated at ten dollars the copy, and lit up. A steward glided across the office from a little food and beverage station. He wiped out the black onyx ashtray on the marble table and asked Leinau, "Drink?"

"Yeah, some coffee. Got espresso?"

"Very good, sir."

Leinau liked the place very much. He liked especially the fact that there was no actual desk in the office, not the sort of imposing piece that he usually encountered, something with enough empty space to serve as a landing strip for troop transport planes, a desk designed for maximum intimidation.

That was style, Leinau thought. No desk. Just a collection of couches and side chairs, a handsome antique table roughly in the middle of the room, covered over with books. Discreet telephones here and there. And an especially interesting wardrobe against the wall, with pegs on the outside to hold Whitson's highly distinctive cane and hat.

The door opened and Whitson walked in. The only adjective Leinau could think of was beautiful.

Whitson was roughly the same size as Leinau, six feet and one inch, but quite another shape and style. His hair was carefully tended, but not fussed over. Thick black with silver, wing-shaped temples. Maybe he was sixty, judging by the character and texture of his face, but he didn't have the scars a man of modest means and tastes accumulates. Whitson's belly was absolutely flat, his skin smooth and tanned, teeth gleaming white and hands that looked as if they belonged on a Greek statue.

Leinau, on the other hand, owned a haircut he hadn't much changed since 1966, save for the length of his sideburns from year to year. He had a thin moustache that got wet every time he ate something, a nose with lots of broken veins, the inevitability of gravity around the waist of a nearly middle-aged man who watched games rather than played them and a shaving rash on a neck that betrayed a fondness for sweets. But Leinau puffed on his Individualé and delighted, without the slightest self-consciousness about it, in the aura of William W. Whitson's good fortune and worldliness. Leinau didn't begrudge Whitson a bit of it and there was only the slightest chance that any of it would rub off on him.

"I like the way you do business, Whitson."

"Thanks." He turned around when he heard the steward, who glided along with a silver tray and an espresso cup and saucer. "Ah, I see Henry has taken care of you."

"Yeah. Just like downtown."

"As I understand it, ah . . ."

"Leinau. Detective."

Whitson smiled and folded his hands in his lap. "Yes, Detective Leinau. As I understand it, you've spoken to the superintendent of my building and you've spoken to the maid. My wife, of course. What have you determined?"

Leinau sipped half the espresso, then puffed the cigar.

"I've determined that you're careless about where you keep your wife's valuable jewelry."

"Yes, we should have had it in the bank. Or here in my office, at least. After all, I'm not very far from home."

"So you've never had any trouble in your building. Is that why you were sort of lax, if you don't mind my sayin' so?"

"I don't mind what you say, Detective Leinau. And you're quite correct. To my knowledge, there has never been a robbery in my building."

"Thought so. I didn't bother checking with the computer. You ever see the people who run computers? All they know how to do is tell you that computers are great when they work, but they never work because people don't know how to run them. They just claim the whole damn world is going to be a wonderful place when we have computers fouling everything up.

"Well, I digress. Anyway, I figured you didn't have problems that way. Of course, you had insurance, I suppose. I don't imagine I have to tell you that, do I?"

"No, sir. I try to attend to business matters as best I can."

"Yeah, I know. I can tell. You got a swell place here, that's for sure. You got to take care of business real good to have a spread like this. Jesus, what's the rent here, anyway?"

Whitson smiled benevolently and said nothing.

"Oh yeah. You don't ask prices. What's wrong with me, huh? Hey, you'd know if we traded places and you saw where I had to work, Mr. Whitson. What a dump!"

Whitson tilted his head back and laughed. "Like Bette Davis in the movies," he said. "She walked into a place and said, 'What a dump!'"

"Yeah, well, I think the writer of that line worked in the Nineteenth PDU for a spell. Say, how come it was half a day before we got the call on this anyway? Did something happen at our end, or what? Boy, if it did I'm sure sorry, Mr. Whitson. We try to stay right on top of things, you know. Man, what a delay if it was our fault! But honest to god, it was like a half day before I knew about it and I was the detective on the catch for new cases then, so I should have gotten word first thing."

"Well," Whitson said, his debonair coolness chipped ever so slightly, "I wanted to have a chance to take a look at things myself. I had to make sure my wife was all right, of course."

"Oh yeah. A guy's got to look after the little woman. Some women need a lot of care. But not yours, Mr. Whitson. She seemed pretty capable to me."

"What?" Whitson turned away from Leinau and called for Henry. "Get me a . . . oh, an anisette with coffee."

"Very good, sir."

"Nice to get to know your undertaker long before the time comes, sir. That Henry's going to do a bang-up job with you."

"What?"

"Henry. The steward. The guy who moves around like an undertaker with—"

"I mean, Detective Leinau, what about my wife?"

"Oh yeah. What's her name, anyway? I don't think I ever got it."

"Tildy. Short for Matilda."

"Would that make it Bill and Tildy? I like that."

"Detective Leinau, I'm a busy man."

"I can well imagine, sir. I'm busy myself, so I know how it is." Leinau smiled benevolently now.

"You said something about my wife. What did you mean?"

"When I got there, sir, I met a woman completely in charge of herself after an event I've seen rattle some pretty tough folks. She didn't have a hair out of place, and I didn't have a sense that anybody had anything to do with it but her. She's the most self-confident person I've come across in a long time."

"Tildy's a game girl."

"And a smart one, and completely honest, in my book."

"She told you about this 'Juan' person?"

"Oh yes. She told me everything. She had it all written down, you know. Everything that everyone said, as best as she could remember it. She wrote it down right away so she wouldn't forget. That's what she told me."

"Well then, I suppose it's true."

"If she said it?"

"Of course."

"That's what I thought. I pegged her honest. She can handle herself pretty well, too, from the way she described what happened. I mean, keeping that one piece of jewelry like she did."

"The wedding band."

"Yeah. I'll bet you're glad about that, eh? In the family so long and all and the sentimental value of it and everything."

"Tildy performed magnificently. I'm sure we're in agreement here. I'm not at all sure what we're accomplishing with this conversation, though." Whitson took a peek at the wristwatch beneath the french cuff on his left wrist.

"You in a hurry to get somewhere, Mr. Whitson? Am I keeping you or something?"

Whitson tried to keep cool. "Tildy told you about the situation with the maid's boy friend, Juan?"

"Yeah, but I figure it's nothing."

"What?"

"I figure that's not the angle here. You don't think Juan has anything to do with it either, do you?"

Whitson stuttered and Leinau knew he was on the right track.

"Mr. Whitson, you've got some troubles here at the office that might have something to do with all this, don't you?"

Henry glided over with Whitson's coffee and anisette and Whitson looked very grateful. Leinau grinned at him and puffed on the Individualé.

Whitson, a quick learner, tried putting Leinau off guard. "Would you like to take one of those cigars for later, Detective Leinau? What about the rest of the squad? Any cigar smokers? These are the best, I hear. I don't smoke them myself, but Henry here has excellent taste and tells me that this is just the thing for a man who loves truly fine tobaccos."

"Hey, thanks a lot, sir." Leinau opened the humidor and took three of the Individualés, which emptied the humidor, and put them into his inside breast coat pocket. He had no intention of sharing them with anyone.

"Enjoy."

"Oh, I will, that's for sure." Leinau picked up the little espresso cup and finished off its contents. "Nice. You got your own machine for this back there? I'd like one for myself. Saw it in the housewares section at

Bloomingdale's once. A hundred and eighty clams! Man, I can't afford that. I suppose you'd be willing to get it for me, though, right?"

"I'd get it. What?"

"An espresso machine. You'd get it for me, right?"

"Well, I might." Whitson grew very red in the face.

"Tell you what would be even cheaper for you, as if that's not cheap enough," Leinau said. "Just come clean for me."

Whitson shook his head. "You win." He stood up, slapping his long, supple thighs as he did so. He walked toward the antique table in the center of the office and slid open a long drawer. He removed a bundle of letters and smacked them against the palm of his hand as he returned to the window where Leinau was waiting for the plain truth.

"You ought to come work for me, Detective Leinau. I could make it quite worth your while. You're quite good at maneuvering a conversation. That's what you'd need with the access I'd give you."

"I'm a cop, Mr. Whitson. It's like being an actor, I think. It's in your blood." He thought of all the times he threatened to take early retirement, open a bait shop on the Sound.

"You could leave for a while."

"What? And quit show business?"

Whitson laughed and sat down. "All right, all right. See these?" He handed Leinau the bundle of letters. "They're demands that I pay up a million dollars."

"What's the point of the shakedown?" Leinau started opening up the letters, all of them, he noticed, postmarked New York.

"The usual."

"Giving the old tap, tap, tap to somebody besides the wife?"

"God, man, you could have some understanding."

"I do."

Whitson sipped the coffee while Leinau looked at the letters. "How did you know about them?" he asked Leinau.

"I didn't. You told me."

"But you knew something."

"Your wife. Tildy. She told me that she thought something was troubling you for a long time. You never had any trouble in the building before, the business with Juan was just too pat. It didn't look to me like the two guys who robbed your wife just waltzed in and knocked on anybody's door.

"There's something more than meets the eye, see. That's why

there's us detectives. The only thing I could figure that couldn't be nailed down was your wife's feeling that there was some sort of trouble with you. That and the fact that there was no way in hell that they could have gotten into your building without the super being involved, right? I mean, you've got half the Third Reich fugitives working that building as security.

"So, usually, you find connections between inside jobs and unseen trouble. I thought your wife's intuition was pretty sound and I figured right away maybe you pulled the strings yourself as an insurance scam. It's that time of year, you know. All over this neighborhood, people are reporting lots of burglaries and robberies and whatnot and getting the little police reports we make out and then making a date with their insurance agents. Helps with the old cash flow."

"But that's not the case."

"Yeah, I can see now. You're being shook."

"They threatened me with a show of force if I didn't come through and this is it."

"You should have come to us a long time ago, Mr. Whitson."

Whitson didn't say anything for a while. Leinau read, once in a while chuckling.

"Detective Leinau, just when did my wife tell you what you say she did? I think she would have told me about such a conversation."

"Oh," Leinau said, raising his head and smiling. "I talked to her on the telephone from the lobby of your building, just before I came up. You don't think I'd want you to be tipped, do you?"

Whitson shook his head. "Amazing. Come work for me."

Leinau said he'd think about it when he was through with the case, but he didn't mean it. He pored through the letters, finished every one of them, and then returned to the latest, dated just a week earlier.

"The writer here says he wants a meeting. Says he'll show you what sort of evidence he's got, what you'd stand to lose in a divorce proceeding."

"Yes."

Leinau looked at the wardrobe against the far wall, distant enough so that a man's features would be blurred, close enough so that his general outline would be recognizable.

"Mr. Whitson, I'm going to ask you to do a favor for me."

"You want the espresso machine after all?"

"Maybe later. Right now, would you just walk over to that clothes rack or whatever?"

"Sure." Whitson rose and walked to the wardrobe. When he got there, he turned to Leinau and said, "All right?"

"Put on the hat."

Whitson put on black felt homburg. He pitched it so that it nearly covered his left eye.

"Okay, now pick up the cane and hold it like you're standing somewhere waiting for your mistress or somebody like that."

Whitson ignored what might have been insolence from a man he couldn't respect. He respected Leinau immensely, and if he ever came out of this alive, he'd buy him an espresso machine for every day of the year.

"Turn around."

Whitson turned around. He spent the next ten minutes taking poses while Leinau considered his next move.

17

Herb Charles floated through the swinging doors of the Nineteenth PDU, all smiles, and popped his head into Lieutenant Stein's office. Detective Charles is not a demonstrative sort and yet he gave a thumbs-up sign to the boss.

"You hit big on Wingo, Herbie?" Stein asked.

"I hit big on a stash of video equipment," Charles said. "We going to get rid of one hell of a lot of paper tonight, Loo."

Stein got up from his desk. "Yeah, what do you have, Herbie?"

"I sweated our boys overnight and what do you know if it didn't work like a charm. You know the boys we got the other day for ripping off apartment lobby TV monitors?"

"Boys is right. They were scared out of their minds."

"Sure were. It worked."

"You recovered yet?" Stein asked.

"I got a confirmed recovery. The stuff's up in a roach hole in the Two-Three. A couple of uniforms opened up the place on a warrant and I'm going on up now."

"Nice work, Herbie. Really nice."

"Okay, Loo. See you."

Charles put on his coat and his trademark hat, an upturned plaid porkpie. He went down to the lobby and signed out for an unmarked car. He took Valentine along with him for the ride up to East Harlem.

"Everybody's involved in crime and drugs these days," Charles said as he drove the car through the early evening traffic up Park Avenue. "And I mean everybody. From the bottom of our society to the top."

He shook his head. "Man, it wasn't always that way. It makes me really feel my age, all this stuff. Sometimes, though, like right now, the fact that we have this big criminal dilettante group sort of works in our favor.

"This is a pretty good case of when sweating your suspects works. We brought these boys in and we popped them right into the slammer on an overnight. You do a little paper delay and you can keep kids like this two nights over.

"Mostly, a night is all it takes. Some have better stomachs than the others. Anyway, after a night or two of seeing what the mental midgets look like who'll be spending most of their lives in the system one way or another and our boys are pretty receptive when we ask, 'How about helping us now?'

"I'll tell you, some of them ask *us* if they can help in any little way. You ever spend a night in the overnight lockup and you'll understand. These guys start thinking about the fact that the creatures they're locked up with have been there years and years all together and they sweat real good.

"So it doesn't do us much good just to lock somebody up and throw away the key. Sweating works. It's better if we can get some of the property back in property crimes like this. So, we're open to deals.

"You manage to work up a pretty good roster of snitches that way, too. Ah, what a system, huh? Sometimes it doesn't always seem right, but I've been at this a long time now and it's better today, that's for sure. A lot better."

Herb Charles was a rookie cop in 1956, then one of so few black police officers that there were only two prospects for him, so it seemed. He would be forever on a foot patrol in Times Square, his precinct assignment, or because he was black he might possibly fall across some unique opportunity for attention—and, hopefully, advancement.

In Charles' case, the latter happened.

Charles' opportunity for attention came on the occasion of a scuffle between Miles Davis, the jazz musician, and New York's finest outside the old Birdland.

A lot of people were calling the cops "New York's Whitest" at that time, an expression given extra coinage the night Miles Davis was beaten up.

For days the marquee of Birdland was ablaze with neon word of Miles Davis' scheduled concert. Outside, there were billboards with Davis' photograph prominently displayed.

On the afternoon of the concert the Birdland management requested a police watch, what with expectations of a large crowd bound to be disappointed when they found there would be no tickets available for day-of-performance rates that night. The musicians had scheduled a rehearsal inside the hall and most arrived early and entered Birdland through the stage door.

Not Miles Davis.

Davis walked up to the police cordon and tried walking through as if he were the star, which he was.

"Nobody through here," a cop said.

Miles Davis ignored the remark and tried getting through anyway and a few more cops told him that nobody was allowed through. So Davis introduced himself.

It was no soap. "Yeah, yeah. Well, I don't care if you're Uncle Remus, you ain't getting through here," a cop said. Something like that.

Davis was highly irritated. He pointed to the billboards right behind the cops, the ones with his photo. What transpired after that is still at issue, as there was never any trial. The word "nigger" came up several times during the melee that pursued. One thing led to another and Miles Davis was hospitalized after being beaten with a nightstick.

The dust hadn't begun to settle when Davis' attorneys filed separate $10,000,000 lawsuits against the following: six cops, personally; the city of New York; the mayor; the music hall; the police commissioner. Quite obviously, lawsuits of this nature are subject to some extensive pretrial negotiation and some are even settled out of court.

The trouble with the Davis case was that the musician refused to talk to anyone connected with the city—most especially the police department—who happened to have a white face. Enter Herbert Charles, rookie police officer of the Times Square precinct.

"This day and age, a rookie would never have the opportunity I had then. It was a freak opportunity, of course, but I sure did run with it," Charles said.

He became the official go-between in the city's negotiations with Miles Davis, a well-known international performer who was beaten senseless by the New York Police Department for behaving like some uppity nigger. Never mind about the big photograph in the billboard right under the noses of the cops who beat him.

Davis settled with the city out of court for what was then a considerable sum, even though it was far short of the fantastical $10,000,000 figure. He settled for $250,000.

"We had one hell of a party," Charles said. "Back then, I had to sort of sneak on over to the party. You know, I was the city representative and the city was the bad guy in the piece. But I'll tell you now I had a great time at that party."

Herbie Charles is still in contact with the jazz musicians he met during that period.

In '56 he was a little worried that his function with the police department might be related strictly to cases involving racial controversy. Charles was and is, after all, a calm, reassuring man, intelligent and quiet and fair. In short, a good man to put into a volatile setting, and during the late 1950s men of such cool stability were rare when it came to racial matters.

Two years after his handling the Miles Davis matter, with a level-headed diplomacy not in the highest councils of government today, let alone in a rookie foot patrolman, Herb Charles would show his superior officers that his temperament was a good police quality across the board. It happened the day before Thanksgiving, 1958.

Officer Herbert Charles was walking his beat in Times Square, as usual. At one point he stood outside a saloon on Seventh Avenue called the Pick-a-Rib, popular with gamblers, journalists and other lowlifes.

Charles stood with his back to the window of the Pick-a-Rib, watching the passing parade of Times Square. It was a peaceable day. The theaters would have matinees that afternoon, a Wednesday, and most New Yorkers would stay away from Times Square in droves in their weekly sharing of the heart of the city with little old ladies from out of town. There would be an early performance that night, then the theaters would close down for the holiday.

Herbert Charles watched the street, said hello to some shopkeepers he knew as they passed him by and he thought about the dinner his wife and his mother were planning, jointly, for tomorrow's holiday. It was a first cooperative effort and, Charles hoped, a pleasant one. Herb Charles liked peace in his household since he had little of that on the job.

He heard a crash of glass behind him, then felt shards of it rip into the exposed skin of his neck. He ducked his head reflexively and a bullet whizzed by, striking a telephone booth.

Suddenly, from the barroom door, came somebody Charles knew— Officer Jimmy McDermott, an Irish cop he'd been friendly with many times after tour.

"There's been a shooting, Herbie," McDermott told Charles. "I'll go turn it in. You take over here."

McDermott, senior to Charles, ran up Seventh Avenue. Charles went into the bar and found five dead men.

"From the position of them, I knew only that someone had just taken shots at these guys, maybe just five to eight shots, and nailed every one. It looked like some plan, except that the five guys were in all different places around the horseshoe bar."

Somebody told Charles that the killer was the guy who just ran out the door.

Jimmy McDermott the cop?

A backup uniform team came into the bar. Charles had them take over and ran up Seventh Avenue in search of the fleeing Jimmy Mc-Dermott, dreading what he might come across, if he was able to catch up to him.

Never in his life had Charles run like he did that November afternoon. He was one of a handful of cops in the city who knew that cops were just as easily brutal as the next guy, just as corruptible and just as redeemable. And that's what made Charles run that day. He was a cop, a black cop when simply that combination made you a controversial man, and he was a believer in the possibility that one honest soul could change a society in need of changing. He'd picked the New York City Police Department to change.

He sighted McDermott, walking along Seventh. He called out. Mc-Dermott spun around and drew a gun out of his pants pocket and fired. Charles ducked and McDermott took off again.

His lungs and legs ached and he was afraid for his life, but Herb Charles knew he was chasing, for whatever reason, a madman who was a threat to innocent people.

From out of nowhere, it seemed, a pair of detectives he knew appeared on a corner. They saw the fleeing McDermott. One of the detectives knew him and called out. McDermott answered with a shot. Then the detectives saw Charles in pursuit.

"We'll radio!" one of them called as Charles passed them by in full sprint.

In a second or two, a squad car jumped the curb and cut off McDermott, who fired on it.

Charles drew his gun, dropped to his knees and assumed the firing stance. But he didn't have to shoot. Another cop did and McDermott fell.

Charles was credited with the capture and he earned a gold shield for it, becoming now Detective Herbert Charles.

"What we found out after all that was a whole lot of nothing," Charles said. "We reconstructed what happened and it played like this:

"McDermott walks into the Pick-a-Rib and takes a spot standing at the bar. There are five guys, all of them very big gamblers, standing around the bar, but they're not talking to one another. They're just there, that's all. McDermott takes a gun out and starts firing. He's got a couple shots that go wild, which I felt with the glass flying out all over me, but he gets all five, one at a time, bing-bang-bing-bang-bing, right in the forehead and they fall backward dead as doornails.

"The only thing we know is that the dead guys are gamblers, that's all. We don't have any hint of any trouble in McDermott's life. Everybody and his brother talked to his widow, trying to figure out what the hell happened and we get exactly nowhere. Nothing makes any sense.

"McDermott, so far as his closest buddies knew, was no gambler. He didn't owe any juice guys money and he never had any reason to borrow so much as a yard in his whole life anyway. He was a good, solid Irish cop and a family man. A straight shooter in more ways than one, as it happened.

"To this day, nobody knows why. No connection was found between McDermott and any of the guys he killed and there was no particular connection that tied the five together. Nothing in McDermott's background gave us a hint.

"It might have been that he would have skipped town or something. That's the only conclusion you could draw. My first instinct was to help a fellow officer and if I hadn't thought about what we call 'worst scenario' now, well maybe he'd have killed someone else."

The way Keenan saw it, the first thing he had to do was get hold of Dory Smith. Maybe she'd be cooled down by now.

He telephoned her apartment from a pay phone on Lexington Avenue. He didn't want anyone hearing at the station house.

She answered on the first ring, which surprised him. For a solid week, all he'd received was her answering machine and she hadn't returned his calls.

"Hi," he said.

She recognized his voice, of course. She'd been waiting to hear from him, hoping desperately to hear.

"Tommy, I'm so glad you called."

"I have to see you."

"When?"

"What about tonight?"

"Tonight's Christmas Eve. What about your family?"

"I'll handle it. I have to see you."

"Good," she said. "I don't feel like being alone for the eighth year in a row."

"I can be there at seven."

Ed Smith and his ex-wife, Ruth, and their daughter, Eve, had dinner at Gage & Tollner in downtown Brooklyn. He'd been seeing Ruth every day since he knocked on her door, wondering every day if it would be possible to step back in time.

Tonight, as they walked through snowy streets and listened to the crunching beneath their feet, each holding a hand of their little girl and hoisting her up into the air between them when she jumped over some imaginary hill, Ruth said to him, "Could you see yourself married to me again?"

How could he answer a question like that? He could only think to ask her the question in reverse. And the answer to that would be no. For the past several days, he'd shown her the face she wanted to see, the face of a man fully possessed of power and confidence. But it wasn't real. Smith had stayed cleaned up for a very long time now and he wasn't growing into it. He felt conspicuous on the street, though his work hadn't suffered particularly. He was just in a different mode, that's all. He could return to being a bum if he wanted, any time.

He was good at it. All that it required to be a man nobody wanted to pay any attention to, especially women, was to take on the look of a man beaten down, saddened beyond repair. People want to move on to others when they encounter such a man.

For a few days, Ed Smith had at least looked like the sort of man Ruth wanted. He hadn't asked a single question about Darryl, though he was burning to know what had happened. More than that, he wanted to get back to his own closed-up little world, God help him.

But there she was, so beautiful in the moonlight of Christmas Eve, proposing to him. Could this have happened last year? Or next?

He struggled to keep in mind two truths he'd developed for himself over the years. Both had to do with women.

The first truth was that women are creatures who operate by a code that no one, to Smith's knowledge, had ever been able to crack. The second was a little more complicated.

Of all the divorced couples Ed Smith knew, there was the common element of a residual struggle to keep the union together. This usually occurred just before the ink had dried on the final decree. Suddenly, there were new statements of undying love and affection.

Smith used to think this crazy because he'd felt the same way twice himself. But when he saw it happen with other people, over and over again, he began to understand the phenomenon for what it was, a basic human need to hang on to the only thing that can be owned or fully known, the past. Probably, it kept the human species alive and well, this urge to stay together.

But there was a requirement that had to be met by all the couples that none fully realized until it was either too late or until they understood themselves to be twice romantically blessed. The requirement was that you had to fall in love with her, or him, all over again, knowing even more than you knew the first time around. It was a difficult trick and most people Smith knew took it far too lightly.

Here was Ruth, though, proposing to him on Christmas Eve, with their little girl bouncing along with the pure joy of the occasion. Ruth, it seemed, had fallen in love with Ed Smith all over again. Or had she fallen in love with the image he'd set out deliberately to project? Was this what he'd been trying to get from her, after all? Just this moment and nothing more?

"I've been thinking about it, if that's what you mean," he said to her.

She smiled. "We've got time to talk later."

They had a fine dinner and went home to Ruth's place on Pineapple Street. Smith stayed over.

He awoke from a sound sleep screaming. The usual nightmare.

Keenan hadn't said anything about dinner. He hadn't said anything at all about why he had to see her, but Dory had a full table set out for him in her little apartment.

The last time he saw her, the night he slept off a drunk in his car and Ciffo had taken him home, Dory had set out dinner, too. She asked him then his intentions and he told her that sounded oddly antique to him, but he didn't believe that; it was just something to say at that moment.

"Are you going to divorce her?" she asked.

Keenan hadn't thought about that. He hadn't thought about marrying Dory Smith, either, which would be a reason for seeking a divorce from Mairead. He told her this.

"I'm to be your mistress, is that it?"

He hardly considered her such. A mistress was a woman who was supported financially, which he couldn't do. A mistress was a woman who provided a married man an extra sexual outlet, but their relationship was only minimally sexual, Keenan reminded Dory.

She began crying then. Keenan reached over to touch her and she made a sort of growling sound. She clawed him and drew blood.

He left her that night and drove around to two or three saloons down in the Seventeenth Precinct. He never remembered driving back up into the Nineteenth and parking near Tony Ciffo's Fuego.

. . . . Now, on Christmas Eve, they were back as they were. Dory said she wanted a "fresh start." Keenan wanted to end it between them, but it sure was going to be hard, what with the giddy mood she was in. She had a present for him, she kept saying.

They looked at each other with very pleasant faces, but they couldn't find much to talk about. When they first started seeing one another, they talked into the night, into many mornings, and Keenan was in his "glory," she had said, so funny and articulate, drunk or no.

It never occurred to Dory Smith what Keenan had in mind in the way of an announcement that evening. Otherwise, she might not have told him midway through their meal that she was pregnant.

Detective Theresa Enterlin was one hour away from quitting her tour to go home on Christmas Eve. So was Detective Herbert Charles. Then came the telephone call from Nadine Weinstock.

Detective Enterlin heard her out, calmed her down as best she could, and said, "You're just going to have to go ahead with it. Don't worry, we'll be right there with you. There's no danger in this and you'll be helping a lot of other young women. Okay?"

She wrote down information on a pad for several minutes, then went to Detective Charles' desk and spoke to him about it.

"Well, you know we're likely to get the collar on this," he said. "And you know that means we'll be stuck here two, maybe three hours longer with the booking and the paper on it."

"What choice do we have?"

"Little. Make that none. How many cases will it wipe away?"

"Over seventy."

"Let's tell the boss. I'm with you."

"Thanks," Enterlin said.

"You're welcome, but I don't think there's any choice here."

"Thanks anyway."

In another ten minutes, Detectives Enterlin and Charles were off in an unmarked car to the corner of Second Avenue and Eighty-ninth Street, a block from a place called Elaine's, the famous watering hole frequented by such celebrities as Woody Allen and Mia Farrow. But the place Enterlin and Charles were concerned with was an all-night laundromat, the suggested rendezvous point.

There, Nadine Weinstock was to meet a man she knew as Peter Michaels, also known by various others as Michael Peters, Peter Michaelson, Peter Mitchell, Peter McMaster and Michael Patterson. Peter was wanted in three states—New York, Connecticut and New Jersey—on a total of seventy-six complaints, some of which had gone as far as the preliminary examination stage, of theft, alienation of affection, unlawful use of automobiles and forgery.

All the charges against Peter involved his prodigious talent for making lonely young single women, most of his victims residents of Manhattan, fall absolutely in love with him. If Nadine Weinstock's story was any indication, his pattern was pretty much unvaried. Detective Enterlin had first heard of the mysterious Peter three years ago. Nadine

Weinstock was the only woman she could manage to keep angry enough to help her engineer an arrest.

About eight months ago, Nadine Weinstock and a girl friend went and did what they vowed, for perhaps the tenth time, they would never stoop to doing again. They dropped into one of the dozens of Upper East Side singles bars.

Peter was smitten with Nadine Weinstock, a slight, pleasant-looking young woman with wavy red hair and brown eyes and a long, slightly crooked nose who bit her nails rather badly and worked as a researcher for a scientific publishing firm. Her parents had staked her to a first apartment in the city, a bright place in a large, well-secured building on York Avenue at Ninety-first Street, and they hoped for the best.

Nadine Weinstock was like a lot of other young men and women on the Upper East Side, migrants from moneyed suburbs who stay in the city for a requisite period, marry as well as they can and then move back to the sort of places they came from in the first place. They are both attracted to the city and repelled by it and the Upper East Side allows for a glimpse of urbanity without having to actually get one's feet too terribly wet. With very little preparation for the urban challenge in the way of character and texture, the Nadines of the Nineteenth Precinct are perfect opportunities for the likes of Peter. His job is achingly simple. He simply talks to them gently in a saloon where the drinks are overpriced and the patrons are overly trustful.

He told her that he worked in the fur trade and he was pleasant and funny and low-keyed. He bought her a drink and then said he had to find a hotel somewhere because the most unbelievable thing had happened to him.

"What?" she asked. They always did.

"Nothing that can't be repaired in a few days, anyway. Maybe a week. It'll set me back, but I'll make it."

"What?"

Peter had been robbed, he said, and he'd ducked into this bar to have himself a drink when he realized that his keys had been stolen along with his billfold and that since he was new to the city he hadn't left keys with anyone. He wouldn't be able to get into his apartment without having the door broken down, since the super didn't have a key for the private dead bolt he'd installed.

"Well, it's a mess. I'm just lucky I'm sort of paranoid and keep some cash in my shoe, that's all."

She bought *him* a drink. Then she had another. And he said he'd really have to be going. But he didn't go and she didn't seem to mind and he knew he had her.

Peter went home with Nadine that night and made love to her and told her she was beautiful, a lie she had been waiting to hear from a man for many years. When she woke, she found him busy in her kitchen. He was so sweet. And a pretty fair hand with breakfast.

He didn't have to go to work that day, he told her. Nadine did.

"Why don't you just take your time? Stay around here as long as you like," she said.

Then just as she left, she asked him, "Will I see you when I get home, I hope?"

"If you want," he said. "I'd like that very much. My God, what a way to meet. What a story we'll have for our grandchildren."

Detective Enterlin had heard this same tale, with only slight alterations, for three years. Peter had been a very busy man. Enterlin personally had twenty-eight young women complainants and there were that many and more in the suburban communities around New York and New Jersey and even more that she would never hear about.

Peter was at home in Nadine Weinstock's apartment when she returned, all right. He said he'd taken care of everything in regard to his own place, but he would be really short on funds until his insurance company paid off.

Nadine loaned him several hundred dollars and wondered the next day where she could have misplaced her diamond earrings.

She didn't see Peter for two days, then he called her and asked if they might get together, his treat. His insurance company had come through early for him.

The dinner was wonderful and Peter was expansive, telling Nadine of his dreams of independence in business, wealth and what he would do with it and with whom he would share it. "It could be you," he told her.

Another lie that chained her to Peter. He spent the night at her place. And again, his day was free. Nadine went off to work, returned to find Peter fussing around her kitchen and fixing the refrigerator, which made too much noise. The next day she was missing cash and another piece of jewelry, a ring of no particular value she had purchased at a crafts show in Maine.

Peter expressed alarm when she told him that she thought someone had been stealing her belongings. He was convincing. She didn't see him for another week, during which time her television set, stereo system, the rest of her jewelry and a mink wrap were stolen on Thursday. The police came and looked around and asked if anyone had a key to her place.

Yes, she said. Her boy friend. But she was sure it couldn't be him.

She replaced her belongings, little by little. But they would be stolen again, promptly after one of Peter's furtive but entirely charming visits.

Then one evening Nadine returned to the singles bar where she'd met Peter. And there he was. She wasn't seen by him. But she watched Peter go through his act, watched him leave the bar with the somewhat homely young woman.

That became her first call to the Nineteenth Precinct and her first contact with Detective Enterlin.

Now, on Christmas Eve, for God knows what reason, Peter had telephoned Nadine and asked her to meet him at this laundromat. For lack of anything better to do, Nadine even brought a bag of laundry along with her. Detective Enterlin sat in a plastic chair inside the laundromat and watched dryers spin around on Christmas Eve. Outside, a few doors down, Herbert Charles looked at a ten-year-old photograph, the only one available, of the man who would make the night pay off, hopefully.

The photo was very blurred and Charles couldn't make very much of it. The profile wasn't much more helpful. White male, approximately thirty-eight, brown hair, brown eyes, even features, five feet and ten inches, medium build.

Charles tried to think how many women this man had bedded in his years and he shook his head. Charles was a man who had every sort of pleasure and every sort of problem he wanted to know about all wrapped up in his wife.

Peter was late.

Fifteen minutes had gone by since the time Peter said he would be at the laundromat. Detective Enterlin told Nadine to continue waiting for him, to walk home with him if he showed. She and Charles would go to her building. Maybe they'd scared him off, she suggested.

Another twenty minutes passed as Enterlin and Charles waited, parked outside Nadine's building on York Avenue. They talked about daughters.

"I can't complain," Enterlin said. "She stayed home the whole time, right through her engagement and all. I remember her saying to me, 'Why should I move out on my own? I want to save up my money and stay right here. Then we'll be able to get a real nice place.' "

"That's exactly the way it was with my older daughter. The same thing," Charles said. "But my younger girl! Oh boy, she just knew it all. She had to have her own place. Well, she did all right."

Enterlin saw him first.

"My God, we've got him," she said.

Charles saw Nadine pulling her laundry in a little cart.

"The guy can't even pull her laundry cart?" he said. He studied the picture he was holding and then looked at Peter, in the flesh, as he made his way around the corner toward the entrance of Nadine's building. "I expected some sort of Adonis, I must say. Look at this guy. Does he have a wart or something on his nose, or am I seeing things?"

"You're not seeing things."

Charles chuckled.

"I'm going to go in right after them," Enterlin said. "Pull up right after they go inside the door. Let me get beyond the second door before you come in."

Nadine and Peter walked through the first door. Enterlin stepped out of the car and walked into the doorway behind the two. A grandmotherly woman with a neat red hairdo was not a suspicious character so far as Peter was concerned. He held the inner door open for her after Nadine had used her key.

Nadine walked ahead toward the elevator and Peter ran a comb through his hair quickly, glancing at himself in a small mirror on the lobby wall.

"Peter?" Detective Enterlin asked the man with the pronounced wart on his nose.

Nadine started crying softly, her face averted.

"Yes?"

"I'm Detective Enterlin, Nineteenth Precinct. This is Detective Charles."

Charles stood behind Enterlin now. She had left a wad of paper stuck in the door so he could get inside.

"We have bench warrants for your arrest, Peter. Now I'm going to read you your rights while Detective Charles puts the handcuffs on you."

"Let's go, pal," Charles said. "Maybe you know the drill?"

Charles placed a hand on the shoulders of a very bewildered Peter Michaels and assorted aliases and guided him to the wall opposite the elevator. He placed a foot between Peter's legs and gently kicked his feet apart.

"Hands on the wall, over your head," he told Peter.

Charles patted down the suspect, pulled his arms behind his waist and snapped on a pair of cuffs. "Too tight?" he asked Peter.

"Yeah."

"Sorry, man. I'll loosen them a bit if I can."

Detective Enterlin read him his rights. He understood.

Nadine Weinstock sobbed and bit her lip and stood near the elevator with her laundry cart while the man she had loved, no matter what he'd done, was taken away from her. She had had him taken away. He didn't look back.

Peter's jeans were awfully tight for a man with a paunch and he had trouble getting into the cramped back seat.

"You're eating too well these days, Peter," Detective Enterlin said. She took the driver's seat while Charles climbed in back with the suspect and tried his best to do something about the tightness of the cuffs.

"It won't be long, man," Charles said. "It's the rules, you know."

"Does Nadine know?" Peter asked.

Enterlin turned around and looked at Peter before she started up the car. "Should she know something, Peter?"

"I don't know."

Detective Charles chuckled. "Peter, my man, you're a legend in your own time."

18

When the holidays had passed, but still long before the air would warm, Cibella Borges was officially dismissed as a police officer of New York City. It was finally over for her and she was happy about that part of it, at least. She talked to reporters in her lawyer's office and hoped that part of it would be over, too.

"I knew they were going to fire me, but I kept hoping and praying," she said. "I liked my job very much."

She didn't think she would, but she sobbed. The newspaper photographers elbowed each other for the best angle at capturing the moment in a picture, the fall of the "nudie cop, Naughty Nina."

Her lawyer, Michael Vecchione, insisted his client had broken neither the law nor the rules of official conduct of the police department as spelled out in the handbook. What else could he say? What would anyone expect him to say?

"When she posed for the magazines," Vecchione said, "she was not a police officer."

It was a defense that had been totally unsuccessful where it counted, which was during Borges' departmental trial. The hearing officer, Departmental Trials Commissioner Jaime Rios, rejected the defense and sided with the prosecuting officer, who simply noted that civilian employees of the police department were subject to the same rules and regulations as sworn personnel and that's just what the handbook said. Cibella Borges was a civilian police employee at the time of the photo sessions with *Beaver* magazine and the call that a judge had to make involved whether her conduct was detrimental to the department and her function as a part of that department—*not* whether she was an officer or a clerk. It was a bit of hair that Vecchione simply could not split, no matter how mightily he tried.

Vecchione's only success came in winning Borges a string of pretrial delays, mostly due, he said, to her schedules for surgery. Now he told the press that he would file appeals.

What else was he expected to say?

But Cibella Borges, for her part, wanted to clear up questions that had nothing to do with lawyers or courts or handbooks. She wanted the reporters to know, for instance, that she did not pose "for the money." She posed, she said, because she had doubts about her sexuality, that she was terribly confused about her femininity and that—rightly or wrongly—she thought that spreading her legs for the pages of a magazine purchased by lonely men might prove her femininity.

"My doctor told me I had to go in for another operation," she said, "and that there was something wrong with my insides. My reaction, like any other female, was I thought I had cancer.

"But I could see it in his face. He told me I could never have kids. I was twenty-two years old."

The reporters wrote down her comments in their notebooks, with neither question nor challenge to whatever she had to say on this, her final day of attention from them.

Even so, this final press confrontation—which had begun with the tabloid headline writers and their delightful tags and with Cibella Borges' pro forma lies—was winding down as a sort of pornography, a very pathetic sort.

"I wanted to feel like a woman!" Cibella declared.

There was a terrible pause and then Cibella's shoulders heaved and she began sobbing uncontrollably and covering her face with her hands. She sat up straight when she had regained some of her control and the photographers danced again. It had been far more dignified posing naked, posing lewdly, for a single photographer in his studio than this. Now dozens of photographers, lenses for faces, pushed and shoved in order to best show the multitudes what Cibella Borges looked like now —stripped of her emotional stability.

Newspaper publishers would always have the best of both worlds. They could profit by pornography by teasing their readers with snappy headlines, they could even show the downfall of the headlined lady.

They could do this and they didn't even have to pay Cibella for the privilege. And they would sell more copies of their newspapers than the likes of *Beaver* or *Pub* or *Girls on Girls* could ever hope.

The cameras clicked.

"I was somewhere else when I met the photographer," she said of Tony Currin, whose testimony helped damn her, "and I thought I had nothing to lose.

"I had an 'I don't care' attitude. I wasn't thinking about the department, I didn't even think of the family. I was nervous and I was scared."

Then Vecchione talked again. Nobody bothered taking his picture.

He went over his defense again, relating how he'd told Commissioner Rios that prior to Borges even thinking of posing in the buff—or not thinking, as the case was, according to his client—she had been officially disqualified for hiring as a cop because of her extensive history of surgery.

Some eighteen months after posing for *Beaver,* as it turned out, though, Cibella Borges was notified that there had been a waiver in her case. Three days after that, she was inducted into training as a cop.

Cibella Borges wept. The image of a dark-haired, dark-eyed, diminutive Dominican beauty who had been a fair cop in her day was transmitted around the world via United Press International and the Associated Press.

Her shame would live, her fame would die quickly.

The late afternoon edition of the New York *Post* would commemorate the event thusly:

I PRAYED FOR MERCY,
SOBS FIRED NUDIE COP

Girl gets boot over
poses in skin mags

Back in the Nineteenth Precinct station house, Cibella Borges' sympathizers were male, her detractors female.

"We felt sorry for her at first," Officer Jean Truta said, "but then, as the story came out, more and more. Well, it's not just that she doesn't belong on the police force because of this, it's much more.

"It's not easy being a woman and a cop at the same time. You can't be just a 'cop.' You're a 'lady cop.' When have you ever read about a 'gentleman cop'? We've got something at stake here.

"I feel sorry for her, but I can't sympathize. There was a defense fund going around once. I didn't contribute. I don't think any of the women did."

On the very same day that Commissioner Rios handed down his ruling against Cibella Borges, two gentlemen cops were arrested in a Times Square bar in the tiny hours.

They had allegedly been performing a striptease. After their strip, it was alleged, the gentleman officers raped and "sodomized," according to the report, a woman on hand at the bar.

The officers were fired.

"We have a hell of a good chance, because the most important thing in something like this is controlling the location. And we've done that."

Detective Charlie Leinau was explaining the finer points of what he hoped would be a sting to his very eager listener, William W. Whitson.

"And just by being able to do that, to set the place, we learned something about who we're dealing with," he said to Whitson. "Know what that is?"

Whitson thought for a moment. On Leinau's instruction, he'd followed the directions of his blackmailer and placed an ad in the personals section of the weekly *Village Voice*. In the ad he acknowledged receipt of the letters and said he would be willing to meet. But he added something, at Leinau's instruction. The meeting place would be of his choosing or else he'd call the police.

"Well, they didn't quibble about it much," Whitson said. "They seemed in a hurry to get it over with."

"And bingo! That's it, exactly. We're dealing with idiots. Not just greenhorns, but idiots. They can be intimidated. When you can intimidate your perps, you've got them by the balls, which is just where you want to have them. It feels so good when you squeeze them hard."

Whitson nodded, smiling with appreciation.

"Lot like business, ain't it?"

"It is, indeed, Detective Leinau. It is indeed."

Leinau sipped his coffee through a hole he'd made in the plastic top.

"I don't know why I'm drinking this stuff out here. I could be in there, where it's nice and warm."

He and Whitson sat in an unmarked squad car across from one of Leinau's favored meeting spots, a large coffee shop on a Park Avenue corner, adjoining a hotel used by Prince Rainier and his sort of crowd. Leinau checked his wristwatch. Still too early.

The restaurant had big glass windows, one facing the avenue, the other the street. That way, squad cars could be situated in at least eight positions for a clear view of the entire dining room.

Besides the door to the avenue, the only other way out of the restaurant was through a smaller doorway connecting the coffee shop with the hotel lobby by way of a small corridor lined with telephone booths, the handiest thing in the world for cops on a stakeout. Leinau had a man from the weekend anticrime squad sitting in one of those booths at this minute.

It was a Saturday and it was twenty minutes to ten o'clock in the morning.

Leinau had wanted a Saturday because there would be just enough people in the coffee shop to make the perps feel comfortable, but not the usual weekday crowd that would make it hard for the cops to maintain a close watch. Leinau also figured that the perps might have jobs. Perps didn't like to take off work. It might create suspicion. It had played this way more than once. The hoods liked things smooth and trouble-free, just like the cops.

"Did you check on Mickey like I told you?" Leinau asked. He was almost ready to make his move.

"Of course. I gave him a twenty and told him I needed work done in the kitchen right away, this morning, as we'll be entertaining tonight."

"And he never complained?"

"Ordinarily, he would, even for the twenty. Not today, though."

"Great."

Mickey thought he was creating himself an alibi, should any little thing go wrong. What Mickey couldn't figure was that the cops wanted to know exactly where he was at a specific time.

"Poor fellow," Leinau said. "Actually, he's a very good super."

"Yeah, when he's not shaking down the tenants."

Leinau picked lint off the lapel of his new topcoat.

"I think I can get the I.R.S. to go along with this," he said. "How do I look?"

Whitson brushed his shoulder.

"Excellent. Top drawer. Really, I'm well pleased."

Beneath the navy cashmere coat, Leinau wore an Irish tweed jacket with soft shoulders, wool gabardine slacks with sharp creases, a lamb-suède vest, a cotton broadcloth shirt and a knit tie. There wasn't an unnatural fiber on his entire body that day.

"Well, here I go," Leinau said. "The final touch."

Leinau used both hands to place Whitson's homburg just so, cocked at the distinctive angle. Whitson handed him the cane—a light maple with dark veins and a huge brass wolf's head.

"Wish me luck," Leinau said.

Whitson saluted and put on his own headgear for the duration of the play. "Easy does it."

Leinau opened the door and stepped out of the car. Then he walked jauntily across the avenue and into the coffee shop, was shown to a table and sat down, wired for sound. He didn't remove his hat and placed the cane on the table in front of him.

Keenan had things figured out.

Sure, Dory Smith was pregnant. And she was right, no doubt. He was the father. At least he assumed she had no other lovers. She was as unskillful, as unsure of sex as he was.

But these days, as far as the world was concerned, how could a reasonably good-looking single woman on the Upper East Side of Manhattan be sleeping with only one man? Well, she could press for a paternity test in some lawsuit. But why?

As for Mairead, well, his wife was completely dependent on him, wasn't she? Even more so, now that the baby was only a month away. How would a girl like Mairead make it in the world without him?

Dory could have an abortion, any time between now and the next forty days or so, and it wouldn't do her a bit of damage, now would it?

Sometimes, when things seem their darkest, the sun comes out. Isn't that the truth?

Well, a body could talk himself into such things.

Keenan had done so. And then he'd talked to the inspector and managed to get himself off the ignoble bow-and-arrow squad. He was back at it, in uniform and on general patrol, his gun back on his hip where it belonged.

And he swore he'd never so much as look at another woman. Mairead was plenty for him, and since he'd been paying a bit of attention to her lately, she was doing what she could to prompt genuine interest beyond his charitable considerations.

This morning he'd left the house early and driven first to Dory's building. He rang her apartment and she came to meet him in the lobby. He handed over an envelope containing six hundred-dollar bills.

"For the operation, I suppose?" Dory asked.

"Are you going to refuse?"

She looked like she might spit in his face. "No, I'm going to take it." She did, turned on him and marched back up the stairway to her apartment.

A bit wobbly in the legs, Keenan left her building, got into his car and drove to his regular parking space. He felt clean and detached, in control. He thanked his lucky stars.

Inside the muster room, Keenan dialed from the pay phone and reached his pal, a cop in the Times Square precinct who could get house tickets to all the Broadway shows. Keenan arranged a pair on the aisle to *Dreamgirls*, a very hot ticket. Mairead would like that. Then he dialed Mama Leone's restaurant and made dinner reservations for two.

Minnie Margoles, seventy-one years old, spent the war years on the Upper East Side watching pasty-faced young men who didn't amount to much march around Yorkville with swastika armbands, which they wore right out in the streets, until the attack on Pearl Harbor anyway and the entry of her beloved United States into the fighting.

"It's an amazing thing about America," she used to say when she told stories about the war years, "how the hatred was paraded around on the streets, openly. And yet this is the safest country in the world."

Her husband joined the Army and died somewhere in France for his troubles.

Then after the war, Minnie went to Europe in search of her parents, who ignored her importunings for so many years. They would stay in Germany. "Why not?" her mother asked in letters. "We were born here. We should come to America, to your New York? Here in Germany, we have read newspapers of Nazis in New York, too."

It had been an easy matter finding her father, or record of him. The Germans kept excellent records when they wished. Nathan Margoles had been among the first to die at Bergen-Belsen, of a heart attack. It probably meant that he had not known a fraction of the terror and the torture that his fellow inmates at the concentration camp knew. She was able to believe this. Her father had a long history of heart trouble.

But it took four months to find her mother. Four months of mystery, until Minnie herself suggested that perhaps her mother was classified under her father's name rather than her husband's.

Finally, Minnie found her, in a sanitorium in the village near Buchenwald. Minnie wished she had died, as her father had; she wished her mother was at peace. Instead, the woman lived in some hideously private, all-encompassing panic, her visions so monstrous they robbed her of the ability to free herself by telling her tale. She could not speak, could not sleep with her eyes shut, could not control her bodily functions. She could not die. The woman who scoffed at the notion of leaving Germany for America—"a civilized nation we have here, not some place where gangsters shoot each other in the streets just to sell some beer"—was now taken to New York, where her daughter would take care of her until her death.

Minnie worked two jobs, one in a bakery and one in a millinery at night, in order to make ends meet. Her mother's care was expensive. Minnie's friends used to tell her that she didn't have to work herself like a horse for her mother, that there were fine homes where her mother would be made comfortable, places that would cost so much less, where she might even get some government help in the expenses.

"No," Minnie said, "I'll take care of her. I should have brought her here. I should have. Now I'll take care."

When her mother finally died, Minnie began losing her health and began to know a fear generally ignored by the young and then suddenly known in the dark of some night when the firm, strong grip of a desperate young man cuts off their breathing, when their arms are twisted and they fall to the street, when their money is stolen, when they are shoved into their apartments and forced to lie helplessly on the floor while their precious things are thrown about in the barbaric search for cash, jewelry, anything valuable and portable.

It had happened to Minnie once, a year after her mother had gone. The short man with the scraggly beard, the blue eyes and the friendly smile was not the delivery man she thought he was. She stepped off the elevator to her floor and walked down the corridor. She'd pushed her key into her door when she heard his footsteps. He hadn't let the elevator door close. He'd waited for her to open her door.

He rushed her, hit her in the neck, knocking her to the floor. He made off with forty dollars in cash, a brass samovar that had been a wedding gift from her husband's parents and a black and white television set badly in need of repair.

It was seven weeks before Minnie lost the pain, then another two weeks before she worked up the courage to leave her apartment.

A friend told her that now it was over. She had been a statistic and the odds against it happening again, especially now that her building had become such a fancy place, were slim.

She believed it, until the day she saw the boy with the swastika on a chain around his neck.

Minnie was returning to her apartment, at York Avenue and Eighty-eighth Street, from grocery shopping. The boy, one of those "punks" with his hair dyed a greasy black, looked at her handbag, then looked behind him.

Minnie trembled and clutched her bag close to her body. There was no one near her, no one but this boy looking at an old lady's handbag. She couldn't take her eyes off the swastika. She tried screaming, but, like her mother, she could not speak.

The boy with the swastika began running toward Minnie.

A young man named Eddie at that very moment came around a corner, just behind Minnie Margoles, a tenant in the building where he worked as a doorman. He didn't plan on making the job a career, not by any means. Eddie's father had been a New York City police officer and Eddie was bound and determined to follow in his footsteps.

Eddie had a cup of steaming coffee in one gloved hand and a slice of pizza in the other. He tossed both on the street when he saw the boy grab Mrs. Margoles' bag.

Eddie made a lunge at the boy as he ran past him, leaving Mrs. Margoles spinning about a little on her feet. Somehow, she found her voice and called to Eddie, "I'm all right."

Then Eddie took flight, screaming loudly at the fleeing boy about a block in front. "Stop him! Stop him, everybody! He mugged an old lady!"

A taxicab driver stepped out of his yellow vehicle and stood in the boy's path, landing a heavy body block that wobbled him, but not enough to stop him. Eddie gained a half block.

"Stop him! Everybody, stop him!"

The boy tossed the handbag.

A Korean greengrocer threw apples at the boy. Two women, waiting for a bus, screamed at him. A man in a suit picked up a brick and threw it at the boy, missing him.

Eddie was gaining. And along with Eddie, four men and a teenage girl were in pursuit of the boy who robbed Mrs. Margoles.

"Stop him! Stop him!" An entire block full of people were shouting.

The boy stumbled and fell.

Eddie was all over him. He picked him up by his jacket and, with one hand and an entire body full of rage, heaved him against a store-front steel grate, opening a big wound in the boy's temple.

Someone shouted, "I'll call the cops. Hold him!"

Eddie pulled the boy's arms behind his back and bent them upward. One of the men who'd joined Eddie's chase started kicking the boy's face. Another man kicked him in the ribs several times.

"Get back, get back!" Eddie yelled. "We don't want him to get off because of what we do."

He managed to persuade the men who were kicking the boy. People in the street behind them pulled the men away.

"Okay, we'll just wait now," Eddie said. "You going to be any trouble?"

The boy shook his head.

In less than a minute, a squad car pulled up at York Avenue and Eighty-second Street. The boy looked at the uniformed officers like they were saviors. He collapsed into their arms, was tossed into the back seat and manacled.

Eddie had taken the police civil service test once before and just missed being hired. He would take it the next time it was offered.

Leinau looked at his watch again. Fifteen minutes past the meeting time.

He looked out the avenue window. The headlights of his car were still off. Whitson would turn them on when he saw it come down.

Another fifteen minutes, Leinau decided. No more. He would rather scrub a meeting than risk being made. Another meeting was a very easy matter when a potential of one million dollars was involved.

"Sir?" the red-jacketed waiter asked him.

"Another coffee."

"I'll have to charge you extra for it, sir. We have a one refill policy here."

"Cheap fucking place. All right, go ahead and gouge me."

The waiter rolled his eyes and went for the service station.

Whitson, waiting in the car and picking up the conversation on the radio receiver, chuckled.

An imposing black man approached Leinau's table.

"The man in the homburg?" he said. "With the cane." His eyes fell to the cane across the table.

Leinau motioned him to sit.

"Would your friend like anything?" the waiter asked when he arrived with Leinau's coffee.

"My friend wants a very great deal," Leinau said. "But he won't be wanting any breakfast." Leinau asked the black man, "Isn't that right, LeRoy?"

If eyes were bullets, the blackmailer sitting across from Leinau would have shot him dead.

"Nothing for me," the black man said to the waiter, who left.

"I want a show, like you said," the black man said.

Leinau reached into the breast pocket of his jacket.

"How much you got in there?" the black man asked.

"Enough for a hell of a show," Leinau said. He pulled out an inch-high stack of hundred-dollar bills and fanned them, then returned them to his pocket. "I've got another pocket. Want to see what's in that one?"

"I have a plan for delivery," the black man said.

"Look here, LeRoy, you're not dealing with a fool. I'm willing to pay off, all right. But not unless I have a guarantee that whatever it is you have becomes mine in its entirety. And I just don't see how in hell you can possibly guarantee that."

"Look here, man. We got video tapes, man. We're selling you video tapes and you'll get it. We could take chump change on this, but you're not dealing with fools, either. Why the hell you think we're asking for the million, man? You think we'd take a million and come back for more once we had a pile like that?"

"Who's to say you won't squirrel away a copy for insurance? Or just for kicks?"

"Look, man, don't be fucking with me. You dip it in and you always

take a chance, you know? Sometimes it don't cost too much and sometimes it cost a lot. Always, it's a risk. No telling what's going to happen."

Leinau looked out the avenue window. The lights were still off.

"Tell me something, how many others has it been?" he asked the
black man.

"Oh, man, you don't want to be knowing that sort of thing. What's
it matter?"

Leinau hung his head. "Believe it or not, I was in love. That's what
matters."

"Oh, shit. I haven't got time for this bullshit. Next thing, you'll be
tellin' me you love your old lady, too."

"Tildy?"

"That her name?"

"She's a saint."

"She's a spooky lady, man. Nobody that cool when they bein'
robbed. Nobody but somebody spooky, that's all."

"She told me about it. She stood right up to you, right?"

The lights were still off on the car. Leinau didn't know how much
longer he could hold out. Maybe he'd just have to wrap it up here.

"I ain't got any more time, man. Let's get down to it."

"To, what?"

"The delivery, man."

"I'm still worried that I might not get all the material."

"Let me tell you somethin', chump. Can't see my hands, can you?"
The black man's hands were under the table.

"No."

"Inside 'em, I got a little cannon trained on your gut. I told you, I
don't have any time. I told you before, we meant business. I told you
we could touch you whenever we wanted, that's why we busted into
your place like we did. Teach you a lesson.

"Man, I know your every move. I could blow you open right now. Or
one time someday when you never think it's comin', away you go."

The lights went on. Leinau saw a tall, auburn-haired woman walk
through the avenue door and sit down at a table across the room. He
could see that she was watching his table.

"You're not going to shoot me, LeRoy, and I'm going to tell you
why. Now don't get excited, but you're busted, man."

"Huh?"

"You heard me."

The black man turned, found the auburn-haired woman across the room and raised his hand to greet her. He placed his other hand on the table. There was no gun.

The auburn-haired woman rose and started for the door. She was stopped by a plainclothes officer from anticrime and invited to walk across the street to where Whitson was waiting.

"What's comin' down?" the black man asked.

"LeRoy, this is your lucky day. Your boss lady is busted and so are you. In a couple of minutes, just as long as it takes for the officer there accompanying your boss lady to our car to make a little call, we're going to pick up your pal Mickey the super."

"Shit. Why you tellin' me this shit?" The black man stood and Leinau shook his head.

"No, no, LeRoy. I wouldn't leave just yet. That would be called resisting arrest. Sit down, sucker."

The black man sat down.

"You have the right to remain silent," Leinau said. "Any statements you make may be used against you in a court of law—"

"Yeah, yeah."

"Shut the fuck up while I'm talking, LeRoy."

"Yeah, yeah."

Leinau finished the Miranda warning.

"Like I said, it's your lucky day, LeRoy. I'm going to give you the opportunity to do the right thing. You're going to tell me all about the boss lady and her business and you're going to finger Mickey for me so I can wrap this case up all nice and neat and you're going to tell me where your little helper is."

"In return for what?"

"Hey, that's not for me to decide."

"Oh shit, man."

"LeRoy, I haven't got time now and you're not the only creep in this I can sweat. Let's go. Up easy on your feet. No commotion."

The black man stood up. The waiter dropped a check on the table.

"Pay the man, LeRoy."

"What?"

"Yeah, pay the check. You think the city's got me on an expense account?"

The black man took out a billfold.

"Jesus, LeRoy, I'm just kidding." Leinau left a ten-dollar bill on the table and walked outside with the black man.

The woman sat in the back of the squad car with the plainclothes officer, her arms behind her in cuffs.

Leinau cuffed the black man after frisking him, then opened the back door. He whispered into his ear, "LeRoy, it's either you or Mickey. We got him and he's going to get the same deal. I can help only one of you."

19

"Best thing you can do to keep yourself sharp to what's going on is to keep your eye on everything and try to profile everything and everybody you see."

Jack Clark wore his tartan-plaid beret with tassel today, the one he likes to wear on wintry gray days. He'd been following a strange act for an hour, but he'd come up empty. "He looked real good, though. Thought I really had something there, but he went down into the subway and that's all she wrote. He's somebody else's problem now."

So he sat resting in the burglary unit car, on Lexington Avenue and Eighty-sixth Street, watching the passing parade.

"Okay, look at that," he said.

Clark pointed to a tall, slender, effeminately dressed man in his mid-twenties looking at a window display of pastries.

"Here we have Bruce Stronghart. He tends bar at a straight place somewhere here on the Upper East Side, so he trades in his Ralph Lauren kerchief for a bow tie. This is the time of year when he's just soooo-ooo bored. He looks with disdain at his customers from those rose-tint glasses in the red horn rims and says, 'Oh, I've seen it all, you know.' And he just can't wait for summer to come so he can go to Fire Island with the boys."

Clark looked at the Korean stacking up fruit outside his shop.

"Now that guy," Clark said. "You'd probably think to look at him like all he wants out of life is just to stack up oranges. Don't you believe it. At home, he's got a huge collection of Marilyn Chambers films on

Betamax. In Korean, yet! He plays them every morning before he goes to work and then he comes here and stacks up fruit. He's got a full life, I'm telling you."

He started up the car.

"Too slow here and I don't like to sit around one place too long," he said.

He drove down Lexington and cut over at Seventy-sixth Street toward Third Avenue. Halfway down the block, he stopped the car, unable to get around a Porsche double-parked in front of a town house. The owner of the car, who stood talking with a young woman on the stoop of the town house, looked over at Clark in the unmarked car, then continued talking to the woman. He wore a sheepskin coat and designer jeans.

"Watch what happens when the driver of a banged-up Chevy toots his horn at the man from Vegas over there," Clark said.

He tapped the horn.

"Hey, what's the problem?" the Vegas man shouted.

"Move the car, huh?"

"I'll be there. Hold on." He continued talking to the woman.

"It's just too easy," Clark said. "I'm not going to do it. I'd just shoot up my blood pressure, you know? The guy wants to look like big shit to pussy there, so why not? Who needs a test of manhood, the guy with the beat-up Chevy or the guy with designer jeans?

"And look at that car, will you? I swear, these assholes think you pay over twenty-five thousand for a damn car and you're allowed by the state of New York to do whatever you want with it. That comes under the Elite Motor Act, I guess."

Mr. Vegas sauntered to his Porsche and waved at Clark, waiting at the head of what was now a long and impatient line of cars trying to make it through the street.

Clark leaned out the window. "Oh, mister, will you come here just a minute?" He crooked a finger. Designer Jeans sauntered over and Clark showed him his shield.

"I didn't want to say anything while you were making time, friendly, but now I'm telling you that I'd like you to move your butt and move it fast, okay? Some cops are real mean about this sort of thing. Me, I'm a lover. I understand. But move it."

"Yes, sir."

"Have a nice day."

"Thanks."

Clark drove through Third Avenue, then turned downtown on Second Avenue. An elderly black man wearing two or three coats was rooting through a trash can.

He pulled the car up next to him, on the east side of the avenue, rolled the window down and called out his name.

"Howard, my man!"

Howard turned slowly around and squinted his eyes at the skinny Irish face with the plaid beret.

"Hey, Jack boy, what's goin', eh?" The old man walked slowly to the car.

"You behavin' yourself, Howard?"

"Sure as shit, Jack. You wouldn't want to help me out a little, would you?"

"Hey, come on, Howard. You know what that'd make me?"

"Chump."

"Yeah."

Clark explained to Valentine, "Howard here taught me a lesson not long ago. I find we have a little problem with old people like him. We tend to overlook them. Human, eh? But you know, you have to think like the victim of a guy like Howard here."

" 'At's right, Jack." Howard's breath filled the front seat of the car.

"Well, you're out with your wife, say, and you get back to your car at the end of the night and it's been robbed. What the hell do you care how old the thief is? You want him nailed, right?"

" 'At's right!" Howard said, pounding the window frame for emphasis.

"Glad to see you agree, Howard," Clark said. He turned back to Valentine. "Howard, here, boosts from cars, you see. I know that because not so long ago I watched him break into a car right along here and take a motorcycle helmet and some gloves."

" 'At's right!"

"Howard, you're getting on my nerves, pal."

"Ooooh. Howard shut his trap."

"Thanks." He spoke to Valentine. "So I bust him and take him in and seeing as how he's an old guy and pretty gentle and what he stole was under two hundred and fifty dollars, we let him go with a desk summons."

Clark turned to Howard. "That about right so far, Howard?"

"Sounds familiar." Howard grinned.

"Then he starts complaining to me that he hasn't got any carfare and he needs to get home and all, so I reach into my pocket and I give him a dollar."

Howard reached into his own pocket now and handed over a dollar bill to Clark, who took it and stuck it into his shirt. "Much obliged, old pal."

"Guess what happened thirty minutes after I'd given him the dollar?" Clark asked Valentine. "I'll tell you. I see him about four blocks from the station house breaking into another car."

" 'At's right. Jack here got me fair and square."

"Howard, what do you know?" Clark asked him.

"Don't know much of nothin', I guess."

"Oh, well, I was hoping here you could help me round up a bad guy or two today."

"I don't hang 'round no trouble, you know that, Jack."

"Yeah, right. Howard, I'll see you now, okay? Take care, man."

"You, too, Jack."

Clark reached into his shirt pocket and retrieved the dollar bill. He handed it to Howard.

"Keep it, man. And keep a warm memory of yours truly, okay?"

"You better believe it, Jack."

Howard stood on the corner waving to the car as Clark drove off.

"I tell you, the great cartoon never stops."

Now for the second time, Mairead Keenan found herself floating through what she believed was a magical evening. The play was a wondrous thing, even Tommy had enjoyed it. And now, with the same strolling violinists, she was sitting in Mama Leone's.

The baby kicked.

While Mairead and Tommy Keenan ordered an antipasto and studied their menus, Dory Smith decided to make a telephone call, her first to Keenan's home up in Riverdale.

The baby-sitter took down her name and number. Dory said she was an old friend of Mairead's.

"And where were the two of them off tonight?" Dory asked.

The baby-sitter told her.

Clark picked up Carl Trani at the corner of Third Avenue and Sixty-ninth Street, then pulled the magnetic flasher-siren out of the glove compartment and set it on top of the car.

"Burglary in progress call," he told Trani. "East Sixty-six, number four-twenty."

"Got it," Trani said.

A couple of uniforms had just arrived on the scene when Clark and Trani drove up.

"One of you here and one in back, if there's a court," Clark said.

He and Trani took the stairway to the fourth floor, where the burglary had been called. They took the stairs two at a time, opened the door slowly on the fourth and walked through the corridor.

Nothing.

They crept up the stairway to the fifth floor, the top of the building, and again found nothing. Clark went up onto the roof, where there were no traces of anyone having left the building. Down below, in a small courtyard, was the uniformed officer, who didn't look like he'd run across anything, either.

"Come and gone, or it's a false alarm," Trani said when Clark rejoined him on the fifth floor.

"We do a floor-by-floor now," Clark said.

Nothing on any floor, no paint chips, no signs of a jimmy being used against a door. The few people at home didn't report seeing or hearing anything.

Down in the lobby, a woman in her early twenties carrying two pies saw Clark's shield on the chain around his neck.

"Oh, my God! What's going on?" she asked.

"Did you call about a burglary, miss?" Clark asked.

"Oh, my God, a burglary now?"

"I didn't say that. I asked you if you called about a burglary."

"Oh, my God, this building sucks. I mean, it really sucks. Here, hold my pies." She placed them in Clark's hands while she rummaged through her handbag, searching for keys. "Oh, the pies are for later."

"I see."

"God, my boy friend was shot in here. This building sucks. You hear me?"

"Yes," Clark said. "The building sucks."

"Did you tell my friend up on the fifth floor?"

"I'm afraid I don't know—"

"That's who the pies are for. God, this building sucks. We all think so."

"Yes, ma'am."

"Oh, my God."

Trani tapped Clark on the shoulder. "Give her back her pies, Jack. That's a hell of a thing for a cop to do, steal a lady's pies."

Clark extended his hands, but the young woman didn't seem interested.

"Who can eat at a time like this?" she asked.

A cab deposited her at the door.

All the way over, she was bound and determined just what she had set out to do. But now that she was here, actually here with all the people around her, she felt hot and her blood raced and her heart pumped.

She sat in the back of the cab fumbling in her purse for the money. Then she held a ten in her hand and just sat there in the seat, looking out the window.

"Lady, you want to pay up or what?" the driver asked.

"Yes. Oh, here," she said. She handed over the ten.

Then she opened the door and left. The fare on the meter was just over five dollars. She didn't care.

She walked past a doorman. Then she encountered the maître d'.

"Yes, madam?"

"I haven't got a reservation," she said.

"You're . . . alone?"

She laughed. "No, I'm here to meet someone," she said. "They're probably already seated. I'll just step in and take a look if you don't mind."

The maître d' seemed greatly relieved.

She stood just inside the huge dining room and saw them toward the back. She had never seen his wife before and she was startled by her appearance. She'd pictured her as a redhead, but she didn't know why. Instead, she was black-haired, with dark brown eyes. And she was laughing at something he said. She thought she somehow never laughed, that she only cleaned and took care of babies and gabbed with housewives in the park. But here she was in a theater restaurant, unchic as it might be, laughing the night away. And maybe for once in his life he'd be all right later that night, maybe for once he wouldn't behave like he was committing some terrible sin just because he was doing something men have been doing ever since the creation.

Again, she was resolute. She would do it, by God, and she would do it up with style.

She reached inside the large handbag she carried and fished out a large piece of folded cardboard. Attached at two ends of the cardboard was a bit of string, so that she could place the cardboard across her chest, as a sign, suspended by the string around her neck.

A startled strolling violinist was the first to notice the sign. He stopped playing and dropped his bow. A busboy stepped on it.

Then a woman with something green in her mouth stopped chewing and gasped, nearly choked.

"Oh Tommy!" she called across the room.

A few hundred heads turned. The violinists stopped, one by one. The conversation died in waves. She waited for almost complete silence and then shouted again.

"Tommy! Tommy Keenan!"

She waved and began walking toward the Keenans' table.

Just before she reached the table, she turned around so all sides of the room could see her and read her sign. She placed her hand on the back of a chair and said, "Tommy, how nice to see you. And you have your lovely wife along as well."

Tommy Keenan's face was scarlet. Mairead Keenan's was stone.

Dory Smith stood at their table, smiling, with a large white sign with big block lettering: "I'm the other woman."

Mairead's voice was cool, quiet but powerful. She said to Dory, "Please sit down, dear."

And Dory Smith did.

"It's been like this all night," Clark said to Trani. "Lots of nothing. Everybody's behaving themselves tonight. That's nice, I guess."

Trani adjusted his vest. It always scratched. Clark drove down Second Avenue.

"What's the guy at the can?" Trani said.

"Jesus, it's just old Howard again. He's only doing garbage tonight. Maybe he's gone straight."

In another block, they snapped to attention. Both had seen the same thing. Clark pulled the car over to the curb, as unobtrusively as possible. Trani slipped out the door and walked nonchalantly toward a young man hurrying from a building, a black bag over his shoulder.

He was perfect. Twenty years old, tops. Hispanic. Didn't belong in the neighborhood. Climbing out a ground-floor window of an apartment building. Seemed in a hurry. Clark stepped out of the car and skipped through the traffic as Trani fell into step behind the perp.

"Hold it!" Trani said. "Police."

The perp turned around fast and dropped the bag.

Clark joined Trani and stepped behind the perp.

"What's going on?" Clark asked.

The perp turned toward Clark.

"Just keep looking at the arresting officer," Clark said. "What's in the bag?"

"My clothes," the perp said.

"Where do you live?" Trani asked him.

"Over there," the perp said. He pointed to the apartment building he'd climbed out of.

"You live there?" Clark said from behind. "Sure you weren't just visiting a little bit?"

"Am I under arrrest?" the perp asked.

"What were you doing climbing out the window?" Trani asked.

"I got a key broken in the door. I live there," the perp said.

"A key broken in the door?"

"Yeah. The super's fixing it from out in the hallway. Meanwhile, I can't get in or out and I've got to do my laundry, which is in that bag."

Clark groaned. "You got some identification?"

"Sure," the perp said. He pulled a billfold from his back pocket. It was jammed with credit cards and two pieces of picture identification. Clark looked it over and then handed it back to him. "Satisfied?"

"What's the super's name?" Clark asked.

"José."

"Let's go," said Trani.

The two officers and the man who was probably telling the truth walked to the lobby of the apartment building. They rang the super's bell and in a few minutes a middle-aged Puerto Rican man responded.

"Your name José?" Clark asked.

"Yes."

"You know this guy?" Clark pointed to the perp with the laundry bag.

"Yes. Mr. Sante."

"Tell me about Mr. Sante's door," Clark said.

"What about his door?"

"Any problems?"

"I'm fixing it."

Clark put his hand on Sante's shoulder. "We're ever vigilant, sir, as you can plainly see. Sorry for the inconvenience. Rest easy tonight, right?"

"Yeah, sure," Sante said.

Clark and Trani walked quickly out the lobby to the street. Clark said to Trani, out of the corner of his mouth, "Let's get the hell out of here as fast as possible. Jesus, I was afraid of something like this sometime."

"I can understand your wanting to spoil my husband's evening," Mairead said to a very stunned Dory Smith, "but why would you do this to me? Have I hurt you in some way?"

"No, I—"

"Do you have some reason for wanting to humiliate me?"

Dory Smith hung her head. Keenan felt the heat of every eye in the place burning through his skin.

"No, of course not," Dory said. "I'm sorry."

"Apology accepted."

Keenan looked at his wife. "What is this?" he asked her.

"That's exactly what I'm hoping to find out," Mairead said. She started to say something to Dory Smith, but the baby kicked and she lost her breath.

"What is it?" Dory asked.

"Oh, it gets you in the windpipe," Mairead said. She took a sip of water. "My baby kicked."

Dory hung her head again and started crying. Keenan wanted desperately to leave the table for the comforts of the men's room.

"What's wrong with *you*, dear? I'm pregnant. That's my excuse."

Mairead stared at the troubled woman. Her crumpled white sign lay on the table in front of her. And Dory Smith didn't look much better than the sign herself.

Mairead turned to her husband. "Tommy, can it be? She's pregnant, too, isn't she?"

The answer yes blazed in Tommy Keenan's face.

"And you're the one who thinks *I'm* a silly twit," Mairead said. "Have you never heard of prevention, Tommy? And you being a cop in Sex Crimes for so long. You should be ashamed of yourself, man."

He was. But more than that, he was amazed by his wife.

"Now then," Mairead said, drawing her hands together below her chin, "we're going to have to figure out what we're going to do about our problem, aren't we?"

On the way back to the house, when they'd decided to call it quits for the tour, Clark and Trani spotted a woman standing near a car on Lexington Avenue at Sixty-third, her hands waving. As they drove closer, they heard her shouting.

Inside the car was a man, also shouting.

"Easy does it, Carl," Clark said. "Looks like a domestic. You know how these things go. They can blow up like nothing else in the business."

"Yeah, I know. Just watch your mouth, Jack."

Clark shrugged. He stopped the car parallel to the black Mercedes. Trani walked slowly around the front of the car, noting the license plate. He pulled his shield from under his shirt and let it hang from the chain.

"Police officers, ma'am," he said.

He thought he heard her snarl.

Clark, meanwhile, motioned for the man at the wheel to roll down the passenger-side window. The procedure in a domestic was to separate the parties and talk calmly, one officer to each in order to defuse the situation.

The man rolled down his window.

"Look, we're just having a little argument here, Officer," he said. "Nothing serious."

"Sure sounds serious, pal. Can I help?" Clark asked.

"Well, no. We just broke up tonight, that's all."

"Oh, that's pretty tough sometimes. You going to be all right? She doesn't sound at all well."

He looked back over his shoulder. Trani was talking to her quietly, hands in the pockets of his jacket.

"She's the nervous type."

Clark laughed.

"What's so funny?" the woman shouted. "I heard that! Whose side you want to be on, anyway? You're all fucking alike. Men! Feh!"

Trani told her to hush.

"Don't tell me to keep my voice down!" she screamed. "This is New York Fucking City and it's the noisiest fucking place on planet Earth and I'll do my part to make it a little fucking noisier if you don't fucking mind!"

Clark said to the man in the Mercedes. "Yeah, see what you mean. Can't you take this someplace else, like your apartment or something?"

"Are you nuts, Officer?"

"Well, hell, look what I'm doing for a living."

The woman walked around Trani to get a better view of Clark in the unmarked police car.

"You two boys having a pretty good fucking laugh about all this, huh?" she shrieked.

"No, ma'am."

"Don't 'no ma'am' me!"

Trani tried talking to her, reached out a hand to touch her arm. "Listen—"

The woman spun around and clawed him. She managed to sink her nails into the top of his wrist, caught them there and squeezed, embedding her nails even deeper into his skin.

"Jesus Christ!" Trani yelled.

The woman clawed at him with her other hand. Blood spattered her coat and face.

Clark jumped out of the car and ran around the front of the car. He grabbed the woman's elbows and pressed them together behind her back. She bucked backward, raised her foot and tried to kick Clark in his testicles.

Trani had the cuffs out, snapped her up and then he and Clark each took an arm and led her, screaming and cursing, to the squad car. They bent her double over the rear deck.

"You're going to have to be quiet if you want to hear your rights, lady," Clark said.

"My God, you're going to actually arrest her?" the man in the Mercedes said.

"You got it, pal," Clark said. "Stick around a minute, we're going to need your name."

"Oh, my God."

"You're telling me," Clark said.

The woman calmed herself. She went completely limp, actually. Clark radioed for a backup unit and when it arrived placed the hand-cuffed woman in back and had her run into the station house and held in the women's lockup until he got there to do the paperwork.

"Carl," he said to Trani, "I think we'd better get a look at that."

After taking the particulars from the man in the Mercedes, Clark took Trani to Lenox Hill Hospital at Park and Seventy-seventh. He radioed over the PTP for Laffey and called him to join the watch at the hospital.

"Doesn't look like much," Laffey said as he held Trani's hand in his, turning it over. "But these things have a way of spreading down to the worst places. Heard of a guy who lost his limbs and it started just this way."

Trani's eyes grew. He was a bit of a hypochondriac, but he lived, after all, in a city where more people are bitten each year by human beings than by rats.

"Listen, Carl. You got clean underwear?" Laffey asked.

Trani pulled his hand away.

"Aw, it's not going to be all that bad," Laffey said. "The doctors will probably tell you you can't jerk off for a few days. What do they know?"

Back at the station house, Clark worked up the paper. Laffey ordered a booking charge of felonious assault, since the victim was a police officer. Otherwise, it would have been simple assault at best.

"But you know what the hell's going to happen," Laffey said. "She'll get it busted down. She'll show up in court with a nice skirt and white gloves and she'll be sugar and spice and everything nice."

But the booking would be good enough to get her jailed overnight, which was the idea.

20

Matty Monahan threw in the towel, which is to say he put through papers to release a police composite sketch of the man he'd hunted for so long—Kano the arsonist and killer. He signed the release and the sketch, along with information advising readers to call detectives at the special number—577-TIPS—that would appear in the *Daily News* and the *Post* tomorrow. With the *Times,* you never knew. A new agrarian research breakthrough in Katmandu could knock a little matter like a killer on the loose in New York right off the page.

Monahan sat hunched over the forms on a desk at the Nineteenth PDU on St. Patrick's Day. He wore his regulation bright green necktie and filled in the blanks: dark-skinned Hispanic male, thirty to forty years old, five feet seven, black hair and moustache.

Someone in the public information office at Police Headquarters downtown would type up the information from Monahan's standard form as a news release and then deliver it immediately to the local press, as if it were hot stuff, which it wasn't. Monahan put the carbons of the form in his inactive file.

Detective Joe Simon, too, pushed a file into inactive status. Absolutely nothing was forthcoming on the Paul McRae murder.

People say you can't get away with murder. You can. Killers do, every day.

An officer named Wisneski poked his head through the door of the detective squad room. The first Irish detective he saw was Theresa Enterlin.

"You hear about the St. Paddy's parade?" he asked her.

"What?"

"They canceled it. Changed it to the St. Pulaski parade."

"Listen, Wisneski. You hear about the Polish car pool?"

"Okay, what?"

"It meets at work."

A private school off Fifth Avenue at East Ninety-fifth Street, and the apartment building that houses Robert and Lola Redford, had trouble during the night.

Robert Redford wasn't much help in the case of his home. He slept through it.

A burglar made his way up a fire escape outside the Redford home, then broke through a bathroom window and climbed inside, probably not knowing whose home he'd just entered and probably caring not a whit.

Lola Redford heard noises.

She crept out of her bed, leaving her husband where he was, slumbering peacefully the last few hours before his run around the Central Park Reservoir.

Lola put on her slippers and made her way to the bedroom door. She peeked through a crack and saw a shadowy form making his way through her home.

Bob would probably just make a whole lot of noise, so she let him alone. She waited until the intruder got into the living room, at the opposite end of the huge apartment.

There was a telephone in a carpeted hallway. If she could make it to the phone, quickly and quietly, she could dial 911 and report the crime in progress.

In less than three minutes, there were two uniformed officers on the rooftop of the Redford building, two in the shadows at the bottom of the fire escape and detectives in the lobby as well as in the rear court, where the burglar was most likely to return—the same way he'd entered, according to Mrs. Redford.

She crept back into bed beside her husband and listened. The burglar returned through the bathroom window and she breathed a deep sigh of relief.

When the officers knocked at the door, she made them coffee and woke her husband.

In the case of the private school, Officers Ciffo and Truta weren't allowed to be of much help.

Sometime during the night or early in the morning, the headmistress told Ciffo and Truta, fully two blocks away from the school lest anyone see police uniforms intruding on the peace and calm of the private school, that whoever it was who had been making violent threats against one of the teachers had struck again.

"Again?" Ciffo asked.

The headmistress, perhaps thirty-five years of age, with dark brown hair and mesh hosiery and green eyes and a silk eyelet blouse that Ciffo particularly enjoyed, said, "Oh yes, again."

"What happened the first time?" he asked.

"Well, you must understand, we have a slight labor relations problem here at the school," she said.

"Yes?"

"The faculty is completely French. We offer our staff one- and sometimes two-year contracts. They have begun circulating a petition demanding a full tenure arrangement instead, as they do not wish to return to France necessarily."

"And who is being threatened?"

"Well," the headmistress said, "the one teacher who apparently refused to sign the petition."

"What's the nature of the threats?"

"One day she arrived in her classroom to find a swastika painted on her desk. Another day it was chicken livers with needles stuck in them. And now . . ."

She handed Ciffo a piece of paper.

Ciffo handed it to Truta. "I can't read this," he said. "It's in French."

"Well, neither can I."

"Oh, I forget in my worry. Here," the headmistress said, "I've made English translations."

Neatly typed on a sheet of crisp white paper was:

We will have your skin. You are on the side of the pigs. You will die. You've been warned!

Officers Dennis MacDonald and Basil Reece were called to a Food Emporium supermarket on Third Avenue at Eighty-second Street, where the store's security personnel had detained a shoplifter. The radio dispatcher called it "Food Euphoria."

MacDonald and Reece followed the store manager down into the basement of the supermarket, where a dejected young man sat on a crate in the middle of a large storeroom, surrounded by the staff of beefy stockmen and three of the store's butchers, all of them with forearms roughly the size of Virginia hams.

The alleged shoplifter wasn't going anywhere.

"Okay, let's have you tell me what he got," MacDonald said to the store manager, a young woman with a clipboard and a paper hat.

"We caught him with three legs of lamb in his shirt," she said.

"Jesus!" MacDonald said. He asked the shoplifter for identification. "So it's Hector?"

Hector nodded.

"You always carry ID with you when you go boosting, Hector?"

Hector didn't seem to understand.

MacDonald took the supermarket manager aside. "Look," he said to her, "you realize we have to have the three legs of lamb if we're going to make a case?"

"You do?"

"Of course. It's material evidence. Where is it?"

"Well, we put it back in the case. We sold one of them."

MacDonald sighed. "What do you want to do here? I don't think we have a case for court if you go and sell the evidence."

"Well, can't you make a report?"

"Sure." MacDonald knew what he would have to do. He would have to try to scare Hector, who looked dumb as a fox.

"I'll have to make a report, too," the manager said. She started scratching something onto a piece of paper in her clipboard. "Officer, how do you spell burglary?"

"Never mind now," MacDonald said wearily.

He went to Hector, took his identification card and copied down the information. The manager would have to decline prosecution.

"Hector," MacDonald said. Doleful brown eyes were raised to the officer. "I'm telling you, next time you get caught at this, it's a felony. Understand? That means one year in the slammer. Got me?"

Hector was marched upstairs between Reece and MacDonald. Customers stared at the three.

Out on the street, MacDonald said to Hector, "Get out of here. Go home and be glad for what you have that's yours fair and square."

Then he and Reece got back inside their squad car.

"So two hours later, I'll bet you, he's uptown doing it again. He knows he can get away with it."

Ed Smith shook the administrator's hand and left the big office. His beard had grown back since Christmas, but he kept it neatly trimmed now, and for the interview he'd worn a blue striped shirt and tie, a navy blazer and gray slacks.

Ruth wanted him to call her immediately, but he wanted to savor the moment alone for a while, so he left the hospital where she worked as head of public relations and walked the streets, going nowhere in particular. Just walking, thinking.

He found himself approaching the Queensboro Bridge and he wondered where Joe might be.

"He's taking a crap behind the piling, since you got to know so bad," a leathery-faced bum said. "Got a spare cigarette or some change or somethin'? What do you think, information's for free around here?"

Smith gave the old man a cigarette and even lit it for him. He waited for Joe to reappear, which he did. Joe didn't recognize Whispering Ed by sight.

"Joe, I need to talk to you," Ed said.

Joe grabbed him by the arm. "Come on then, not here. What do you think, I want to be seen with you? Look at you. My pals will think I'm a fink or somethin' and they'll damn sure tag you now for a cop."

"That's what I got to talk to you about."

"Come on, then."

Joe and Smith walked along the bridge's south pilings. Overhead, the traffic roared and whooshed.

"I might be leaving, Joe."

"What, New York?"

"No, just the police department."

"You, not a cop?" Joe scratched his face. "Well, that's a kick, ain't it? Finally, you start looking like a nice young clean-cut cop instead of some smelly old bum and you right away start thinking of quitting."

"Well, there are reasons."

"Women."

Smith nodded.

"They're always trying to bend us out of shape. She wants you to quit, right?"

"Right."

"So what do you think?"

"I'm sort of neutral about the whole thing."

"That's the trouble with the world today. Everybody's neutral. There's guys in charge, and that's damn few. They run Russia and the U.S. and a few other places. Then there's guys like me at rock bottom. Guys like you and ninety-nine and three-quarters percent of the rest of the world are in the middle and most of the time you're all neutral."

"This doesn't help me much, Joe."

"Nothing can. Walk around with it a few days, that's all I'd say. Course, I got time for that sort of thing."

On the way back to the station, Ciffo had Truta stop at a travel agency on Lexington.

He returned to the car with a dozen brochures on Caribbean destinations. He flipped through them all the way back.

"Listen to this," he said. "The Cayman Islands, a scuba diver's paradise . . . coconut trees . . ."

"You couldn't stay away from your mother's cooking long enough to put on a scuba tank," Truta said.

"One more crack like that and I won't take you along with me."

"Yeah, fat chance." Truta pulled the car up to a rare spot right in front of the precinct house.

Upstairs, in the detective squad room, they gave the case to Detective Mensch.

"You're going to love this one, Mensch," Ciffo said.

"Tony did. The headmistress was pretty cute," Truta said.

"Oh yeah? You talking about the one with the good legs and that white blouse and the green eyes? I didn't notice."

"What do we got?" Mensch said.

"Fingerprints, death threats and a fancy-schmancy school."

Mensch read over the material. "What's these fingerprints?"

"They had a private detective come and make fingerprints of the desk where the threat was found, the letter itself and the doorknob to the teacher's classroom. The originals of all this stuff are with the private detective," Truta said.

"Hey, wish I was a private dick right about now," Mensch said. "A couple of hundred bucks for a useless piece of work. They're still trying to push that fingerprint nonsense, aren't they? The guy'll end up finger-printing the whole damn school and then what? He's got a bunch of fingerprints and some nice billings.

"Jesus, we would have done it for free—if we'd have done it. Seems kind of a wasted effort to me."

Ciffo said, "Well, that's what I told the headmistress. I said we had some pretty good experience with taking fingerprints and that we had an actual resident graphologist on the detective squad. That's true, isn't it?"

Mensch shook his head. "What can I do about this?"

"I guess they want to talk to a city detective. No uniforms, though. You're supposed to go there and not say anything about being from the police, either."

"Oh, good lord no. We wouldn't want to dirty up their premises."

Ciffo met Tommy Keenan on the steps outside the station.

"What's the good word, Tommy?"

"It's a boy."

"No kiddin'?"

"His name's Tony. Anthony Keenan."

"For me?"

"Why not?"

"Tommy, how is it going back on real duty, huh? You got things straightened out, or what?"

"I'm getting a transfer, Tony."

"To what?"

"Desk job downtown. Regular hours, home for dinner every night, weekends off."

"What about the Nineteenth?"

"I'll probably never be around."

"This all your idea?"

Keenan shrugged. "There was a time when I thought I could never give up this stuff. Now I got to get used to it and I am. Funny how you can adapt. But to answer your question, no it's not all my idea."

Ciffo waited, said nothing.

"Tony, I had to get out of the life or I'd lose Mairead and the kids and it's as simple as that. She told me I was killing myself and maybe I was. Maybe I'm not supposed to be a cop. It's not what I planned on, God knows."

"What's the desk job?"

"I'll be in public information at Police Plaza. Brochures, community meetings, press releases, that sort of thing."

"Think you'll like it?"

"It's indoors and there's no heavy lifting."

"Yeah, well," Ciffo said, "but will you be happy?"

"Like I was here? Hell, man, I was miserable. More miserable and self-destructive than I've ever been in my life."

"Mairead pointed this out to you?"

"Of course. Shouldn't she?"

"Sure." Ciffo lit a cigarette. "What about the other one, the hobby cop we don't see around here anymore?"

"She's over with."

"Mairead know?"

Keenan smiled. "Mairead knows."

"Well," Ciffo said, glancing at his watch, "it's your muster. Happy trails. When do you leave?"

"This is it, my last day in the One-Nine."

Ed Smith and Ruth had lunch in an Italian restaurant near the United Nations. Ruth arrived first, bursting with curiosity.

"Well, did he offer the job?" she asked. Ed hadn't managed to sit down yet.

"How hard did you have to work on him?"

"He likes my work. I had to lobby some, but he pretty much goes on my recommendation on most things."

"Well, he did this time, too, apparently."

"Oh, Ed, I'm so proud of you."

Ed Smith, director of security at a hospital. Big salary, big office, no sweat.

"We'd be working at the same place. What would you think of that?"

"What would I think of it? I was the one who suggested it." She had to touch his face to make him look at her. "What's wrong with you? You're happy, aren't you? Didn't we talk all of this all the way through?"

"We talked about us, what we thought about our divorce and what happened to each of us over the years," Smith said. "I'm not sure we did any listening, either of us."

"I thought you were in the same place I was," Ruth said. "You seemed to be. It seems to me that we were pretty objective about this situation for the first time in our lives."

"Maybe that's just what the problem was."

"What problem?"

"The problem of objectivity. I'm not sure it has anything to do with human relationships."

"Look, are you going to take the job or aren't you?"

"Ruth, if I take the job, I'm doing something I don't want to do except for what will make you happy. If I take the job, I'm saying that you're right about my future and I'm not so sure you're entitled to make that decision any more than I'm entitled to decide something like that for you."

"You're not going to take it."

Smith looked past her, out to the East River that glimmered an oily blue between the buildings lining the street to the water's edge.

"Let me tell you something. I don't believe I fit in some objective world. I happen to think that one person is just as likely to be right, or wrong, as another."

"You're not going to take the job?"

"No. Shall we order now?"

Ruth sighed. "Well, I really didn't think so. I hoped a hell of a lot, but I knew it wasn't realistic. What'll you do now? Go back to your bums?"

"Probably not. I need a change. I'll see what's around."

"But you're staying with the department?"

"Yep."

"And I'm supposed to get used to that?"

"That's up to you. I've waited."

"I love you, Ed."

21

"Mrs. Rotare?"

"Yes?"

"It's your secret admirer."

"My secret admirer? Who can that be? I'm just an overweight old lady. I haven't had any beaux in years."

"How the hell are you today?"

"Well, I'm feeling pretty good, Tony. How are you?"

"It's May and May is one of my favorite months of the whole year and I'm going off to the Cayman Islands to scuba dive and I deserve every minute of it."

"I'm happy for you. But you be careful with those island girls down there."

"Hey, I ain't misbehavin' and I'm savin' all my love for you. Like the song, right?"

"Tony, I want to tell you something maybe you already know because lots of other people tell you this."

"Shoot."

"You're a good cop, Tony Ciffo. And a good man. So why don't you find yourself a nice girl and marry her and make yourself some little boys just like you?"

"This city isn't big enough, that's why."

"Oh, I suppose it's none of my business. Tony, you're good to call

me like you do. I got to go now and so do you. 'Bye for now and say
hello to Jeanie."

"I will. 'Bye, love."

He pulled the Fuego into a very tight spot on East Sixty-seventh
between Lexington and Park.

"Here we are, Jeanie. Another day of savage amusement in store for
us."

They climbed out of the car, a little stiff after running on the beach
pretty much the entire afternoon. The first beach trip of the season.
The water had been far too cold to enter, but the sun was hot.

There was an hour's worth of paperwork to do and then Ciffo and
Truta hit the street. The early evening would be one of the year's best.

After an especially long winter season and a freak snowstorm in
April, New Yorkers walked about the streets as if they were mole people
trapped for years in darkness.

They were driving west on Seventy-third Street, past a block of ter-
raced apartment houses. Ciffo looked up and saw a couple seated at a
table, a candle between them.

"Look at that!" he shouted. Truta slammed on the brakes.

"What?"

"Up there. I think I'm going to go up and serenade them."

"Jesus, you'll drive them back inside. You want to ruin everything for
them?"

"Yeah, maybe you're right."

They drove on toward Park Avenue.

". . . three, four . . . five," Ciffo said.

"What are you counting?"

"The number of couples walking along holding hands. That's what I
like to see. Love in the city. Makes my job one whole hell of a lot
easier, love does."

z